To the Instructor

Thank you for your interest in the Townsend Press vocabulary series—the most widely-used vocabulary books on the college market today. Our goal in this series has been to produce nothing less than excellent books at nothing more than reasonable prices.

About the Book

Notice that the introduction to students (page 1) immediately makes clear to them just why vocabulary study is important. Students are motivated to learn by the four compelling kinds of evidence for word study. The back cover as well convinces students that "a solid vocabulary is a source of power."

You may want to look then at the preface, starting on page vii, which describes in detail the nine distinctive features of the book.

Paging through the text, you'll see that a second color is used throughout to make material as inviting as possible. You'll note, too, that each eight-page chapter contains a great deal of hands-on practice to help ensure that students master each word. And you'll find that the practice materials themselves are far more carefully done, and more appealing, than the run-of-the-mill items you typically find in a skills text. The quality and interest level of the content will help students truly learn the words, without either boring them or insulting their intelligence.

Supplements to the Book

Adding to the value of *Groundwork for a Better Vocabulary*, which has a net price of only $7.90, is the quality of the supplements:

• An *Instructor's Edition*, which you hold in your hand. The Instructor's Edition is identical to the student text except that it includes the answers to all of the practices and tests.

• A combined *Instructor's Manual and Test Bank*, free with adoptions of 20 or more copies. This booklet contains a general vocabulary placement test as well as a pretest and a posttest for the book and for each of the five units in the text. It also includes teaching guidelines, suggested syllabi, an answer key, and an additional mastery test for each chapter.

• *Computer disks,* which provide additional testing materials for the words in the book. Free with adoptions of 200 or more copies, the disks contain a number of user- and instructor-friendly features: 1) actual pronunciations of each word; 2) brief explanations of answers; 3) frequent mention of the user's first name; 4) a running score at the bottom of the screen; and 5) a record-keeping file.

Adopters of the book can obtain any of these supplements by calling our toll-free number, 1-800-772-6410, or by writing or faxing Townsend Press at the numbers shown on page iv.

(Continues on next page)

New Features of the Book

Among the changes in a book that has undergone significant revision are the following:

- The book has been greatly expanded in size (it is now 8½ by 11 inches), in the number of vocabulary words (from 150 to 250), and in the number of activities (over twice as many).

- Each chapter now begins with a multiple-choice format that gets students interacting immediately with each word.

- To provide more review and reinforcement, most of the words in each chapter are repeated in context in later chapters of the book.

- The print in the book has been enlarged, a pronunciation key now appears on the inside front cover, a crossword puzzle has been added as a unit review, and the introduction to the book has been expanded to include an explanation of the different types of context clues.

- Answer spaces can now be marked either with the word itself or with a number or letter— so that a Scantron machine or answer key can be used for easy grading.

A Comprehensive Vocabulary Program

There are eight books in the Townsend Press vocabulary series:

- *Vocabulary Basics* (reading level 4–6)
- *Groundwork for a Better Vocabulary, 2/e* (reading level 5–8)
- *Building Vocabulary Skills, 2/e* (reading level 7–9)
- *Improving Vocabulary Skills, 2/e* (reading level 9–11)
- *Advancing Vocabulary Skills, 2/e* (reading level 11–13)
- *Building Vocabulary Skills, Short Version, 2/e* (reading level 7–9)
- *Improving Vocabulary Skills, Short Version, 2/e* (reading level 9–11)
- *Advancing Vocabulary Skills, Short Version, 2/e* (reading level 11–13)

Note that the short versions of the *Building, Improving,* and *Advancing* books are limited to 200 words, as opposed to the 260 words and 40 word parts in each of the long versions. For some students and classes, the short versions of these books will provide an easier, more manageable approach to vocabulary development.

GROUNDWORK FOR A BETTER VOCABULARY

SECOND EDITION

R. KENT SMITH
UNIVERSITY OF MAINE

BETH JOHNSON

CAROLE MOHR

TOWNSEND PRESS   Marlton, NJ 08053

Books in the Townsend Press Vocabulary Series:

VOCABULARY BASICS
GROUNDWORK FOR A BETTER VOCABULARY, 2/e
BUILDING VOCABULARY SKILLS, 2/e
IMPROVING VOCABULARY SKILLS, 2/e
ADVANCING VOCABULARY SKILLS, 2/e
BUILDING VOCABULARY SKILLS, SHORT VERSION, 2/e
IMPROVING VOCABULARY SKILLS, SHORT VERSION, 2/e
ADVANCING VOCABULARY SKILLS, SHORT VERSION, 2/e

Books in the Townsend Press Reading Series:

GROUNDWORK FOR COLLEGE READING, 2/e
KEYS TO BETTER COLLEGE READING
TEN STEPS TO BUILDING COLLEGE READING SKILLS, FORM A, 2/e
TEN STEPS TO BUILDING COLLEGE READING SKILLS, FORM B, 2/e
TEN STEPS TO IMPROVING COLLEGE READING SKILLS, 3/e
IMPROVING READING COMPREHENSION SKILLS
TEN STEPS TO ADVANCING COLLEGE READING SKILLS, 2/e

Supplements Available for Most Books:

Instructor's Edition
Instructor's Manual, Test Bank, and Computer Guide
Set of Computer Disks (IBM or Macintosh)

Copyright © 1998 by Townsend Press, Inc.
Printed in the United States of America
ISBN 0-944210-74-0
9 8 7 6 5 4 3 2 1

Send book orders to:

Townsend Press
1038 Industrial Drive
West Berlin, New Jersey 08091

For even faster service, call us at our toll-free number:

1-800-772-6410

Or FAX your request to:

1-609-753-0649

ISBN 0-944210-74-0

Contents

Note: For ease of reference, the titles of the reading selections in each chapter are included.

UNIT FOUR

UNIT FIVE

APPENDIXES

Preface

The problem is all too familiar: *students just don't know enough words.* Reading, writing, and content teachers agree that many students' vocabularies are inadequate for the demands of courses. Weak vocabularies limit students' understanding of what they read and the clarity and depth of what they write.

The purpose of *Groundwork for a Better Vocabulary* and the other books in the Townsend Press vocabulary series is to provide a solid, workable answer to the vocabulary problem. In the course of 25 chapters, *Groundwork for a Better Vocabulary* teaches 250 important basic words. Here are the book's distinctive features:

1   **An intensive words-in-context approach.**   Studies show that students learn words best by reading and using them repeatedly in different contexts, not through rote memorization. The book gives students an intensive in-context experience by presenting each word in nine different settings. Each chapter takes students through a productive sequence of steps:

   • Students infer the meaning of each word by considering two sentences in which it appears and then choosing from multiple-choice options.

   • On the basis of their inferences, students identify each word's meaning in a matching test. They are then in a solid position to deepen their knowledge of a word.

   • Finally, they strengthen their understanding of a word by applying it in five different words-in-context passages, including sentence-completion activities and high-interest fill-in-the-blank passages.

   • Last, to lock in their mastery of the new words, students are asked to apply those words in a variety of speaking and writing situations.

   Each encounter with a word brings it closer to becoming part of the student's permanent word bank. *No comparable vocabulary book gives such sustained attention to the words-in-context approach.*

2   **Abundant practice.**   Along with extensive practice in each chapter, there are a crossword puzzle and a set of unit tests at the end of every five-chapter unit. The puzzle and tests reinforce students' knowledge of the words in each chapter. In addition, most chapters reuse several words from earlier chapters (such repeated words are marked with small circles, like this°), allowing for more reinforcement. Last, there are supplementary tests in the *Test Bank* and the computer disks that accompany the book. All this practice means that students learn in the surest possible way: by working closely and repeatedly with each word.

3 Controlled feedback. The opening activity in each chapter gives students three multiple-choice options to help them decide on the meaning of a given word. The multiple-choice options also help students to complete the matching test that is the second activity of each chapter. A limited answer key at the back of the book then provides answers for the third activity in the chapter. All these features enable students to take an active role in their own learning.

4 Focus on essential words. A good deal of time and research went into selecting the 250 words featured in the book. Word frequency lists were consulted, along with lists in a wide range of vocabulary books. In addition, the authors and editors each prepared their own lists. A computer was used to help in the consolidation of the many word lists. A long process of group discussion then led to final decisions about the words that would be most helpful for students on a basic reading level.

5 Appealing content. Dull practice materials work against learning. On the other hand, meaningful, lively, and at times even funny sentences and selections can spark students' attention and thus enhance their grasp of the material. For this reason, a great deal of effort was put into creating sentences and selections with both widespread appeal and solid context support. We have tried throughout to make the practice materials truly enjoyable for teachers and students alike. Look, for example, at the selections on page 16 that serve as the Final Check in Chapter 1.

6 Clear format. The book has been designed so that its very format contributes to the learning process. Each chapter consists of four two-page spreads. In the first two-page spread (the first such spread is on pages 10–11), students can easily refer to all ten words in context while working on the matching test, which provides a clear meaning for each word. The other two-page spreads allow students to see the words in a variety of contexts as they work through the fill-in activities.

7 Helpful supplements.

a A convenient *Instructor's Edition* is available at no charge to instructors using the book. It is identical to the student book except that it contains answers to all of the activities and tests.

b A combined *Instructor's Manual and Test Bank* is also offered at no charge to instructors who have adopted the book. This booklet contains a general vocabulary placement test as well as a pretest and a posttest for the book and for each of the five units in the text. It also includes teaching guidelines, suggested syllabi, an answer key, and an additional mastery test for each chapter.

c Finally, *computer disks* accompany the book. The disks provide additional tests for each vocabulary chapter and have a number of user- and instructor-friendly features: brief explanations of answers, a sound option, frequent mention of the user's first name, a running score at the bottom of the screen, a record-keeping file, and actual pronunciation of each word. The disks are free to adopters of 200 or more copies of the book.

To obtain a copy of any of the above materials, instructors may write to the Reading Editor, Townsend Press, Pavilions at Greentree—408, Marlton, NJ 08053. Alternatively, instructors may call our toll-free number: 1-800-772-6410.

8 Realistic pricing. As with the first edition, the goal has been to offer the highest possible quality at the best possible price. While *Groundwork for a Better Vocabulary* is comprehensive enough to serve as a primary text, its modest price also makes it an inexpensive supplement.

9 **One in a sequence of books.** *Vocabulary Basics* is the most fundamental book in the Townsend Press vocabulary series. It is followed by *Groundwork for a Better Vocabulary* (a slightly more advanced basic text)*, Building Vocabulary Skills* (an even more advanced basic text), *Improving Vocabulary Skills* (an intermediate text), and *Advancing Vocabulary Skills* (an advanced text). There are also short versions of the last three books. Suggested reading levels for the books are included in the *Instructor's Manual.* Together, the books create a strong vocabulary foundation that will make any student a better reader, writer, and thinker.

NOTES ON THE SECOND EDITION

Major changes have been made to the second edition of the book.

- It has been greatly expanded in size (it is now 8½ by 11 inches), in the number of vocabulary words (from 150 to 250), and in the number of activities (over twice as many).

- The activities now include "Related Words," a practice that will help students learn other common words related to the core words. In addition, a practice titled "Word Work" asks students to infer the meanings of words based on examples provided; in a trial run of the book, students found this activity to be especially entertaining. A third new page in the chapter offers practice on one of the following: (1) word parts, (2) synonyms and antonyms, or (3) analogies. And a new final page uses speaking and writing activities to further ensure students' ownership of the words in the chapter.

- Instead of an opening preview, each chapter now begins with a new format that uses a multiple-choice question to get students interacting immediately with each word. Teachers' and students' responses to this change have been extremely favorable.

- For ease of grading, including with the use of Scantron machines, answer spaces can now be marked either with the letter or number of the word or with the word itself.

- The print in the book has been enlarged, a pronunication key now appears on the inside front cover, a crossword puzzle has been added as a unit review, and the student introduction to the book has been expanded.

- Thanks to feedback from reviewers and users, many of the words in each chapter are now repeated in context in later chapters (and marked with small circles). Such repetition provides students with even more review and reinforcement.

ACKNOWLEDGMENTS

We are grateful for the enthusiastic comments provided by users of the Townsend Press vocabulary books over the life of the first edition. Particular thanks go to the following reviewers for their many helpful suggestions: Barbara Brennan Culhane, Nassau Community College; Carol Dietrick, Miami-Dade Community College; Larry Falxa, Ventura College; Jacquelin Hanselman, Hillsborough Community College; Shiela P. Kerr, Florida Community College at Jacksonville; John M. Kopec, Boston University; Belinda E. Smith, Wake Technical Community College; Daniel Snook, Montcalm Community College; and William Walcott, Montgomery College. We appreciate as well the editing help of John Langan and Paul Langan; the proofreading of Susan Gamer; and the remarkable design, editing, and proofreading skills of the indefatigable Janet M. Goldstein.

R. Kent Smith   *Beth Johnson*   *Carole Mohr*

To the Student

WHY VOCABULARY DEVELOPMENT COUNTS

You have probably often heard it said, "Building vocabulary is important." Maybe you've politely nodded in agreement and then forgotten the matter. But it would be fair for you to ask, "Why is a good vocabulary so important? Can you prove it?" Here are four convincing reasons.

1 Common sense tells you what many research studies have also shown: vocabulary is a basic part of understanding what you read. A word here and there may not stop you, but if there are too many words you don't know, comprehension will suffer. The content of textbooks is often difficult enough; you don't want to work as well on understanding the words which express that content.

2 Vocabulary is a major part of almost every standardized test, including reading achievement tests, college entrance exams, and armed forces and vocational placement tests. Test developers know that vocabulary is a key measure of both one's learning and one's ability to learn. It is for this reason that they include a separate vocabulary section as well as a reading comprehension section. The more words you know, then, the better you are likely to do on such important tests.

3 Studies have shown that students with strong vocabularies are more successful in school. And one widely known study found that a good vocabulary, more than anything else, was common to people enjoying successful careers. Words are, in fact, the tools not just of better reading, but of better writing, speaking, listening, and thinking as well. The more words you have at your command, the more effect you can have on the people around you.

4 In today's world, a good vocabulary counts more than ever. Far fewer people work on farms or in factories. Far more are in jobs that provide services or process information. More than ever, words are the tools of our trade: words we use in reading, writing, listening, and speaking. In addition, experts say that workers of tomorrow will be called on to change jobs and learn new skills at an ever-increasing pace. The keys to survival and success will be the abilities to read, write, speak, and learn in a quick and skillful way. A solid vocabulary is essential for all of these skills.

Clearly, there is powerful proof that building vocabulary is a key to success. The question then becomes "What is the best way of going about it?"

WORDS IN CONTEXT: THE KEY TO VOCABULARY DEVELOPMENT

Memorizing lists of words is a traditional method of vocabulary development. However, a person is likely to forget such memorized lists quickly. Studies show that to master a word, you must see and use it in various contexts—that is, different real-life sentences and paragraphs. By working actively and repeatedly with a word, you greatly increase the chance of really learning it.

The following activity will make clear how this book is organized and how it uses a words-in-context approach. Answer the questions or fill in the missing words in the spaces provided.

Inside Front Cover and Contents

Turn to the inside front cover.

- The inside front cover provides a _____*pronunciation guide*_____ that will help you pronounce all the vocabulary words in the book.

Now turn to the table of contents on pages v–vi.

- How many chapters are in the book? __*25*__

- Three short sections follow the last chapter. The first of these sections is a limited answer key, the second gives helpful information on using _____*the dictionary*_____, and the third is a list of the 250 words in the book.

Vocabulary Chapters

Turn to Chapter 1 on pages 10–17. This chapter, like all the others, consists of nine parts:

- The **first part** of the chapter, on pages 10–11, is titled _____*Ten Words in Context*_____.

    The left-hand column lists the ten words in the chapter. Under each **boldfaced** word is its _____*pronunciation*_____ (in parentheses). For example, the pronunciation of *challenge* is _____*chăl′ĭnj*_____. For a guide to pronunciation, see the inside front cover as well as "Dictionary Use" on pages 251–252.

    Below the pronunciation guide for each word is its part of speech. The part of speech shown for *challenge* is _____*noun*_____. The vocabulary words in this book are mostly nouns, adjectives, and verbs. **Nouns** are words used to name something—a person, place, thing, or idea. Familiar nouns include *boyfriend, city, hat,* and *truth.* **Adjectives** are words that describe nouns, as in the following word pairs: *former* boyfriend, *large* city, *red* hat, *whole* truth. All of the **verbs** in this book express an action of some sort. They tell what someone or something is doing. Common verbs include *read, drive, discover,* and *imagine.*

    To the right of each word are two sentences that will help you understand its meaning. In each sentence, the **context**—the words surrounding the boldfaced word—provides clues you can use to figure out the definition. There are four common types of context clues—examples, synonyms, antonyms, and the general sense of the sentence. Each is briefly described on the pages that follow.

Common Context Clues

1 Examples

A sentence may include examples that show what an unfamiliar word means. For instance, take a look at the following item from Chapter 2 for the word *category*:

> When I was in high school, I didn't seem to fit into any **category**. I wasn't an athlete, a scholar, or a rebel.

The second sentence gives three examples of *category*—being "an athlete, a scholar, or a rebel." To figure out what *category* means, think about those examples. What is the speaker saying he or she doesn't fit into? Look at the answer choices below, and in the space provided, write the letter of the answer you feel is correct.

  _c_ *Category* means   a. goal.   b. feeling.   c. group.

Since the speaker is talking about the types of groups in high school, you may have correctly guessed that answer *c* is the right choice.

2 Synonyms

Synonyms are words that mean the same or almost the same as another word. The words *joyful, happy*, and *pleased* are synonyms—they all mean about the same thing. A synonym serves as a context clue by telling the meaning of an unknown word that is nearby. For instance, the sentence below from Chapter 1 includes a synonym clue for the vocabulary word *peculiar*.

> My brother thinks my chip-and-dip sandwiches are **peculiar**, but I don't think they're as strange as the peanut-butter-and-tuna sandwiches he eats.

Rather than repeat *peculiar* in the second part of the sentence, the author used a synonym. Find that synonym, and then from the choices below, write in the letter of the meaning of *peculiar*.

  _b_ *Peculiar* means   a. attractive.   b. unusual.   c. innocent.

In the sentence from Chapter 1, *strange* is used as a synonym for *peculiar*. Since another word for *strange* is *unusual*, the answer is *b*.

3 Antonyms

Antonyms are words with opposite meanings. For example, *help* and *harm* are antonyms, as are *work* and *rest*. An antonym serves as a context clue by telling the opposite meaning of a nearby unknown word. The sentence below from Chapter 2 provides an antonym clue for the word *deliberate*.

> Manny's pushing me was quite **deliberate**; it wasn't accidental at all.

To underline the point, the author used an antonym of *deliberate*. Find the antonym, and use it to help you figure out what *deliberate* means. Then write in the letter of the meaning you choose.

  _c_ *Deliberate* means   a. easy.   b. fair.   c. planned.

The sentence suggests that *deliberate* pushing and *accidental* pushing are very different things. So we can guess that *deliberate* means the opposite of *accidental*. Another word that is the opposite of *accidental* is *planned*, so *c* is the correct answer—*deliberate* means "planned."

4 General Sense of the Sentence

Even when there is no example, synonym, or antonym clue in a sentence, you can still figure out the meaning of an unfamiliar word. For example, look at the sentence below from Chapter 1 for the word *surplus*.

> More and more restaurants are donating their **surplus** food to homeless people.

After thinking carefully about the context, you should be able to figure out what kind of food restaurants would be giving to homeless people. Write the letter of your choice.

   _b_ *Surplus* means   a. strange.   b. extra.   c. main.

From the general sense of the sentence from Chapter 1 plus your own common sense, you probably guessed that the restaurants are donating "extra" food. Answer *b* is correct.

By looking closely at the pair of sentences provided for each word, as well as the answer choices, you should be able to decide on the meaning of a word. As you figure out each meaning, you are working actively with the word. You are creating the groundwork you need to understand and to remember the word. Getting involved with the word and developing a feel for it, based upon its use in context, is the key to word mastery.

It is with good reason, then, that the directions at the top of page 10 tell you to use the context to figure out each word's _____*meaning*_____. Doing so deepens your sense of the word and prepares you for the next activity.

• The **second part** of the chapter, on page 11, is titled _____*Matching Words with Definitions*_____.

According to research, it is not enough to see a word in context. At a certain point, it is important to see the meaning of a word. The matching test provides that meaning, but it also makes you look for and think about that meaning. In other words, it continues the active learning that is your surest route to learning and remembering a word.

Note the caution that follows the test. Do not proceed any further until you are sure that you know the correct meaning of each word as used in context.

Keep in mind that a word may have more than one meaning. In fact, some words have quite a few meanings. (If you doubt it, try looking up in a dictionary, for example, the word *make* or *draw*.) In this book, you will focus on one common meaning for each vocabulary word. However, many of the words have additional meanings. For example, in Chapter 1, you will learn that *challenge* means "a test of one's abilities," as in the sentence "My new job is a real challenge." If you then look up *challenge* in the dictionary, you will discover that it has other meanings—for example, "a call to take part in a contest or fight," as in "Ted never turns down a challenge to play any kind of game." After you learn one common meaning of a word, you will find yourself gradually learning its other meanings in the course of your school and personal reading.

- The **third and fourth parts** of the chapter, on page 12, are titled _____*Check 1*_____ and _____*Check 2*_____.

  The first check consists of ten sentences that give you an opportunity to test your understanding of the ten words. After filling in the words, check your answers in the limited key at the back of the book. (Be sure to use the answer key as a learning tool only. Doing so will help you to master the words and to prepare for the remaining activities and the unit tests, for which answers are not provided.) The second check on page 12 then gives you another chance to deepen your understanding of the words.

- The **fifth part** of the chapter, on page 13, is titled _____*Related Words*_____. Here you will have a chance to learn words that are related to many of the ten main words in the chapter. Look on page 13, for example, and write down the three words that are related to *dependent* (one of the words in the chapter): _____*dependence*_____   _____*independent*_____   _____*dependable*_____.

- The **sixth part** of the chapter, on page 14, is titled _____*Word Work*_____. The practices on this page will make the meanings of the words come more alive through the use of vivid examples. Chances are you may find this activity to be one of the most enjoyable in the book.

- The **seventh part** of the chapter, on page 15, offers practice in one of three areas: word parts, synonyms and antonyms, or analogies. Each is explained below.

Word Parts, Synonyms-Antonyms, and Analogies

Word Parts

The first and third chapters in each unit contain word-part practices.

Word parts are building blocks used in many English words. Learning word parts can help you to spell and pronounce words, unlock the meanings of unfamiliar words, and remember new words.

This book covers twenty word parts. You will learn two types: prefixes and suffixes. A **prefix** is a word part that is found at the beginning of words. When written separately, a prefix is followed by a hyphen to show that something follows it. For example, the prefix *sur* is written like this: *sur-*. *Sur-* can mean "beyond" or "additional," as in *surpass* (to go beyond) and *surcharge* (an additional charge).

A **suffix** is a word part that is found at the end of words. To show that something always comes before a suffix, a hyphen is placed at the beginning. For instance, the suffix *ly* is written like this: *-ly*. One common meaning of *-ly* is "in a certain way," as in the words *gratefully* (in a grateful way) and *angrily* (in an angry way).

Each word-part practice begins with the meaning of a word part and examples. Fill-in items then help you remember and recognize the word parts. To see what these items are like, try the one below from Chapter 1 for the word part *sur.* On the answer line, write the word that best completes the sentence.

surcharge   surface   surpass   surplus   surtax

_____*surtax*_____   In addition to the usual taxes, people who earn over a certain amount will have to pay a ___.

The sentence suggests that people who earn over a certain amount will have to pay an additional tax. Since you now know that *sur-* can mean "additional," you probably wrote the correct word on the line: *surtax* (an additional tax).

(There is a third type of word part—a root. You will not be working with roots in this book. Roots are word parts that carry the basic meanings of words. For example, one common root is *vis*, which means "to see," as in the words *visit* and *vision*.)

Synonyms and Antonyms

The second and fourth chapters in each unit contain synonym-antonym practices. You have already learned in this introduction that a **synonym** is a word that means the same or almost the same as another word and that an **antonym** is a word that means the opposite of another word. These practices will deepen your understanding of words by getting you to think about other words with the same or opposite meanings.

To see what the synonym questions are like, do the example below. Write the letter of the word that most nearly means the same as the first word, *hard*.

___b___ **hard**

    a. new   b. difficult

    c. far   d. bad

Since *difficult* is another way of saying *hard,* the correct answer is *b*. Now, to see what the antonym questions are like, do the example item below. Write in the letter of the word that most nearly means the opposite of *kind*.

___d___ **kind**

    a. silly   b. busy

    c. young   d. cruel

The opposite of *kind* is *cruel,* so *d* is the correct answer.

Analogies

The last chapter in each unit contains an analogy practice, yet another way to deepen your understanding of words. An **analogy** is a similarity between two things that are otherwise different. Doing an analogy question is a two-step process. First you have to figure out the relationship in a pair of words. Those words are written like this:

LEAF : TREE

What is the relationship between the two words above? The answer can be stated like this: A leaf is a part of a tree.

Next, you must look for a similar relationship in a second pair of words. Here is how a complete analogy question looks:

LEAF : TREE ::

    a. pond : river   b. foot : shoe

    c. page : book   d. beach : sky

And here is how the question can be read:

_c_ LEAF is to TREE as

    a. *pond* is to *river.*   b. *foot* is to *shoe.*

    c. *page* is to *book.*   d. *beach* is to *sky.*

To answer the question, you have to decide which of the four choices has a relationship similar to the first one. Check your answer by seeing if it fits in the same wording as you used to show the relationship between *leaf* and *tree:* A ___ is part of a ___. Which answer do you choose?

The correct answer is *c.* Just as a *leaf* is part of a *tree,* a *page* is part of a *book.* On the other hand, a *pond* is not part of a *river,* nor is a *foot* part of a *shoe,* nor is a *beach* part of the *sky.*

We can state the complete analogy this way: *Leaf* is to *tree* as *page* is to *book.*

Here's another another analogy question to try. Begin by figuring out the relationship between the first two words.

_d_ COWARD : HERO ::

    a. soldier : military   b. infant : baby

    c. actor : famous   d. boss : worker

Coward and *hero* are opposite types of people. So you need to look at the other four pairs to see which has a similar relationship. When you think you have found the answer, check to see that the two words you chose can be compared in the same way as *coward* and *hero:* ___ and ___ are opposite types of people.

In this case, the correct answer is *d*; *boss* and *worker* are opposite kinds of people. (In other words, *coward* is to *hero* as *boss* is to *worker.*)

By now you can see that there are basically two steps to doing analogy items:

1) Find out the relationship of the first two words.
2) Find the answer that expresses the same type of relationship as the first two words have.

Now try one more analogy question on your own. Write the letter of the answer you choose in the space provided.

_a_ SWING : BAT ::

    a. drive : car   b. run : broom

    c. catch : bat   d. fly : butterfly

If you chose answer *a,* you were right. *Swing* is what we do with a *bat,* and *drive* is what we do with a *car.*

- The **eighth part** of the chapter, on page 16, is titled _____*Final Check*_____. Here you have the context of two interesting passages in which to practice applying the words. The first two such passages, on page 16, are titled _____*"Johnny Appleseed"*_____ and _____*"The Lovable Leech?"*_____.

- The **final part** of the chapter, on page 17, is made up of two sections: _____*Questions for*_____ _____*Discussion*_____ and _____*Ideas for Writing*_____. To ensure mastery and "ownership" of the words, you are given a chance to use them in a series of specific speaking and writing situations.

FINAL NOTES

1   You now know, in a nutshell, how to proceed with the words in each chapter. Make sure that you do each page very carefully. Remember that as you work through the activities, you are learning the words.

How many times in all will you use each word? If you look, you'll see that each chapter gives you the opportunity to work with each word at least nine times. Each time that you work with a word adds to the likelihood that the word will become part of your active vocabulary. You will have further opportunities to use the word in the crossword puzzle and tests that end each unit and on the computer disks that are available with the book.

In addition, many of the words are repeated in context in later chapters of the book. Such repeated words are marked with small circles, like this°. For example, what word from Chapter 1 is repeated in the second Final Check passage on page 24 of Chapter 2? _____*challenge*_____

2   At the bottom of the last page of each chapter is a "Check Your Performance" box where you can enter your score for five of the practices. Note that these scores should also be entered into the vocabulary performance chart located _____*on the inside back cover*_____.

To get your score, take 10% off for each item wrong. For example, 0 wrong = 100%, 1 wrong = 90%, 2 wrong = 80%, 3 wrong = 70%, 4 wrong = 60%, and so on.

3   The facts are in. A strong vocabulary is a source of power. Words can make you a better reader, writer, speaker, thinker, and learner. They can dramatically increase your chances of success in school and in your job.

But words will not come without effort. They must be learned in a program of regular study. If you commit yourself to learning words, and you work actively and honestly with the chapters in this book, you will not only enrich your vocabulary—you will enrich your life as well.

Unit One

Chapter 1

challenge	principal
dependent	solitary
fertile	suitable
peculiar	surplus
preference	transform

Chapter 2

analyze	deliberate
attitude	excessive
category	fragile
contrast	frustration
critical	indicate

Chapter 3

accompany	preserve
desperate	pursue
determine	rejection
dispose of	restore
evident	scarce

Chapter 4

abundant	distinct
betray	exaggerate
comparison	inhabit
demonstrate	neutral
dispute	reduction

Chapter 5

aggravate	intentional
cease	interference
coincide	obnoxious
considerable	unstable
humane	utilize

challenge	principal
dependent	solitary
fertile	suitable
peculiar	surplus
preference	transform

Ten Words in Context

In the space provided, write the letter of the meaning closest to that of each **boldfaced** word. Use the context of the sentences to help you figure out each word's meaning.

1 **challenge**
(chăl′ĭnj)
– *noun*

- Ginny enjoys rock climbing. It's a difficult **challenge**, but she feels very proud after making a climb.
- When the baby sitter arrived, he stared at the four active little boys he was expected to watch. "This will be quite a **challenge**," he sighed.

_c_ *Challenge* means   a. reason.   b. something boring.   c. something requiring effort.

2 **dependent**
(dĭ-pĕn′dənt)
– *adjective*

- Some animals can take care of themselves as soon as they are born, but human babies are **dependent** upon their parents for years.
- Tyrone's father said to him, "You are still much too **dependent** on me. It's about time you got a job and supported yourself."

_a_ *Dependent* means   a. relying.   b. leading.   c. puzzling.

3 **fertile**
(fûr′tl)
– *adjective*

- Because its soil is so **fertile**, Iowa has many farms.
- Our daughter's pet hamsters were so **fertile** that we ended up selling many baby hamsters back to the pet store.

_c_ *Fertile* means   a. common.   b. large.   c. able to produce.

4 **peculiar**
(pĭ-kyool′yər)
– *adjective*

- Jack didn't know why people were giving him **peculiar** looks until he realized there was a large hole in his pants.
- My brother thinks my chip-and-dip sandwiches are **peculiar**, but I don't think they're as strange as the peanut-butter-and-tuna sandwiches he eats.

_b_ *Peculiar* means   a. attractive.   b. unusual.   c. innocent.

5 **preference**
(prĕf′ər-əns)
– *noun*

- There are Chinese, Italian, and Indian restaurants nearby. What's your **preference** for dinner tonight?
- What is your color **preference** for the living room? Do you like cool blues and greens or warm oranges and yellows?

_a_ *Preference* means   a. choice.   b. skill.   c. effect.

6 **principal**
(prĭn′sə-pəl)
– *adjective*

- The **principal** cause of most success is hard work, not luck or talent.
- The queen of England has no real power. The **principal** leader of England is the prime minister.

_c_ *Principal* means   a. most recent.   b. false.   c. chief.

7 solitary
(sŏl′ĭ-tĕr′ē)
– *adjective*

- After taking a **solitary** vacation in my cabin for two weeks, I was ready to return to the company of other humans.
- In the mood to be by herself, Melba looked forward to spending the evening in such **solitary** activities as reading and taking a long bubble bath.

_c_ *Solitary* means
   a. friendly.
   b. proper.
   c. done alone.

8 suitable
(soo′tə-bəl)
– *adjective*

- Sharon asked her mother if her blue dress was **suitable** for a funeral, or if she had to wear black.
- Because the prices and food are so good, we decided that the Red Lion Inn would be **suitable** for our bowling banquet.

_a_ *Suitable* means
   a. right.
   b. too expensive.
   c. important.

9 surplus
(sûr′plŭs)
– *adjective*

- More and more restaurants are donating their **surplus** food to homeless people.
- The Barkleys had more kitchen supplies than they needed, so they gave their **surplus** pots and pans to their son, who had just gotten his own apartment.

_b_ *Surplus* means
   a. strange.
   b. extra.
   c. main.

10 transform
(trăns-fôrm′)
– *verb*

- I plan to **transform** this messy attic into an attractive office.
- The magician seemed to **transform** a chicken's egg into an egg the size of a basketball.

_c_ *Transform* means
   a. to accept.
   b. to repeat.
   c. to change.

Matching Words with Definitions

Following are definitions of the ten words. **Print** each word next to its definition. If you look closely at each word in context, you will be able to figure out its meaning.

1. _fertile_   Producing or able to produce much fruit, large crops, or many children
2. _principal_   Most important; main; leading
3. _dependent_   Relying on others for aid or support
4. _surplus_   Extra; more than what is used or needed
5. _peculiar_   Odd; strange
6. _challenge_   A test of one's abilities; anything that calls for a special effort
7. _solitary_   Happening or done alone
8. _transform_   To change in form or appearance
9. _suitable_   Right for a certain purpose; proper; fitting
10. _preference_   Choice; first choice; something preferred

CAUTION: Do not go any further until you are sure the above answers are correct. Then you can use the definitions to help you in the following practices. Your goal is eventually to know the words well enough so that you don't need to check the definitions at all.

➤ *Check 1*

Using the answer line, complete each item below with the correct word from the box.

| a. **challenge** | b. **dependent** | c. **fertile** | d. **peculiar** | e. **preference** |
| f. **principal** | g. **solitary** | h. **suitable** | i. **surplus** | j. **transform** |

_____*transform*_____ 1. Just one can of spinach ___s Popeye from a weakling into a hero.

_____*fertile*_____ 2. If land is always planted with the same crop, it will become less ___. Changing crops from one year to the next keeps the soil rich.

_____*preference*_____ 3. Although my ___ is for a daytime job, I will work at night if necessary.

_____*surplus*_____ 4. Max and Helen had more clothes than they needed, so they donated their ___ clothes to a thrift store.

_____*peculiar*_____ 5. I can't imagine what that ___ odor is from—it's like a mixture of burning tires and freshly cut grass.

_____*solitary*_____ 6. A man lived by himself in a cave most of his life—yes, his was a ___ life.

_____*principal*_____ 7. I know you have reasons for quitting school. What's the ___ reason?

_____*challenge*_____ 8. Baby-sitting with a lot of children isn't easy—it's a ___.

_____*suitable*_____ 9. My neighbors are looking for ___ homes for the eight puppies their collie gave birth to. They want homes where the pups will be well cared for.

_____*dependent*_____ 10. Sometimes Estela felt like giving up, but she knew she couldn't because she had three young children and an elderly mother who were ___ on her.

NOTE: Now check your answers to these questions by turning to page 249. Going over the answers carefully will help you prepare for the remaining practices, for which answers are not given.

➤ *Check 2*

Using the answer lines, complete each item below with **two** words from the box.

_____*preference*_____
_____*solitary*_____ 1–2. When I'm not feeling well, my ___ is to have lots of company, but when my husband is sick, he prefers to be ___.

_____*transform*_____
_____*principal*_____ 3–4. In the last year, our neighbors have ___ed their unattractive yard into something beautiful. The ___ change they made was to put in some lovely flowering plants; all of the other changes were small ones.

_____*suitable*_____
_____*dependent*_____ 5–6. Ben is happy to live at home, pay no rent, and use his mother's car, but I don't think it's ___ for a grown man to be so ___ on his parents.

_____*fertile*_____
_____*challenge*_____ 7–8. Our tomato plants are almost too ___. It is a ___ to use or give away all the tomatoes before they spoil.

_____*peculiar*_____
_____*surplus*_____ 9–10. We had so many tomatoes that we ended up inventing some ___ recipes to use up the ___ fruit; perhaps the strangest was "Peanut Butter Tomato Pie."

➤ *Related Words*

Once you learn a new word, you can more easily understand many related words. Below are ten words related to the core words of this chapter. Use their definitions to help you write in the word that best completes each item.

a. **dependence**, *noun*	The state of relying on others for help or support
b. **independent**, *adjective*	Not needing help from others
c. **preferable**, *adjective*	Deserving to be chosen over another; more desirable
d. **suit**, *verb*	To be right for; fit
e. **transformation**, *noun*	A striking change

_____*suit*_____   1. A part-time job in the evenings would ___ my school schedule perfectly.

_____*dependence*_____   2. A baby's ___ on its parents is complete; it needs them to do everything for it.

_____*independent*_____   3. By the age of 2, most children have moments of wanting to be ___, and they will push their parents away, saying, "Me do it!"

_____*preferable*_____   4. There are two hotels in town—the Burke and the Oakwood Towers—but in my opinion, the Burke is ___ because it is quieter and has a swimming pool.

_____*transformation*_____   5. At my ten-year high-school reunion, I saw several people who had gone through an amazing ___ —one quiet, shy girl had become an outgoing beauty, and one of the wildest boys in the class had become a priest.

f. **challenging**, *adjective*	Difficult; requiring special effort
g. **dependable**, *adjective*	Able to be trusted or relied upon
h. **fertilize**, *verb*	To make soil richer by adding material to it
i. **infertile**, *adjective*	Unable to produce children
j. **peculiarity**, *noun*	Something odd or strange

_____*fertilize*_____   6. Many gardeners save old food scraps and grass clippings and use them to ___ the garden.

_____*peculiarity*_____   7. Myrna is a nice person, but she does have one ___: she won't eat anything that she hasn't prepared herself.

_____*challenging*_____   8. My beginning math course was easy enough, but I found algebra much more ___.

_____*dependable*_____   9. Jaime is the most ___ friend I have—he's always there when I need him.

_____*infertile*_____   10. When my sister and her husband realized they were ___, they decided to adopt three children who were brothers and sisters.

➤ *Word Work*

A. In the space provided, write the letter of the choice that best completes each item.

_c_ 1. A boy who is too **dependent** on his friends
    a. pays little attention to them.
    b. is too bossy with them.
    c. won't make any decisions without them.

_b_ 2. Someone who enjoys **solitary** work would probably like a job
    a. selling a product that he or she believed in.
    b. working in a one-person office, rarely seeing other people.
    c. meeting people and answering their questions.

_c_ 3. We knew for sure that our dog was **fertile** when she
    a. bit the mailman.
    b. did very well in training class.
    c. had puppies.

_a_ 4. Most people would think it was **peculiar** if a teacher
    a. came into class dressed as Bozo the Clown.
    b. punished a student for cheating.
    c. dropped a piece of chalk on the floor.

_a_ 5. If a friend came to you and sadly said, "I just lost my job," what would be the most **suitable** response for you to make?
    a. "That's awful. I'm really sorry."
    b. "That's nothing; wait until you hear about my day."
    c. "Can you lend me some money?"

B. In the space provided, write the letter of the word that most closely relates to the situation in each item.

_a_ 6. I like Pepsi more than I like Coca-Cola.

    a. preference   b. fertile   c. transform

_b_ 7. The long-jumper is going to try to beat her own best record.

    a. dependent   b. challenge   c. surplus

_c_ 8. Cream is the main ingredient in butter.

    a. challenge   b. dependent   c. principal

_a_ 9. These pieces of cloth were left over after I made myself a shirt.

    a. surplus   b. fertile   c. preference

_c_ 10. Cinderella's fairy godmother will change her rags into a beautiful gown, a pumpkin into a carriage, and mice into horses.

    a. solitary   b. principal   c. transform

➤ *Word Parts*

A. The prefix *trans-* can mean "across" or "change to."

Examples: *transport* — to take from one place across to another
translate — to change from one language to another

On each answer line, write the word from the box that best completes the item.

a. **transatlantic**	b. **transform**	c. **translate**
d. **transplant**	e. **transportation**	

translate	1. Trina's job is to ___ business letters from Spanish into English.
transform	2. You can ___ a room simply by painting it a different color.
transplant	3. The doctor ___ed one of Mark's kidneys into his sister.
transportation	4. Since my grandmother doesn't drive and there is no public ___ in her area, she depends on me to take her shopping.
transatlantic	5. The ship will cross the Atlantic Ocean next week. The ship's ___ trip begins in New York City and ends in England.

B. The prefix *sur-* means "over," "upon," beyond," or "additional."

Examples: *surpass* — to go beyond
surtax — an additional tax

On each answer line, write the word from the box that best completes the item.

f. **surcharge**	g. **surface**	h. **surpass**
i. **surplus**	j. **surtax**	

surface	6. I like to protect and shine the ___s of my wooden tables with wax.
surplus	7. My garden produced so much zucchini that I gave big bagfuls of ___ squash to all of my neighbors.
surtax	8. In addition to the usual taxes, people who earn over a certain amount will have to pay a ___.
surpass	9. The drive to raise money for the children's hospital was so successful that the money raised ___ed the goal that was set.
surcharge	10. Because we brought so much luggage on our trip, we had to pay the airline a ___.

➤ *Final Check*

Read the passages carefully. Then fill in each blank with the word that best fits the context.

A. Johnny Appleseed

a. **fertile**	b. **peculiar**	c. **solitary**
d. **surplus**	e. **transform**	

John Chapman, who is known to the world as Johnny Appleseed, must have been a strange sight. His (1)_____*peculiar*_____ clothing included cloth sacks for shirts and a tin pot for a hat.

In western Pennsylvania, where Johnny lived, many people grew apples. But there weren't any apples in the lands further west, which were just then being cleared and settled. So Johnny wandered among his neighbors, asking them for their (2)_____*surplus*_____ apple seeds. During his lifetime, Johnny walked thousands of miles, making many long trips from his home to the valleys of Ohio and Indiana. Everywhere he went, he scattered seeds. Many of those seeds fell on (3)_____*fertile*_____ ground and grew into strong trees.

Johnny often wandered through areas where Native Americans fought with the white settlers. Since Johnny was a loner, his travels were always (4)_____*solitary*_____, and he carried no weapon—yet he was never harmed. The Indians believed that the Great Spirit especially loved people like Johnny, who was not like other people. In his own quiet way he (5)_____*transform*_____ed the American wilderness, filling it with thousands of flowering, fruit-filled trees.

B. The Lovable Leech?

f. **challenge**	g. **dependent**	h. **preference**
i. **principal**	j. **suitable**	

As highly developed as we human beings like to think we are, the fact is that we are still (6)_____*dependent*_____ upon many lower forms of life. The (7)_____*principal*_____ way that this is true, of course, is our use of meat to eat and skins to wear. But there are other ways, sometimes strange ways, that we rely on other creatures. Take, for example, the leech. It would be a (8)_____*challenge*_____ for anyone to really like a leech. It is a disgusting-looking worm that lives in freshwater ponds and streams. As many people have discovered when they've gone swimming, a leech's (9)_____*preference*_____ for dinner is human blood. It loves to attach itself to a swimmer's foot and sink in its teeth—as many as three hundred of them. The bite does not cause any pain. But the leech can suck out eight times its own weight in blood. "How disgusting," you are probably thinking. But listen to this. In recent years, doctors have found that leeches are the most (10)_____*suitable*_____ way to remove extra blood from a person after an injury, especially around the eyes. Yes, leeches are honored guests in many modern hospitals.

➤ *Questions for Discussion*

1. Everyone has some personal habits that might seem odd to others. For instance, one person might put all her books in alphabetical order, while another might constantly jingle the change in his pocket. Describe something that you do or that someone you know does which might seem **peculiar** to other people.

2. If you could **transform** one room in your home, which one would it be and how would you change it?

3. Think of a friend of yours and decide, from what you know of that person, what a really **suitable** job would be for him or her. Take into account the person's talents, likes, and dislikes.

4. Who is a person you feel is **dependent** upon you in some way? That is, who relies on your physical or emotional assistance? Describe how that person relies on you.

5. Some people feel strongly that they should have their dogs and cats "fixed" so that they are no longer **fertile**. Others think they should let their pets have babies at least once, or even many times. What is your opinion about letting pets reproduce?

➤ *Ideas for Writing*

1. Write about a **challenge** that you have faced and dealt with successfully. What was the **principal** reason that this challenge was difficult for you? How did you go about dealing with it?

2. When you are feeling blue or depressed, which is your **preference**: to cheer yourself up by being with people or to be **solitary**? In other words, at such a time do you need the company of others or quiet time alone? Tell about a time that makes your preference clear.

Check Your Performance			CHAPTER 1
Activity	*Number Right*	*Points*	*Total*
Check 2	_____	× 10 =	_____
Related Words	_____	× 10 =	_____
Word Work	_____	× 10 =	_____
Word Parts	_____	× 10 =	_____
Final Check	_____	× 10 =	_____

Enter your scores above and in the vocabulary performance chart on the inside back cover of the book.

analyze	deliberate
attitude	excessive
category	fragile
contrast	frustration
critical	indicate

Ten Words in Context

In the space provided, write the letter of the meaning closest to that of each **boldfaced** word. Use the context of the sentences to help you figure out each word's meaning.

1 **analyze**
(ăn′ə-līz)
– *verb*

- Someone in the laboratory will **analyze** the blood sample to see if the patient has an illness.
- Before we can suggest solutions, we must carefully **analyze** the city's money problems.

_b_ *Analyze* means   a. to plan.   b. to study.   c. to create.

2 **attitude**
(ăt′ĭ-to͞od′)
– *noun*

- Athletes need to have a positive **attitude**. Even if they have lost the previous game, they need to come into the next one ready to win.
- Rudy came to the party with a poor **attitude**; he was sure that he'd be bored and wouldn't have any fun.

_c_ *Attitude* means   a. set of rules.   b. background.   c. way of thinking.

3 **category**
(kăt′ə-gôr′ē)
– *noun*

- When I was in high school, I didn't seem to fit into any **category**. I wasn't an athlete, a scholar, or a rebel.
- The small store had many jazz and rock recordings, but not much in the **category** of country music.

_c_ *Category* means   a. goal.   b. feeling.   c. group.

4 **contrast**
(kən′trăst′)
– *noun*

- Everyone is surprised to see that there's a **contrast** between Peggy's eyes—one eye is brown, and the other is green.
- I was struck by the **contrast** between the fancy cars and houses west of Main Street and the poor neighborhoods to the east.

_c_ *Contrast* means   a. disappointment.   b. place.   c. difference.

5 **critical**
(krĭt′ĭ-kəl)
– *adjective*

- My boss can be very **critical** of me when I don't do my best work, but she's also quick to praise me when I do well.
- My aunt is **critical** of her neighbors. She calls them lazy because their house needs painting and their yard is overgrown with weeds.

_a_ *Critical* means   a. fault-finding.   b. jealous.   c. proud.

6 **deliberate**
(dĭ-lĭb′ər-ĭt)
– *adjective*

- Manny's pushing me was quite **deliberate**; it wasn't accidental at all.
- I'm sure our neighbor knew that the tall tree he was planting would keep the sun from our flowers. It was a **deliberate** dirty trick.

_c_ *Deliberate* means   a. easy.   b. fair.   c. planned.

7 excessive
(ĭk-sĕs′ĭv)
– *adjective*

- **Excessive** speed caused the accident; the truck driver was going nearly eighty miles an hour.
- Mrs. Hill's concern about her little boy's health is **excessive**. She rushes him to the doctor every time he gets the sniffles or scrapes his knee.

a *Excessive* means   a. overly great.   b. off and on.   c. normal.

8 fragile
(frăj′əl)
– *adjective*

- The lamp is **fragile**, so when you pack it, please put it in a deep box with plenty of newspaper around it.
- When our daughter was little, we kept our **fragile** dishes and glasses out of her reach. We knew she would break them.

c *Fragile* means   a. broken.   b. strong.   c. breakable.

9 frustration
(frŭs-trā′shən)
– *noun*

- Trying to learn to roller-blade, I fell down twenty times and then crashed into a wall. Feeling more **frustration** than pain, I finally gave up.
- Elaine felt great **frustration** when she failed her driving test for the third time.

b *Frustration* means   a. relief.   b. discouragement.   c. pleasure.

10 indicate
(ĭn′də-kāt′)
– *verb*

- Jeff's frown seemed to **indicate** that he was unhappy with our plan.
- The parking-lot attendant pointed to **indicate** that I should drive the car all the way up to the fence.

b *Indicate* means   a. to hide.   b. to show.   c. to plan.

Matching Words with Definitions

Following are definitions of the ten words. **Print** each word next to its definition. If you look closely at each word in context, you will be able to figure out its meaning.

1. _____*frustration*_____   A feeling of anger and helplessness that comes from bad luck, defeat, or failure; disappointment

2. _____*attitude*_____   A point of view; state of mind; way of thinking or feeling

3. _____*category*_____   A group of people or things having something in common; type

4. _____*excessive*_____   Too much; more than is reasonable

5. _____*deliberate*_____   Done on purpose; carefully planned

6. _____*contrast*_____   An obvious difference

7. _____*critical*_____   Disapproving; tending to find fault

8. _____*fragile*_____   Easily broken or damaged

9. _____*analyze*_____   To examine carefully; study closely

10. _____*indicate*_____   To show; serve as a sign or signal

CAUTION: Do not go any further until you are sure the above answers are correct. Then you can use the definitions to help you in the following practices. Your goal is eventually to know the words well enough so that you don't need to check the definitions at all.

➤ *Check 1*

Using the answer line, complete each item below with the correct word from the box.

a. **analyze**	b. **attitude**	c. **category**	d. **contrast**	e. **critical**
f. **deliberate**	g. **excessive**	h. **fragile**	i. **frustration**	j. **indicate**

frustration   1. To avoid the ___ of failing the driving test again, Elaine has decided to take driving lessons.

deliberate   2. A planned action is ___.

Excessive   3. ___ eating over the holidays led to my gaining three pounds.

indicate   4. A road sign with a picture of a leaping deer ___s that deer often cross the road at that spot.

attitude   5. After losing every game last season, the soccer players began training this year with a poor ___. If they don't transform° their outlook, they will have another losing season.

fragile   6. Something that is ___ can be easily damaged.

category   7. Which ___ of movie do you prefer, comedy or action-adventure?

analyze   8. When Maggie ___d her reasons for wanting to marry Joe, she realized that they were not good ones.

critical   9. Many teenagers feel their parents are too ___ of their clothing, music, and friends.

contrast   10. I was surprised by the ___ between kind, gentle Bill and his impatient, bad-tempered brother.

NOTE: Now check your answers to these questions by turning to page 249. Going over the answers carefully will help you prepare for the remaining practices, for which answers are not given.

➤ *Check 2*

Using the answer lines, complete each item below with **two** words from the box.

contrast
category   1–2. There is a large ___ between things that fit in the ___ of junk food and those foods needed for basic nutrition.

attitude
critical   3–4. When a child is learning to play a musical instrument, parents should have an encouraging ___. Rather than being ___ of the child, parents should find things to praise.

deliberate
fragile   5–6. When we broke three glasses while washing the dishes, it wasn't ___. They were just too ___.

frustration
excessive   7–8. Most people can deal with some ___, but if discouragement becomes ___, it can actually cause illness.

analyze
indicate   9–10. When we ___ the citywide election returns, they will ___ how each neighborhood voted.

➤ *Related Words*

Once you learn a new word, you can more easily understand many related words. Below are ten words related to the core words of this chapter. Use their definitions to help you write in the word that best completes each item.

a. **analysis**, *noun*	A careful study of something, especially by looking at its parts
b. **contrasting**, *adjective*	Showing a noticeable difference
c. **deliberately**, *adverb*	Purposely
d. **excess**, *noun*	An amount that is greater than needed
e. **indication**, *noun*	A sign of something

indication _____ 1. A fever is one ___ of illness. Headache and an upset stomach are other signs of being sick.

deliberately _____ 2. No matter how many times Mike says it was an accident, I believe he ___ tried to knock me down.

excess _____ 3. Our garden is growing more vegetables than our family can eat, so we're giving the ___ to neighbors.

analysis _____ 4. The laboratory's ___ of the blood sample showed that the patient was quite healthy.

contrasting _____ 5. We painted our living room in ___ colors—one wall is pale yellow and the others are dark green.

f. **categorize**, *verb*	To put into groups
g. **criticism**, *noun*	Comments about faults
h. **excessively**, *adverb*	To a point that goes beyond what is reasonable or wise
i. **frustrated**, *adjective*	Feeling discouragement
j. **uncritical**, *adjective*	Accepting of faults

frustrated _____ 6. When the candy machine didn't return my change, I was so ___ that I kicked it.

categorize _____ 7. My parents ___ their books by subject—mysteries, health, humor, and so on.

criticism _____ 8. My instructor's ___ of my paper was tough, but helpful. In addition to pointing out the paper's faults, he suggested ways to correct them.

uncritical _____ 9. I'm completely ___ when it comes to pizza. Frozen or fresh-baked, crisp or soggy, thick crust or thin—I love it all.

excessively _____ 10. Even though her son is now in college, Mrs. Hill is still ___ concerned about him. She calls him every day to be sure he's eating right and getting enough sleep.

➢ *Word Work*

A. In the space provided, write the letter of the choice that best completes each item.

___c___ 1. A piano teacher who was very **critical** of the child's playing would

    a. not pay attention.   b. praise the child.   c. point out every mistake.

___a___ 2. When the boss advised Jim to improve his **attitude**, he meant that Jim should

    a. have a better   b. be neater.   c. speed up his typing.
       outlook about work.

___c___ 3. If a rash **indicates** an allergy, the rash

    a. has nothing to do   b. causes the allergy.   c. is a sign of the allergy.
       with the allergy.

___a___ 4. My grandmother's lace wedding veil is too **fragile** for me to wear at my own wedding. The veil

    a. might get torn.   b. is too old-fashioned.   c. is stained.

___b___ 5. There is a big **contrast** in the twins' personalities. Their personalities

    a. are very much alike.   b. are very different.   c. aren't very pleasant.

B. In the space provided, write the letter of the word that most closely relates to the situation in each item.

___b___ 6. The fire that destroyed the store was no accident—someone set it on purpose.

    a. category   b. deliberate   c. uncritical

___a___ 7. Did the murdered man's coffee contain poison? The police laboratory will examine a sample of the coffee to find out.

    a. analyze   b. contrast   c. attitude

___b___ 8. When the swimming class was divided into sections, I was put with the "beginners."

    a. excessive   b. category   c. fragile

___c___ 9. The little girl can't get her snow boots off. She pulls and tugs, pulls and tugs, and finally bursts into tears.

    a. deliberate   b. contrast   c. frustration

___b___ 10. The servings at the restaurant are much too large. Plates are heaped with more food than anyone could eat.

    a. indicate   b. excessive   c. fragile

➤ *Synonyms and Antonyms*

A. Synonyms. Write the letter of the word or phrase that most nearly means the **same** as each boldfaced word.

_b_   1. **analyze**

    a. remember   b. examine
    c. find fault with   d. use

_b_   2. **attitude**

    a. height   b. outlook
    c. knowledge   d. skill

_a_   3. **category**

    a. group   b. purpose
    c. reaction   d. problem

_d_   4. **critical**

    a. absent   b. frightened
    c. nervous   d. disapproving

_c_   5. **indicate**

    a. plan   b. conceal
    c. show   d. disappoint

B. Antonyms. Write the letter of the word or phrase that most nearly means the **opposite** of each boldfaced word.

_d_   6. **contrast**

    a. difference   b. environment
    c. enjoyment   d. sameness

_a_   7. **deliberate**

    a. accidental   b. harmful
    c. helpful   d. fortunate

_b_   8. **excessive**

    a. not real   b. not enough
    c. unexpected   d. required

_b_   9. **fragile**

    a. damaged   b. unbreakable
    c. unnecessary   d. beautiful

_c_ 10. **frustration**

    a. showing ignorance   b. feeling hatred
    c. being satisfied   d. expressing surprise

➤ *Final Check*

Read the passages carefully. Then fill in each blank with the word that best fits the context.

A. Finding Fault—And What to Do About It

a. **attitude**	b. **category**	c. **critical**
d. **excessive**	e. **frustration**	

Are you one of those people who are constantly finding fault? Are you very (1)_____*critical*_____ of everyone else's mistakes? If the washing machine or the stereo breaks down, is your reaction (2)_____*excessive*_____ anger and (3)_____*frustration*_____? If so, beware! Too much bad temper and discouragement could be harming your health. Scientists say that faultfinders and those who are often angry actually seem to have more heart attacks. So if you fall into this (4)_____*category*_____ of people, it's a smart idea to try to change your outlook. Learn to take things more calmly; learn to be more patient when someone or something disappoints you. If your (5)_____*attitude*_____ improves, your health may improve too.

B. What Do Your Hobbies Reveal About You?

f. **analyze**	g. **contrast**	h. **deliberate**
i. **fragile**	j. **indicate**	

Mira, Pat, and Celia are sisters, close in age and similar in looks—but what a (6)_____*contrast*_____ there is in their leisure activities! Mira loves an exciting challenge° and often takes (7)_____*deliberate*_____ risks. She has mastered the skateboard, she drives in stock-car races, and she's even tried boxing. In fact, she says she'd go skydiving if only she could afford it. Pat is a collector. She spends her spare time searching for old crystal and china—and taking care of it. She never minds the hours it takes her to wash and dust her precious, (8)_____*fragile*_____ treasures. Then there's Celia, who wants to spend every possible minute reading—and that's all! You've never met Mira, Pat, and Celia, but doesn't this tell you a lot about them? If we (9)_____*analyze*_____ how people spend leisure time, their interests and hobbies can reveal a great deal about their personalities. What do you think your hobbies and other activities would (10)_____*indicate*_____ about you?

➤ *Questions for Discussion*

1. What do your favorite leisure activities reveal about you? Tell about one or more of your principal° interests and what they **indicate** about your personality.

2. Many people feel that a positive, hopeful **attitude** is more likely to lead to success than a negative one. Do you agree? Explain your answer.

3. What are you most **critical** about in other people? What are you most critical about in yourself? Is your answer the same in both cases? Or is there a **contrast** between the faults you focus on in someone else and in yourself?

4. If you like to read, what is your favorite **category** of reading material? If you hate to read, what type of reading do you hate the least?

5. We are likely to think that if someone hurts us **deliberately**, it is worse than doing the same harm by accident. But why? Aren't we hurt just as much either way?

➤ *Ideas for Writing*

1. Write about something in your life that causes you **excessive frustration**. It might be a personal relationship, a chore you hate, or a problem that keeps coming up. Explain why it makes you feel so discouraged.

2. In a paper, **analyze** what your favorite leisure activities **indicate** about your personality. Use examples to illustrate your points.

Check Your Performance			CHAPTER 2
Activity	*Number Right*	*Points*	*Total*
Check 2	_____	× 10 =	_____
Related Words	_____	× 10 =	_____
Word Work	_____	× 10 =	_____
Synonyms and Antonyms	_____	× 10 =	_____
Final Check	_____	× 10 =	_____

Enter your scores above and in the vocabulary performance chart on the inside back cover of the book.

CHAPTER

3

accompany	preserve
desperate	pursue
determine	rejection
dispose of	restore
evident	scarce

Ten Words in Context

In the space provided, write the letter of the meaning closest to that of each **boldfaced** word. Use the context of the sentences to help you figure out each word's meaning.

1 accompany
(ə-kŭm′pə-nē)
– *verb*

- The Myers asked my sister to **accompany** them to the seashore to help take care of their young children.
- In popular music, words usually **accompany** the tune. In much classical music, there are no words to go with the notes.

__c__ *Accompany* means   a. to go before.   b. to go after.   c. to go with.

2 desperate
(dĕs′pər-ĭt)
– *adjective*

- Extremely ill people may be so **desperate** for a cure that they will try anything.
- The earthquake victims are **desperate** for food and clothing.

__b__ *Desperate for* means   a. harmed by.   b. in great need of.   c. surprised by.

3 determine
(dĭ-tûr′mĭn)
– *verb*

- The doctor in the emergency room **determined** from an x-ray that Chen's ankle was sprained, not broken.
- Using a calculator, I **determined** that the "super-giant" box of laundry soap was a better buy than the "family economy" box.

__c__ *Determine* means   a. to regret.   b. to remember.   c. to discover.

4 dispose of
(dĭ-spōz′ ŭv)
– *verb*

- The sign said, "Lungs at work. Please **dispose of** all cigarettes, cigars, and pipes before entering."
- After losing forty pounds, Herb decided to **dispose of** all the clothes that reminded him of his old size. He never wanted to see them again.

__a__ *Dispose of* means   a. to get rid of.   b. to pay for.   c. to use up.

5 evident
(ĕv′ĭ-dənt)
– *adjective*

- The fact that my aunt dyes her hair is **evident**—her gray roots show.
- To make it **evident** that she didn't want to go out with James again, Crystal sent him back all his letters and gifts.

__b__ *Evident* means   a. useful.   b. easy to see.   c. unlikely.

6 preserve
(prĭ-zûrv′)
– *verb*

- Steps are being taken to **preserve** the remaining giant redwood trees of California and Oregon for future generations.
- To **preserve** its valuable old fabrics, the museum keeps them away from bright lights and extreme temperatures.

__a__ *Preserve* means   a. to keep safe.   b. to sell off.   c. to seek.

7 pursue
(pər-sōō′)
– *verb*

- At the age of 49, the woman decided to **pursue** a degree in social work and become a social worker.
- Victor plans to **pursue** an acting career in New York City. His goal is to become a great actor, not a great star.

_b_ *Pursue* means   a. to avoid.   b. to work toward.   c. to replace.

8 rejection
(rĭ-jĕk′shən)
– *noun*

- My brother was upset when he received a letter of **rejection** from a college he wanted to attend.
- Nita wasn't too disturbed when she didn't get the job she had interviewed for. "If you can't handle **rejection**, you have some growing up to do," she said.

_b_ *Rejection* means   a. respect.   b. not being accepted.   c. bad taste.

9 restore
(rĭ-stôr′)
– *verb*

- During the 1980s, the Statue of Liberty was **restored**. The damaged torch and the 1,600 iron bands that hold the copper skin to the frame were replaced.
- Surprisingly, there have been cases where a bump on the head has **restored** the sight of a blind person.

_a_ *Restore* means   a. to fix.   b. to harm.   c. to give away.

10 scarce
(skârs)
– *adjective*

- Since 1909 pennies are **scarce**, the one I own may be worth a lot of money.
- In the book *The Long Winter*, the author tells about a time when food was so **scarce** that she and her family lived on little more than bread for weeks.

_c_ *Scarce* means   a. common.   b. clear.   c. hard to find.

Matching Words with Definitions

Following are definitions of the ten words. **Print** each word next to its definition. If you look closely at each word in context, you will be able to figure out its meaning.

1. _____evident_____   Obvious; clear
2. _____determine_____   To find out exactly; figure out
3. _____dispose of_____   To throw or give away; get rid of
4. _____desperate_____   Having a great need or desire
5. _____scarce_____   Rare; hard to get; not enough to meet demand
6. _____restore_____   To bring back to a normal or former condition; repair
7. _____preserve_____   To protect; keep in good condition
8. _____rejection_____   A saying "no" (to a request or desire); refusal
9. _____pursue_____   To try to get or succeed in; seek
10. _____accompany_____   To go along with; be together with

CAUTION: Do not go any further until you are sure the above answers are correct. Then you can use the definitions to help you in the following practices. Your goal is eventually to know the words well enough so that you don't need to check the definitions at all.

➤ *Check 1*

Using the answer line, complete each item below with the correct word from the box.

a. **accompany**	b. **desperate**	c. **determine**	d. **dispose of**	e. **evident**
f. **preserve**	g. **pursue**	h. **rejection**	i. **restore**	j. **scarce**

_____ desperate _____ 1. If you are ___ for food, that means you are in great need of it.

_____ evident _____ 2. When we say that something is ___, we mean that it can be clearly seen or clearly understood.

_____ accompany _____ 3. Do you like ketchup to ___ your french fries, or do you prefer them plain?

_____ scarce _____ 4. The opposite of "plentiful" is "___."

_____ dispose of _____ 5. There are several ways to ___ things you no longer want: put them in the garbage, recycle them, or give or sell them to someone who can use them.

_____ rejection _____ 6. The opposite of "acceptance" is "___."

_____ preserve _____ 7. To _____ a piece of furniture, protect it from too much heat, sun, and moisture.

_____ determine _____ 8. A good way to ___ which twin is which is to look for the mole on Beth's forehead.

_____ pursue _____ 9. Many athletes ___ an Olympic medal by practicing hours a day for years, but only a few athletes can actually win one.

_____ restore _____ 10. To _____ an old table, you must begin by removing all of the old varnish and paint.

NOTE: Now check your answers to these questions by turning to page 249. Going over the answers carefully will help you prepare for the remaining practices, for which answers are not given.

➤ *Check 2*

Using the answer lines, complete each item below with **two** words from the box.

_____ evident _____
_____ preserve _____
1–2. It is ___ that this old movie theater has been very well taken care of—the original seats and wallpaper have been ___d since 1924.

_____ scarce _____
_____ pursue _____
3–4. Jill wants to be a zookeeper, but since such jobs are ___, she may need to ___ another kind of work.

_____ desperate _____
_____ determine _____
5–6. The woman was ___ for money, so she decided to sell her grandmother's diamond ring. She was disappointed when the jeweler ___d that the diamond was a cheap imitation.

_____ restore _____
_____ dispose of _____
7–8. The owners of the old car are trying to decide if they will ___ it with new parts and a lot of body work, or ___ it by giving it away.

_____ accompany _____
_____ rejection _____
9–10. I offered to ___ my friend to the tryout for the play, thinking that if she did not get the part, she might need help in dealing with the ___.

➤ *Related Words*

Once you learn a new word, you can more easily understand many related words. Below are ten words related to the core words of this chapter. Use their definitions to help you write in the word that best completes each item.

a. **desperately**, *adverb*	In a way that shows a great need or desire
b. **disposal**, *noun*	The act of getting rid of something
c. **evidence**, *noun*	Something that helps prove a fact or belief; proof
d. **pursuit**, *noun*	The act of seeking or chasing
e. **reject**, *verb*	Refuse

evidence   1. The ___ found by firefighters—matches and a gasoline can—prove that someone set the fire on purpose.

desperately   2. The runner tried ___ to be the first to cross the finish line, but he failed by inches.

pursuit   3. Our silly dog spends hours in ___ of her own tail—which, of course, she never catches.

reject   4. Why did Amy ___ the job that was offered to her? Did she take another one instead?

Disposal   5. ___ of nuclear waste is very difficult—people don't want such dangerous garbage near them.

f. **accompaniment**, *noun*	A musical part that provides the background for a soloist
g. **determination**, *noun*	The act of finding out something
h. **evidently**, *adverb*	Obviously; clearly
i. **preservation**, *noun*	Protection; the act of keeping something safe or in good condition
j. **scarcity**, *noun*	A shortage

determination   6. After a ___ of just exactly why the car is squealing, the mechanics can figure out how to repair it.

scarcity   7. Because of freezes in Florida and California, there is a ___ of oranges this year.

accompaniment   8. The only ___ to the jazz singer was played on the flute.

preservation   9. If the town doesn't start working on the ___ of some open space, soon there won't be a spot that isn't covered with a house or shopping center.

evidently   10. Jerome and his cousin Theo go everywhere together; ___, they are very good friends.

➤ *Word Work*

A. In the space provided, write the letter of the word that most closely relates to the situation in each item.

___c___ 1. Keep your wedding gown carefully wrapped in plastic and stored in a box.

   a. restore   b. determine   c. preserve

___a___ 2. In my opinion, waffles go best with butter and maple syrup.

   a. accompany   b. restore   c. dispose

___b___ 3. It was clear where the missing brownie went—my son's face was full of chocolate.

   a. desperate   b. evident   c. preserve

___c___ 4. To find out what was wrong with his patient, the doctor had to do several tests.

   a. dispose   b. accompany   c. determine

___b___ 5. Annamarie worked hard to reach her goal of owning her own restaurant.

   a. preserve   b. pursue   c. evidence

B. In the space provided, write the letter of the choice that best completes each item.

___a___ 6. **Dispose of** clothes that

   a. are old and no longer fit.   b. you just bought.   c. you will wear next summer.

___c___ 7. Ernie experienced **rejection** when he

   a. was invited   b. moved into   c. was turned down
      to a party.   a new house.   for a date.

___b___ 8. When tomatoes are **scarce**, they are

   a. in season.   b. hard to find.   c. cheap.

___c___ 9. You could **restore** an old piano with

   a. a large truck.   b. beautiful music.   c. new keys, strings,
                                                      and woodwork.

___a___ 10. You might feel **desperate** if you were

   a. stuck on a   b. wearing attractive   c. standing in a long line
      desert island.   new clothes.   at the supermarket.

➤ *Word Parts*

A. One meaning of the suffix *-ly* is "in a certain way."

Examples: *desperate* — in great need   *grateful* — thankful
desperately — in a way that shows great need   *gratefully* — in a thankful way

On each answer line, write the word from the box that means the same as the *italicized* words.

| a. **angrily** | b. **deliberately°** | c. **desperately** |
| d. **excessively°** | e. **skillfully** | |

_____*deliberately*_____   1. Eva *in a deliberate° way* stuck her foot out as her little brother came by. As he fell, he yelled, "Hey, you did that on purpose!"

_____*skillfully*_____   2. The doctor sewed up the wound so *in a skillful way* that it did not even leave a scar.

_____*excessively*_____   3. I guess I have been spending *in an excessive way* on clothes and eating out; I haven't saved a cent for the last year.

_____*desperately*_____   4. Many neighbors stayed up all night, searching *in a desperate way* for the missing child.

_____*angrily*_____   5. The principal said to the class *in an angry way,* "There's no good reason for such rude behavior toward a substitute teacher."

B. One meaning of the prefix *re-* is "back."

Examples: *reflect*—to bend light back
recall—to call back to mind; remember

On each answer line, write the word from the box that best completes the item.

| f. **recall** | g. **reflect** | h. **remove** |
| i. **repay** | j. **restore** | |

_____*restore*_____   6. To ___ this old lamp, you'll need to put in new electrical wiring.

_____*repay*_____   7. When I get my next paycheck, I will ___ the ten dollars you lent me.

_____*recall*_____   8. I remember the man's face, but I cannot ___ his name.

_____*reflect*_____   9. The truck's headlights hit my rearview mirror, which ___ed the light right into my eyes.

_____*remove*_____   10. "Please ___ your hand from my car," said the young man.

➤ *Final Check*

Read the passages carefully. Then fill in each blank with the word that best fits the context.

A. Fixing Up Furniture

a. **determine**	b. **dispose**	c. **evident**
d. **preserve**	e. **restore**	

I feel proud when I can fix up furniture that other people have (1)_____*dispose*_____d of. Rather than spend a lot on new furniture, I like the challenge° of taking an old chair thrown out by a relative or an ugly bureau I've found in a neighbor's trash pile and trying to (2)_____*restore*_____ it to its original condition. I often find a beautiful piece of furniture hidden under many coats of paint or varnish. At first it is hard to (3)_____*determine*_____ how good or bad the piece underneath really is. I must carefully remove the old paint or varnish. If it becomes (4)_____*evident*_____ that the quality of the piece of furniture is good, I sand it until it is smooth. Then I stain it to bring out the wood's natural lines and colors. Finally, I apply new varnish to (5)_____*preserve*_____ the wood from damage by water or heat. Fixing other people's "junk" has been an inexpensive way for me to get some beautiful furniture.

B. Barbara's Date with Her Cousin

f. **accompany**	g. **desperate**	h. **pursue**
i. **rejection**	j. **scarce**	

Barbara can finally laugh about the time twenty years ago when she was so (6)_____*desperate*_____ for a date that she paid her cousin twenty-five dollars to go with her to the senior prom. She admits that dates were pretty (7)_____*scarce*_____ for her in high school. However, when the prom tickets first went on sale, Barbara hoped that some handsome fellow would fall for her charms and ask her to the prom, and maybe even ask her to go steady. It didn't happen.

Back then, people didn't think it was very "ladylike" behavior to actively (8)_____*pursue*_____ a date with a boy, but Barbara really wanted to go to the prom. Despite her fear of (9)_____*rejection*_____, she got up her nerve to ask Gary. He already had a date. So she asked Emilio and then Chuck. They also said no.

One week before the prom, she called her cousin. He said, "Okay, but it will cost you." He said ten dollars was for being willing to (10)_____*accompany*_____ her to the dance and fifteen dollars was for not telling anyone at the prom that they were related.

➤ *Questions for Discussion*

1. Do you have a special belonging that you hope to **preserve** throughout your life? What is it, and how could you keep it in good condition?

2. What kind of items do you frequently use that other people **dispose of**, and what do you use them for? What would you have to do if such items were no longer available?

3. If a visitor went shopping with you, what would become **evident** to him or her about your taste in clothes?

4. What career do you plan on **pursuing**? What ways can you pursue it in addition to going to school?

5. Who is the actor or actress you would most like to **accompany** to the Academy Awards ceremony? Why?

➤ *Ideas for Writing*

1. What is one goal in life that is important for you to **pursue**? When did it become **evident** to you that this was a meaningful goal for you? Write about that goal and its meaning in your life.

2. Write about a time when you experienced a feeling of **rejection**. How did you feel? After you were rejected, did you do anything to **restore** your feeling of self-confidence?

Check Your Performance			**CHAPTER 3**
Activity	*Number Right*	*Points*	*Total*
Check 2	_____	× 10 =	_____
Related Words	_____	× 10 =	_____
Word Work	_____	× 10 =	_____
Word Parts	_____	× 10 =	_____
Final Check	_____	× 10 =	_____

Enter your scores above and in the vocabulary performance chart on the inside back cover of the book.

CHAPTER 4

abundant	**distinct**
betray	**exaggerate**
comparison	**inhabit**
demonstrate	**neutral**
dispute	**reduction**

Ten Words in Context

In the space provided, write the letter of the meaning closest to that of each **boldfaced** word. Use the context of the sentences to help you figure out each word's meaning.

1 abundant
(ə-bŭn′dənt)
– *adjective*

- Our apple tree bore such an **abundant** crop this year that we'll have plenty of applesauce all winter.
- Mom's energy is so **abundant** that the rest of us can't keep up with her. After a day's work, she'll bike ten miles and then say, "Let's shoot a few baskets before dinner!"

__b__ *Abundant* means   a. different.   b. great.   c. reasonable.

2 betray
(bĭ-trā′)
– *verb*

- The prisoners refused to **betray** their country by telling its secrets.
- I didn't mean to **betray** my brother by telling our parents he was using drugs—I wanted to help him.

__a__ *Betray* means   a. to turn against.   b. to give aid to.   c. to argue with.

3 comparison
(kəm-păr′ĭ-sən)
– *noun*

- I decided which car to buy after making a **comparison** of all the cars in my price range.
- A **comparison** of Marty's two wives makes his second wife seem like a saint.

__a__ *Comparison* means   a. check of what is alike and different.   b. argument.   c. explanation.

4 demonstrate
(dĕm′ən-strāt′)
– *verb*

- I asked the salesman to **demonstrate** how to use the camera, but it was clear he didn't know how.
- When the new copying machine arrives in our office, someone who knows how to use it will **demonstrate** how all its features work.

__c__ *Demonstrate* means   a. to remember.   b. to imagine.   c. to show.

5 dispute
(dĭ-spyo͞ot′)
– *noun*

- My **dispute** with my brother about who would get the last piece of pie was settled when our father ate it.
- Business at the store was so slow that the salespeople had a **dispute** over who would get the next customer.

__b__ *Dispute* means   a. answer.   b. disagreement.   c. explanation.

6 distinct
(dĭ-stĭngkt′)
– *adjective*

- The faces of the people in the faded old photo were not **distinct**—we couldn't identify anyone.
- Although the two bowls of onion dip looked the same, there was a **distinct** difference in their taste.

__a__ *Distinct* means   a. definite.   b. healthy.   c. hard to notice.

7 exaggerate
(ĭg-zăj′ə-rāt′)
– verb

- Dad, reminding us not to stretch the truth, always jokes, "I've told you a million times never to **exaggerate**!"
- I didn't **exaggerate** when I called Randall a musical genius. He really does play the guitar amazingly well.

_b_ *Exaggerate* means   a. to ask questions.   b. to overstate.   c. to explain.

8 inhabit
(ĭn-hăb′ĭt)
– verb

- Six billion people **inhabit** the Earth.
- Bats often **inhabit** the attics of houses, barns, and other buildings.

_b_ *Inhabit* means   a. to show.   b. to live in.   c. to check.

9 neutral
(nōō′trəl)
– adjective

- If you ever go to a marriage counselor, don't expect him or her to take sides in your problems with your spouse. A counselor must remain **neutral**.
- Switzerland has been a **neutral** country since 1648. It doesn't participate or support either side in wars.

_b_ *Neutral* means   a. clear.   b. not taking sides.   c. not loyal.

10 reduction
(rĭ-dŭk′shən)
– noun

- When our company offered to pay us for sick time we didn't use, there was a sudden **reduction** in the number of sick days taken.
- It seems everyone who runs for public office promises a **reduction** in taxes.

_c_ *Reduction* means   a. order.   b. quarrel.   c. cut.

Matching Words with Definitions

Following are definitions of the ten words. **Print** each word next to its definition. If you look closely at each word in context, you will be able to figure out its meaning.

1. _inhabit_ — To live in
2. _abundant_ — Very plentiful; more than enough
3. _comparison_ — The act of checking or judging how two or more things are alike or different
4. _exaggerate_ — To say that something is larger or greater than it really is; overstate
5. _distinct_ — Clear; obvious; easy to see or notice
6. _neutral_ — Not taking sides in a quarrel
7. _dispute_ — An argument; a quarrel
8. _betray_ — To be disloyal to; turn against
9. _reduction_ — A decrease; cutback
10. _demonstrate_ — To explain or teach by showing

CAUTION: Do not go any further until you are sure the above answers are correct. Then you can use the definitions to help you in the following practices. Your goal is eventually to know the words well enough so that you don't need to check the definitions at all.

➤ *Check 1*

Using the answer line, complete each item below with the correct word from the box.

| a. **abundant** | b. **betray** | c. **comparison** | d. **demonstrate** | e. **dispute** |
| f. **distinct** | g. **exaggerate** | h. **inhabit** | i. **neutral** | j. **reduction** |

_____*reduction*_____ 1. If someone's new job pays less than the old job, he or she has taken a ___ in pay.

_____*betray*_____ 2. Benedict Arnold was an American officer who secretly helped the British during the American Revolution; he is remembered as a man who ___ed his country.

_____*exaggerate*_____ 3. You ___ a point when you overstate it, as in saying, "I'm dying of hunger."

_____*abundant*_____ 4. We had such an ___ crop of tomatoes this year that we had enough to give to our neighbors.

_____*neutral*_____ 5. If you want to remain friends with two people who are quarreling, it is best to stay ___ and keep out of the fight.

_____*comparison*_____ 6. A ___ of our backgrounds and interests revealed we had a lot in common.

_____*demonstrate*_____ 7. The uncooperative salesman refused to ___ how to use the VCR, saying, "Just read the manual and figure it out yourself."

_____*distinct*_____ 8. Even though I was only 3 at the time, I have a ___ memory of the first time I saw the ocean.

_____*inhabit*_____ 9. The people who ___ Canada are called Canadians.

_____*dispute*_____ 10. When we say that two people had a ___, we mean that their fight consisted of words, not punches.

NOTE: Now check your answers to these questions by turning to page 249. Going over the answers carefully will help you prepare for the remaining practices, for which answers are not given.

➤ *Check 2*

Using the answer lines, complete each item below with **two** words from the box.

_____*dispute*_____
_____*neutral*_____ 1–2. My roommates are having a ___ over whether to paint the kitchen yellow or tan. I'm remaining ___; I don't care what color it is.

_____*reduction*_____
_____*comparison*_____ 3–4. There has been a ___ in crime in our city this year. In ___ with last year, far fewer crimes were committed.

_____*abundant*_____
_____*exaggerate*_____ 5–6. I'll admit that ants were ___ at our picnic, but let's not ___. There really were not a trillion of them.

_____*demonstrate*_____
_____*distinct*_____ 7–8. Although I'd never sent E-mail on a computer before, Corey ___d how it works so clearly that I now have a ___ idea of how to do it myself.

_____*inhabit*_____
_____*betray*_____ 9–10. Homeless people secretly ___ed the abandoned building, but when someone ___ed them and told the police, they were thrown out.

➤ *Related Words*

Once you learn a new word, you can more easily understand many related words. Below are ten words related to the core words of this chapter. Use their definitions to help you write in the word that best completes each item.

a. **compare**, *verb*	To check on what is the same and different
b. **demonstration**, *noun*	An act of showing; presentation
c. **distinctly**, *adverb*	Clearly
d. **inhabitant**, *noun*	Someone who lives in a particular place; resident
e. **reduce**, *verb*	To make smaller or fewer

_____demonstration_____ 1. The juggling class began with a ___ by the instructor, who juggled six cups and saucers, a teapot, and three muffins.

_____inhabitant_____ 2. Tokyo, Japan, has the largest population of any city in the world—over 26 million ___s.

_____distinctly_____ 3. I ___ remember asking you to buy bread and milk on your way home.

_____compare_____ 4. If you ___ what it costs to serve homemade foods and prepared foods, you will see that you can save money by doing your own cooking.

_____reduce_____ 5. Scientists are telling Americans to ___ the amount of fat in our diets. They say we eat much more fat than is healthy.

f. **abundance**, *noun*	A great or plentiful supply
g. **betrayal**, *noun*	Lack of loyalty
h. **disputed**, *adjective*	Being debated, or argued, about; being a subject of debate
i. **exaggeration**, *noun*	An overstatement; act of stating that something is larger or greater than it actually is
j. **habitat**, *noun*	The place where an animal or plant lives or grows

_____exaggeration_____ 6. After the holidays, Elena complained, "I've gained a ton!" This was a slight ___, since she had actually gained three pounds.

_____betrayal_____ 7. "I have never experienced such ___," said Tom, after finding out that his best friend was having an affair with his wife. "It may be impossible to restore° my faith in either of them."

_____habitat_____ 8. The tropical areas of Africa and Asia are the elephant's natural ___. We need to preserve° those areas so that elephants will have places to live.

_____disputed_____ 9. The death penalty and abortion are two hotly ___ topics in the United States today.

_____abundance_____ 10. There was an ___ of food at the party: platters were heaped high with cold cuts, salads, breads, and desserts.

➣ *Word Work*

A. In the space provided, write the letter of the choice that best completes each item.

_b_   1. Polar bears **inhabit**
    a. fish.
    b. the North Pole.
    c. white fur.

_c_   2. The neighbors had a **dispute**
    a. to celebrate a birthday.
    b. because they got along so well together.
    c. over where the property line between them was.

_c_   3. The king's most trusted advisers **betrayed** him by
    a. giving him a surprise party.
    b. checking to be sure his food was safe.
    c. planning to kill him.

_a_   4. Surprisingly, there was a **reduction** in the prices of houses in our area. The prices were
    a. lowered.
    b. raised.
    c. kept the same.

_b_   5. In a **comparison** at the supermarket, Annie learned that
    a. it takes her forty-five minutes to shop.
    b. Wheatsies cereal is a better buy than Oatsies.
    c. her friend Cara shops at the same store.

B. In the space provided, write the letter of the word that most closely relates to the situation in each item.

_c_   6. "My grandchildren are the smartest youngsters in the world, and as for their behavior —
they're perfect, that's all. They're angels."
    a. neutral   b. betray   c. exaggerate

_b_   7. In the the woods and fields around my hometown, blueberries grow everywhere. You
can pick them by the bucketful.
    a. neutral   b. abundant   c. betray

_c_   8. The view of the moon through the new telescope was extremely clear and sharp.
    a. abundant   b. reduction   c. distinct

_a_   9. When my husband and I have an argument, my mother-in-law never takes sides.
    a. neutral   b. demonstrate   c. abundant

_b_ 10. To show the new soldiers how to take a rifle apart and put it together again, the
instructors go through the whole process themselves.
    a. inhabit   b. demonstrate   c. neutral

➤ *Synonyms and Antonyms*

A. Synonyms. Write the letter of the word or phrase that most nearly means the **same** as each boldfaced word.

d 1. **betray**

    a. encourage   b. annoy

    c. escape   d. be disloyal

b 2. **comparison**

    a. thoughts and feelings   b. check of how things are alike or different

    c. questions and answers   d. time and effort

a 3. **demonstrate**

    a. show   b. confuse

    c. entertain   d. judge

a 4. **dispute**

    a. argument   b. agreement

    c. fact   d. condition

c 5. **inhabit**

    a. go away from   b. approach

    c. live in   d. explore

B. Antonyms. Write the letter of the word or phrase that most nearly means the **opposite** of each boldfaced word.

a 6. **abundant**

    a. not enough   b. effective

    c. lucky   d. great

d 7. **distinct**

    a. quiet   b. not constant

    c. large   d. not clear

c 8. **exaggerate**

    a. admire   b. destroy

    c. understate   d. defend

b 9. **neutral**

    a. unusual   b. taking sides

    c. frightened   d. possible

b 10. **reduction**

    a. comment   b. increase

    c. agreement   d. answer

➤ *Final Check*

Read the passages carefully. Then fill in each blank with the word that best fits the context.

A. The Vacuum-Cleaner Salesman

a. **abundant**	b. **demonstrate**	c. **distinct**
d. **exaggerate**	e. **reduction**	

I'll never forget the day a salesman (1)_____*demonstrate*____d his vacuum cleaner on my living room rug. I know some salespeople (2)_____*exaggerate*_____ their product's good qualities, so I didn't believe everything he said. But I let him show me what his machine could do.

The first thing he did was deliberately° wipe his muddy feet on my rug. Next, he dumped an (3)_____*abundant*_____ amount of ashes onto it. Then he vacuumed the mess up. In no time, there was a difference between the rest of the rug and the part he had dirtied and then cleaned. A clear light stripe now ran down the middle of my rug. The machine was great. He told me how lucky I was to have the chance to buy it then, because of a great (4)_____*reduction*_____ in the price. Sadly, I had to tell him that even the lower price was too high for me. He then quickly thanked me and left.

Then I realized that he hadn't finished cleaning up all of the mess he had made. So I used my own vacuum cleaner, which did not do a very good job. As a result, I'm reminded of the frustration° of that day every time I walk through my living room. It still has a (5)_____*distinct*_____ light stripe right down the middle.

B. Peace at Last

f. **betray**	g. **comparison**	h. **dispute**
i. **inhabit**	j. **neutral**	

My new apartment is so nice and quiet in (6)_____*comparison*_____ with my last one. In my old building, the people who (7)_____*inhabit*_____ed the apartments on both sides of me were always having (8)_____*dispute*_____s. For example, the woman in 401 and the man in 403 would argue all the time about politics. Once she yelled that she had trusted him to keep her secrets, but that he had (9)_____*betray*_____ed her by telling everyone in the building. He then loudly insisted that she was the one with the big mouth. In addition, his wife sometimes screamed at the woman for flirting with her husband. Although they tried to get me to take sides, I remained completely (10)_____*neutral*_____. I don't know who was right or wrong. I just know that the excessive° number of noisy arguments was too much for me to bear, and I'm glad to be out of there.

➤ *Questions for Discussion*

1. If you found out that someone you love very much had committed a crime, would you **betray** him or her and tell the police?

2. Suppose that your company needs to save money, so it gives its employees this choice: Everyone takes a **reduction** in pay, or half of the workers will lose their jobs. You don't know, of course, who will be fired and who won't. Would you take the cut in pay?

3. When trouble strikes, do you tend to **exaggerate** it ("This is the end of the world!") or do you tend to play it down ("It's no big deal")? What different results might each of those attitudes° toward trouble have?

4. Describe a **dispute** in which you feel strongly about one side, and a debate in which you feel **neutral**. Why do you care about the first issue but not about the second one?

5. Do you think human beings will ever **inhabit** another planet?

➤ *Ideas for Writing*

1. If you could make one thing on Earth more **abundant**, what would it be, and why? Write about your choice.

2. Write about how you would **demonstrate** to others something you know how to do very well, such as baking a cake or riding a bike. How would you give your audience a **distinct** idea of the process?

Check Your Performance			CHAPTER 4
Activity	*Number Right*	*Points*	*Total*
Check 2	_____	× 10 =	_____
Related Words	_____	× 10 =	_____
Word Work	_____	× 10 =	_____
Synonyms and Antonyms	_____	× 10 =	_____
Final Check	_____	× 10 =	_____

Enter your scores above and in the vocabulary performance chart on the inside back cover of the book.

aggravate	intentional
cease	interference
coincide	obnoxious
considerable	unstable
humane	utilize

Ten Words in Context

In the space provided, write the letter of the meaning closest to that of each **boldfaced** word. Use the context of the sentences to help you figure out each word's meaning.

1 **aggravate**
(ăg′rə-vāt)
– *verb*

- If you walk on your sprained ankle, you'll only **aggravate** the injury: the pain and swelling will get worse.
- If your next-door neighbors hate your dog, it's a difficult situation—so don't **aggravate** the problem by walking the dog on their lawn.

  b *Aggravate* means   a. to make use of.   b. to make worse.   c. to create.

2 **cease**
(sēs)
– *verb*

- After the police warned him twice, our landlord **ceased** burning trash in the backyard, an illegal activity in our town.
- When the snowfall finally **ceased**, we went out to shovel the driveway.

  c *Cease* means   a. to repeat.   b. to start.   c. to quit.

3 **coincide**
(kō′ĭn-sīd′)
– *verb*

- My best friend from high school and I have moved to different states. We try to make our visits to our hometown **coincide** so that we can see each other.
- My roommate is getting married on the same day as my cousin. I wish the weddings were not going to **coincide** because I'd really like to go to both.

  a *Coincide* means   a. to happen at the same time.   b. to be stopped.   c. to be interesting.

4 **considerable**
(kən-sĭd′ər-ə-bəl)
– *adjective*

- After two hours and **considerable** effort, I finally found Vernon's apartment.
- Elena loves gardening, so she spends a **considerable** amount of time caring for flowers, vegetables, and herbs.

  c *Considerable* means   a. too little.   b. gentle.   c. quite a bit.

5 **humane**
(hyōō-mān′)
– *adjective*

- When our cat developed a fatal blood disease, we didn't want her to suffer. We felt it was more **humane** to have her painlessly "put to sleep."
- For years, mentally retarded people were often poorly cared for in large institutions. Happily, many now receive more **humane** treatment in small group homes.

  c *Humane* means   a. wasteful.   b. fast.   c. caring.

6 **intentional**
(ĭn-tĕn′shə-nəl)
– *adjective*

- The police believe the fire was **intentional**, although they don't know why someone would purposely burn down the library.
- I know I'm an hour late, but it wasn't **intentional**. A huge traffic accident held me up.

  b *Intentional* means   a. important.   b. planned.   c. late.

7 interference
(ĭn′tər-fēr′əns)
– *noun*

- Because the street workers outside our classroom window were such an **interference**, the class was moved to the library.
- I'm very fond of my mother-in-law, but I do not like her **interference** in arguments between me and my wife.

b *Interference* means   a. help.   b. getting in the way.   c. silence.

8 obnoxious
(əb-nŏk′shəs)
– *adjective*

- The children visiting the chicken farm held their noses because of the **obnoxious** smell.
- I won't go to the party if Lester is there. He always makes himself **obnoxious** by insulting and making fun of people.

c *Obnoxious* means   a. not interesting.   b. popular.   c. not pleasant.

9 unstable
(ŭn-stā′bəl)
– *adjective*

- The ladder felt so **unstable** that I was afraid to climb any higher than the third step.
- The young man's personality was **unstable**. One minute he seemed quiet and satisfied, and the next minute he was angry about something.

a *Unstable* means   a. not steady.   b. useful.   c. easy to break.

10 utilize
(yōōt′l-īz′)
– *verb*

- Don't throw bread away just because it's stale. Stale bread can be **utilized** to make bread crumbs and croutons.
- Last summer, Cindy **utilized** her swimming skills as a camp lifeguard.

c *Utilize* means   a. to sell.   b. to replace.   c. to use.

Matching Words with Definitions

Following are definitions of the ten words. **Print** each word next to its definition. If you look closely at each word in context, you will be able to figure out its meaning.

1. ___obnoxious___   Very unpleasant; distasteful; disgusting

2. ___cease___   To stop; discontinue

3. ___unstable___   Unsteady; wobbly; not reliable

4. ___intentional___   Done on purpose; planned ·

5. ___aggravate___   To make worse

6. ___humane___   Kind; sympathetic; merciful; gentle

7. ___coincide___   To happen at the same time

8. ___considerable___   Rather great; rather large

9. ___interference___   The act of getting in the way of something; meddling in someone else's business; something that gets in the way

10. ___utilize___   To make use of; put to use, especially to good use

CAUTION: Do not go any further until you are sure the above answers are correct. Then you can use the definitions to help you in the following practices. Your goal is eventually to know the words well enough so that you don't need to check the definitions at all.

➤ *Check 1*

Using the answer line, complete each item below with the correct word from the box.

a. **aggravate**	b. **cease**	c. **coincide**	d. **considerable**	e. **humane**
f. **intentional**	g. **interference**	h. **obnoxious**	i. **unstable**	j. **utilize**

unstable   1. It's no wonder the vase fell over; the flowers were so top-heavy that the whole arrangement was ___.

utilize   2. My brother is glad he'll be able to ___ his skills as a mechanic in his new job at a garage.

aggravate   3. Surprisingly, going to bed and taking it easy can actually ___ back pain. Gentle movement is often more helpful.

considerable   4. A ___ amount of time is the opposite of a rather small amount of time.

obnoxious   5. You may feel that slurping with straws is ___, but my kids don't find it disgusting at all.

intentional   6. The young man was charged with arson—the ___ setting of a harmful fire.

coincide   7. The two funerals will ___; that is, they will take place on the same day.

interference   8. My nosy neighbor calls what she does just "taking a healthy interest in people's lives," but I call what she does "___."

humane   9. It really isn't ___ to give small children chicks and baby ducks as presents—the poor little birds are almost sure to die soon.

cease   10. The opposite of "begin" is ___.

NOTE: Now check your answers to these questions by turning to page 249. Going over the answers carefully will help you prepare for the remaining practices, for which answers are not given.

➤ *Check 2*

Using the answer lines, complete each item below with **two** words from the box.

aggravate
cease   1–2. "No pain, no gain" is bad advice when it comes to sports injuries. You can easily ___ an injury by playing before the pain has ___d.

unstable
interference   3–4. If a couple's marriage seems ___, family members may try to get involved. But ___ from relatives sometimes does more harm than good.

considerable
obnoxious   5–6. It may take ___ effort to get along with an ___ coworker, but learning how to deal with difficult people is a valuable skill.

utilize
humane   7–8. Animal-rights activists say it is not right to ___ cats, dogs, and monkeys in medical experiments. However, many researchers argue that their treatment of the animals is ___.

coincide
intentional   9–10. The vocabulary skills class and the study skills class ___ this semester. Scheduling them for the same day and time probably wasn't ___, but students who wanted to take them both are annoyed.

➤ *Related Words*

Once you learn a new word, you can more easily understand many related words. Below are ten words related to the core words of this chapter. Use their definitions to help you write in the word that best completes each item.

a. **aggravation**, *noun*	A worsening
b. **coincidence**, *noun*	A striking chance happening of events at the same time, as if they had been planned
c. **considerably**, *adverb*	To a rather large extent; in a rather large amount
d. **humanitarian**, *noun*	A person who helps further human welfare
e. **ceaseless**, *adjective*	Constant; never stopping

_____*ceaseless*_____ 1. When Tania picked up her old friend at the airport, they were both so excited about seeing one another that they couldn't stop talking—the car was filled with their ___ chatter until they reached home.

_____*humanitarian*_____ 2. If you won the lottery, would you be a ___ and give some of the money to charity? Or—be honest—would you keep it all for yourself?

_____*aggravation*_____ 3. The patient's refusal to take his medicine led to an ___ of his illness— in fact, he nearly died.

_____*considerably*_____ 4. My husband is one of those people who get the blues over the Christmas holidays, but his spirits brighten ___ after New Year's Day.

_____*coincidence*_____ 5. My roommate and I discovered a funny ___: our mothers had been roommates at the hospital where we were both born.

f. **intention**, *noun*	A plan to do something
g. **interfere**, *verb*	To become involved in other people's business
h. **noxious**, *adjective*	Very harmful to health
i. **stable**, *adjective*	Steady; reliable
j. **utility**, *noun*	Usefulness; the quality of serving a use or purpose

_____*stable*_____ 6. To make the ladder more ___ while Luis climbed up to the roof, Andy and I held onto the sides.

_____*noxious*_____ 7. The children had to be taken from the school building quickly when ___ fumes began escaping from the furnace. Luckily, none of them got sick.

_____*intention*_____ 8. The old saying "The road to hell is paved with good ___s" means that just planning to do good things is not enough; we must also do them.

_____*utility*_____ 9. We purchase most of our household items for their ___—to sit on, to cook with, and so on. However, we buy works of art for their beauty, not their usefulness.

_____*interfere*_____ 10. If children are quarreling, should parents ___? Or is it better to stay out of the quarrel and let kids work things out for themselves?

➤ *Word Work*

A. In the space provided, write the letter of the word that most closely relates to the situation in each item.

__c__ 1. Mom doesn't like to dispose of° anything. She uses the comics as wrapping paper, cuts up worn-out rubber gloves to make rubber bands, and saves old stockings to use as dust cloths.

    a. interference   b. humane   c. utilize

__a__ 2. My grandmother took in foster children and also gave much of her time to a program for pregnant teenagers.

    a. humane   b. aggravate   c. obnoxious

__c__ 3. The drunken man at the restaurant was loudly critical° of other customers and tried to start a fight.

    a. utilize   b. coincide   c. obnoxious

__b__ 4. My cold got much worse when I went ice skating on the coldest day of the winter.

    a. intentional   b. aggravate   c. utilize

__c__ 5. Our restaurant table was distinctly° rocking back and forth, so we put a matchbook under one leg to steady it.

    a. coincide   b. humane   c. unstable

B. In the space provided, write the letter of the choice that best completes each item.

__c__ 6. According to the weather report, the rain should **cease** tonight. Tonight the rain should

    a. start, after a period   b. get much worse, with   c. stop, probably after raining
       of dry weather.   flooding in some areas.   most or all of the day.

__b__ 7. I work at home, and sometimes there is a great deal of **interference** from my children. My children

    a. help me with my work.   b. bother me when I'm   c. leave for long
                       trying to work.   periods of time.

__c__ 8. The bus strike **coincided** with a blizzard, so many offices downtown were closed. The strike

    a. took place a week   b. was called off because   c. happened at the same time
       after the blizzard.   of the blizzard.   as the blizzard.

__c__ 9. "If I hurt your feelings, you can be sure it was not **intentional**." I

    a. tried to hurt   b. have hurt you before.   c. did not mean to
       your feelings.   hurt your feelings.

__a__ 10. The cost of getting my wisdom teeth removed was **considerable**. It was

    a. quite expensive.   b. much cheaper than I expected.   c. free.

➤ *Analogies*

Each item below starts with a pair of words in CAPITAL LETTERS. For each item, figure out the relationship between these two words. Then decide which of the choices (*a*, *b*, *c*, or *d*) expresses a similar relationship. Write the letter of your choice on the answer line. (All the repeated words in these items are from this unit.)

Note: To review analogies, see pages 6–7.

_a_ 1. AGGRAVATE : WORSEN ::

    a. improve : make better   b. improve : make worse
    c. heal : injure   d. raise : lower

_c_ 2. CEASE : BEGIN ::

    a. continue : go on   b. stop : quit
    c. stop : start   d. hurry : rush

_d_ 3. PRESERVE° : FURNITURE ::

    a. restore° : repair   b. chair : furniture
    c. find : lose   d. analyze° : problem

_c_ 4. OBNOXIOUS : PLEASANT ::

    a. harmful : unpleasant   b. annoying : irritating
    c. annoying : nice   d. pleasure : enjoyment

_d_ 5. UTILIZE : TOOL ::

    a. catch : run   b. shaky : wobbly
    c. ship : car   d. swing : bat

_b_ 6. UNSTABLE : STEADY ::

    a. large : big   b. evident° : unclear
    c. abundant° : plentiful   d. busy : happy

_a_ 7. INTENTIONAL : ON PURPOSE ::

    a. untrue : false   b. accidental : on purpose
    c. planned : prevented   d. hoped for : feared

_d_ 8. REJECTION° : ACCEPTANCE ::

    a. hour : time   b. child : children
    c. school : college   d. contrast° : similarity

_d_ 9. INTERFERENCE : ASSISTANCE ::

    a. reduction°: decrease   b. garbage : bag
    c. teacher : subject   d. dispute° : agreement

_a_ 10. SCARCE° : GOLD ::

    a. fragile : glass   b. new : old
    c. diamond : ruby   d. excessive° : deliberate°

➤ *Final Check*

Read the passages carefully. Then fill in each blank with the word that best fits the context.

A. Study Skills to the Rescue!

a. **aggravate**	b. **coincide**	c. **considerable**
d. **interference**	e. **utilize**	

College students say that one of their biggest headaches is what to do when several exams and assignments (1)_____*coincide*_____; for example, when they have an exam and a quiz the same week that a paper and a report are due. To deal with this situation, don't panic—that will only (2)_____*aggravate*_____ your problem. Instead, (3)_____*utilize*_____ some study skills that will make you a better manager of your time. First, you can get (4)_____*considerable*_____ help simply by planning well. Figure out what will take the most time; probably the exam will need more study time than the quiz, and a long report might take more time than a short paper. Setting aside the right amounts of time will give you a sense of control. Second, be sure you get the most out of the time you've planned. Find a quiet place to work, and don't allow any (5)_____*interference*_____ from your friends or roommates, TV, radio, or the CD player. And third? Well, try adding your own ideas to the list. The more you add, the more self-confident you'll feel.

B. How to Control Children

f. **cease**	g. **humane**	h. **intentional**
i. **obnoxious**	j. **unstable**	

For many years, there was little question about how to treat children who misbehaved— they were hit, sometimes beaten. That seemed natural and suitable° to parents, to teachers, and maybe even to the children. In our own time, though, many people have tried to find more (6)_____*humane*_____ methods, gentle ways to help children learn self-control. Of course, they recognize that children's behavior is often (7)_____*obnoxious*_____. Kids can be noisy, rude, and destructive. Although that behavior isn't always done on purpose, sometimes it is (8)_____*intentional*_____. But many adults believe that spanking and other physical violence won't make a child's bad behavior (9)_____*cease*_____. Indeed, hitting children may make them act even worse, as they learn to meet violence with more violence. Their willpower becomes weak and (10)_____*unstable*_____; in other words, their ability to control themselves is shaky, rather than strong and firm. Some adults still believe that spanking is the best way to teach children, but this other approach certainly deserves consideration.

➢ *Questions for Discussion*

1. Think of several things that upset you, disturb you, or make you angry or annoyed. These things may happen in the world, in your community, or in your family. Now suppose that you can make one of them, but only one, **cease**. Which would you stop, and why?

2. Have you ever experienced an interesting **coincidence**—two things that happened at the same time, as if they had been planned? For example, someone may have called you on the phone just as you were beginning to think of that person. Tell about an interesting coincidence in your life.

3. Some people argue that the death penalty is actually more **humane** than life imprisonment—that it is more merciful to be killed than shut up in prison for life. What do you think of this idea?

4. What do you think makes the difference between a solid, lasting relationship—in a marriage, for example—and an **unstable**, troubled one? Do you think one single thing is most important, or is it a combination of many things?

5. Recycling is an important concern to many people today. Do you or your family members save and **utilize** anything out of the ordinary, something that other people might not have thought to put to use? If so, what is it, and how do you use it?

➢ *Ideas for Writing*

1. People sometimes **aggravate** an already bad situation by well-meant but harmful **interference**. Write about a time in your own experience when someone (perhaps even you!) caused worse trouble in this way, even though the harm wasn't **intentional**.

2. Everyone has faults, of course, but have you ever known someone whose fault or faults were especially **obnoxious**? Write about what it was like to know this person, and how you reacted to his or her unpleasant qualities.

Check Your Performance			**CHAPTER 5**
Activity	*Number Right*	*Points*	*Total*
Check 2	_____	× 10 =	_____
Related Words	_____	× 10 =	_____
Word Work	_____	× 10 =	_____
Analogies	_____	× 10 =	_____
Final Check	_____	× 10 =	_____

Enter your scores above and in the vocabulary performance chart on the inside back cover of the book.

UNIT ONE: Review

The box at the right lists twenty-five words from Unit One. Using the clues at the bottom of the page, fill in these words to complete the puzzle that follows.

accompany
attitude
betray
cease
challenge
coincide
critical
deliberate
dispute
evident
fertile
fragile
humane
indicate
inhabit
neutral
preference
preserve
reduction
rejection
scarce
solitary
surplus
unstable
utilize

ACROSS

1. To live in
4. Rare; hard to get; not enough to meet demand
6. A decrease; cutback
12. To protect; keep in good condition
13. To show; serve as a sign or signal
15. Done on purpose
17. Extra; more than what is used or needed
18. Not taking sides in a quarrel
19. A test of one's abilities
20. Happening or done alone
21. To happen at the same time
22. Unsteady; wobbly; not reliable
23. Producing or able to produce much fruit, large crops, or many children

DOWN

2. A point of view; state of mind; way of thinking or feeling
3. To be disloyal to; turn against
5. A saying "no" (to a request or desire); refusal
7. To make use of; put to use, especially to good use
8. Disapproving; tending to find fault
9. Easily broken or damaged
10. Obvious; clear
11. Kind; sympathetic; merciful; gentle
14. Choice; first choice; something preferred
15. An argument; a quarrel
16. To go along with; be together with
21. To stop; discontinue

50

UNIT ONE: Test 1

PART A

Choose the word that best completes each item and write it in the space provided.

_____transform_____ 1. A bucket of paint can ___ a room's looks.

      a. transform   b. accompany   c. challenge   d. utilize

_____unstable_____ 2. Jenna was afraid to climb up the ___ ladder—it was too wobbly.

      a. scarce   b. distinct   c. neutral   d. unstable

_____deliberate_____ 3. Kwan thought my not inviting her to my party was a ___ insult. In reality, her invitation slipped under a book, so it never was mailed.

      a. deliberate   b. suitable   c. humane   d. scarce

_____aggravate_____ 4. Don't scratch a mosquito bite! You'll only ___ the itching and end up feeling even worse.

      a. analyze   b. aggravate   c. indicate   d. utilize

_____principal_____ 5. My ___ aim in going to college is to get a good job when I graduate, but I hope to have a good time while I'm there as well.

      a. abundant   b. obnoxious   c. principal   d. desperate

_____determine_____ 6. It took a long time for doctors to ___ what Felicia was allergic to, but they finally figured out that it was her lipstick.

      a. utilize   b. preserve   c. determine   c. restore

_____solitary_____ 7. After hours of ___ work at my desk, I am ready to spend some time with other people.

      a. abundant   b. solitary   c. humane   d. dependent

_____fragile_____ 8. My grandmother's old china doll is much too ___ for my daughter to play with; it would soon be broken.

      a. fragile   b. suitable   c. distinct   c. scarce

_____betray_____ 9. "Your secret is safe with me," said the handsome prince to the fair maiden. "I swear I will never ___ you!"

      a. restore   b. demonstrate   c. preserve   d. betray

_____peculiar_____ 10. The students in history class noticed a ___ odor coming from the chemistry lab across the hall. The odor smelled like a mixture of rotten eggs and gasoline.

      a. suitable   b. scarce   c. fertile   d. peculiar

(Continues on next page)

_____evident_____ 11. It is ___ that Wayne is interested in Shawna; he can't stop looking at her.

        a. humane   b. evident   c. dependent   d. critical

_____inhabit_____ 12. Animals that ___ a desert region are able to live there because they can go a long time without water.

        a. analyze   b. indicate   c. dispose of   d. inhabit

_____demonstrate_____ 13. A salesperson came to our office to ___ how the new copier worked, but he didn't explain very clearly how to use the machine.

        a. preserve   b. restore   c. demonstrate   d. utilize

PART B
Write **C** if the italicized word is used **correctly**. Write **I** if the word is used **incorrectly**.

_C_ 14. Suddenly, the music *ceased*, and the room was very quiet.

_I_ 15. That jigsaw puzzle is a *challenge* because it is too easy. It's meant for very young children and has only six pieces.

_C_ 16. Because of *interference* by a fan who ran onto the playing field, the game was temporarily stopped by a referee.

_I_ 17. Punishments for criminals in the Middle Ages were *humane*. They included being burned alive, beaten to death, branded, and torn apart.

_C_ 18. Maya's elderly parents are too *dependent* on her. They constantly call her for help and advice.

_I_ 19. The bare, dry, stony fields look very *fertile*.

_I_ 20. Raspberries are so *abundant* in our city that when you can find them at all, they cost as much as five or six dollars for a tiny box.

_I_ 21. My *preference* is to go to an Italian restaurant tonight because I dislike spaghetti and pizza.

_C_ 22. The notice in the airplane said, "Seat cushions can be *utilized* for flotation"—or, in other words, you can use the cushions to float on if the plane crashes in water.

_I_ 23. The teenagers on the subway were especially *obnoxious*—they gave up their seats so some elderly people and a pregnant woman could sit down.

_I_ 24. Stone fences are common on New England farms because stones in the fields are so *scarce*.

_C_ 25. Teenage boys are sometimes nervous about asking a girl for a date because they fear *rejection*.

| *Score*   (Number correct) _____ × 4 = _____% |

UNIT ONE: Test 2

PART A

Complete each item with a word from the box. Use each word once.

a. **accompany**	b. **analyze**	c. **category**	d. **coincide**	e. **comparison**
f. **desperate**	g. **dispose of**	h. **intentional**	i. **neutral**	j. **reduction**
k. **restore**	l. **suitable**	m. **surplus**		

intentional   1. The man who stepped on my foot on the bus said, "Sorry! It wasn't ___. I didn't mean to do it!"

surplus   2. Darin's vegetable garden grew so well and produced so much that he didn't know what to do with the ___ tomatoes and zucchinis.

comparison   3. A ___ between the two jobs didn't make it much easier for Marnie to decide; one paid better, but the other was more interesting.

coincide   4. Why do Easter and Passover ___ in some years, while in other years they are weeks apart rather than at the same time?

neutral   5. My middle child hates to fight. When his brother and sister get into a quarrel, he always stays ___.

reduction   6. Americans think too much about weight ___. There is more to life than just losing weight!

analyze   7. The town will ___ traffic patterns to find out if more traffic lights are needed.

category   8. Some psychologists think there are two types of people: type A's, who are hard-working and uptight, and type B's, who are relaxed and easygoing. Which ___ do you belong in?

desperate   9. If a poor man is ___ for money to buy medicine for his sick wife, do you think he should steal?

dispose of   10. Don't ___ the comic section of the Sunday paper. Save it and use it as wrapping paper—it's colorful and fun!

accompany   11. When Josie had a tooth pulled, she asked Mark to ___ her to the dentist and see that she got home all right afterward.

suitable   12. Cut-off jeans might be ___ to wear to a ball game, but they would be out of place at a funeral.

restore   13. The town wants to ___ the old firehouse instead of tearing it down and building a new one.

(Continues on next page)

PART B
Write **C** if the italicized word is used **correctly**. Write **I** if the word is used **incorrectly**.

_C_ 14. Ronda has an unusual *attitude* towards weekends, vacations, and holidays; she doesn't like them much and would just as soon go to work every day of the year.

_I_ 15. Corey's fame as a football player is *considerable*—nobody has ever heard of him.

_I_ 16. Imagine my *frustration* when I learned I had earned straight A's for the semester!

_I_ 17. Helen is far too *critical* of her husband. She adores him and never finds fault with him no matter how badly he treats her.

_C_ 18. To *preserve* the seat covers in his car, Denny had slipcovers put on. Then he put plastic over the slipcovers. Then he spread old sheets over the plastic.

_C_ 19. Denny's concern for his car's seat covers seems to be *excessive*. Who ever heard of using so many layers of covers at once?

_I_ 20. The old photograph was so *distinct* that the faces of the people in it were just a blur.

_C_ 21. "If you get robbed on the street," said the police officer, "never try to *pursue* the thief yourself. Call us and let us do the chasing!"

_I_ 22. There is a real *contrast* between the twins. They look so much alike that sometimes even their mother can't tell them apart.

_C_ 23. Don't *exaggerate* when you fill out a job application. If you were a store clerk, for instance, don't say you were the manager.

_C_ 24. When President Calvin Coolidge wanted to *indicate* that he was not a candidate for reelection, he said, "I do not choose to run."

_I_ 25. Lupe and Jorge are such lovebirds that they agree about everything, so they have one *dispute* after another.

Score   (Number correct) _____ × 4 = _____ %

Enter your score above and in the vocabulary performance chart on the inside back cover of the book.

UNIT ONE: Test 3

PART A: Synonyms
In the space provided, write the letter of the choice that is most nearly the **same** in meaning as the **boldfaced** word.

_d_ 1. **accompany**   **a**) go   **b**) seek   **c**) figure out   **d**) go with

_c_ 2. **analyze**   **a**) worry about   **b**) argue about   **c**) study   **d**) change

_c_ 3. **attitude**   **a**) height   **b**) disappointment   **c**) point of view   **d**) skill

_a_ 4. **category**   **a**) type   **b**) book   **c**) difference
    d) check for similarities and differences

_b_ 5. **challenge**   **a**) quarrel   **b**) something needing effort   **c**) change   **d**) use

_c_ 6. **coincide**   **a**) change   **b**) live in   **c**) happen at the same time   **d**) show

_a_ 7. **comparison**   **a**) check for what is alike and different   **b**) increase
    c) feeling of anger   **d**) first choice

_c_ 8. **considerable**   **a**) unpleasant   **b**) typical   **c**) quite large   **d**) producing much

_c_ 9. **critical**   **a**) kind   **b**) hard to get   **c**) disapproving   **d**) harmful

_a_ 10. **demonstrate**   **a**) show   **b**) get rid of   **c**) turn against   **d**) overstate

_b_ 11. **desperate**   **a**) relying on others   **b**) in great need   **c**) clear   **d**) alone

_c_ 12. **determine**   **a**) prevent   **b**) explain   **c**) figure out   **d**) protect

_c_ 13. **evident**   **a**) hard to get   **b**) fitting   **c**) clear   **d**) too much

_d_ 14. **fertile**   **a**) careful   **b**) helpful   **c**) fearful   **d**) fruitful

_b_ 15. **indicate**   **a**) disapprove of   **b**) show   **c**) turn against   **d**) protect

_c_ 16. **inhabit**   **a**) make a habit of   **b**) seek   **c**) live in   **d**) leave

_a_ 17. **interference**   **a**) getting in the way   **b**) difference   **c**) decrease   **d**) refusing

_a_ 18. **preference**   **a**) first choice   **b**) disappointment   **c**) extra   **d**) test

_d_ 19. **preserve**   **a**) teach   **b**) turn against   **c**) destroy   **d**) protect

_a_ 20. **principal**   **a**) main   **b**) on purpose   **c**) plentiful   **d**) unusual

_b_ 21. **pursue**   **a**) examine   **b**) chase   **c**) get rid of   **d**) stop

_d_ 22. **restore**   **a**) remove   **b**) seek   **c**) give away   **d**) repair

_c_ 23. **solitary**   **a**) rare   **b**) alike   **c**) done alone   **d**) not reliable

_c_ 24. **transform**   **a**) bring back   **b**) send   **c**) change   **d**) end

_b_ 25. **utilize**   **a**) protect   **b**) use   **c**) show   **d**) stop

(Continues on next page)

PART B: Antonyms
In the space provided, write the letter of the choice that is most nearly **opposite** in meaning to the **boldfaced** word.

_c_ 26. **abundant**   a) healthy   b) unplanned   c) rare   d) unkind

_d_ 27. **aggravate**   a) attack   b) learn   c) move   d) make better

_d_ 28. **betray**   a) grow   b) be happy   c) keep   d) be loyal to

_d_ 29. **cease**   a) give   b) learn   c) ruin   d) start

_a_ 30. **contrast**   a) similarity   b) help   c) agreement   d) success

_c_ 31. **deliberate**   a) unusual   b) unclear   c) unplanned   d) unnecessary

_a_ 32. **dependent**   a) relying on oneself   b) working alone   c) knowing oneself   d) not obvious

_b_ 33. **dispose of**   a) like   b) keep   c) leave   d) remember

_b_ 34. **dispute**   a) test   b) agreement   c) group   d) choice

_c_ 35. **distinct**   a) helpful   b) broken   c) unclear   d) well-known

_a_ 36. **exaggerate**   a) understate   b) go away from   c) think about   d) support

_b_ 37. **excessive**   a) not clear   b) not enough   c) strong   d) not able

_d_ 38. **fragile**   a) not proper   b) unhappy   c) unpleasant   d) unbreakable

_d_ 39. **frustration**   a) failure   b) kindness   c) too much   d) satisfaction

_a_ 40. **humane**   a) cruel   b) forgotten   c) important   d) too little

_d_ 41. **intentional**   a) proper   b) done poorly   c) plentiful   d) accidental

_b_ 42. **neutral**   a) paying attention   b) taking sides   c) proper   d) pleasant

_c_ 43. **obnoxious**   a) approving   b) common   c) pleasant   d) intelligent

_b_ 44. **peculiar**   a) difficult   b) ordinary   c) weak   d) excellent

_b_ 45. **reduction**   a) last choice   b) increase   c) start   d) answer

_a_ 46. **rejection**   a) approval   b) addition   c) lack   d) loss

_d_ 47. **scarce**   a) helpful   b) recent   c) too little   d) plentiful

_c_ 48. **suitable**   a) improved   b) unkind   c) improper   d) immediate

_b_ 49. **surplus**   a) success   b) lack   c) luck   d) trouble

_a_ 50. **unstable**   a) steady   b) easy   c) usual   d) quite small

Score   (Number correct) _____ × 2 = _____ %

Enter your score above and in the vocabulary performance chart on the inside back cover of the book.

Unit Two

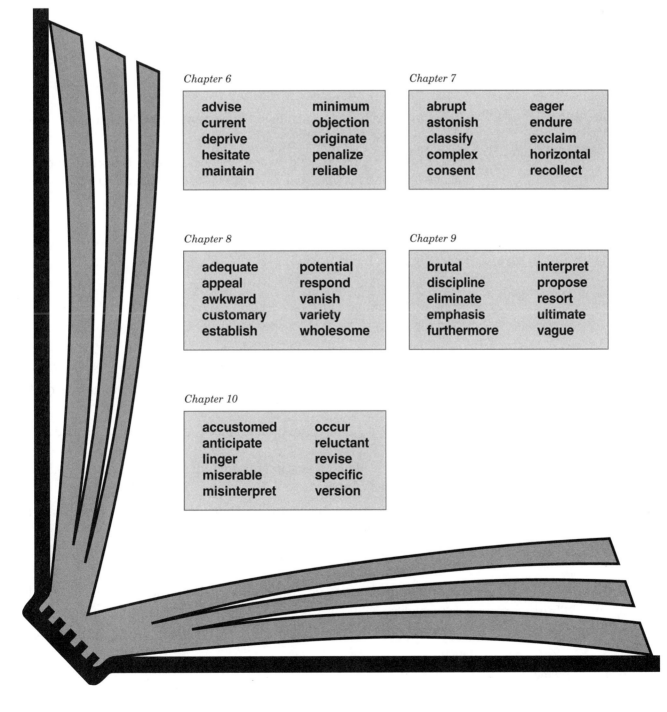

Chapter 6

advise	minimum
current	objection
deprive	originate
hesitate	penalize
maintain	reliable

Chapter 7

abrupt	eager
astonish	endure
classify	exclaim
complex	horizontal
consent	recollect

Chapter 8

adequate	potential
appeal	respond
awkward	vanish
customary	variety
establish	wholesome

Chapter 9

brutal	interpret
discipline	propose
eliminate	resort
emphasis	ultimate
furthermore	vague

Chapter 10

accustomed	occur
anticipate	reluctant
linger	revise
miserable	specific
misinterpret	version

CHAPTER 6

advise	minimum
current	objection
deprive	originate
hesitate	penalize
maintain	reliable

Ten Words in Context

In the space provided, write the letter of the meaning closest to that of each **boldfaced** word. Use the context of the sentences to help you figure out each word's meaning.

1 **advise**
(ăd-vīz′)
– verb

- I'd like to **advise** Alan to break up with Elaine, but I know he'll get angry if I offer my opinion.
- The park ranger said, "I **advise** you to hang your food from a tree if you don't want the bears to get it."

_b_ *Advise* means   a. to punish.   b. to suggest to.   c. to follow.

2 **current**
(kûr′ənt)
– adjective

- Rita keeps up with fashion and buys the **current** styles, but her sister wears the same basic style, year after year.
- Doctors once suggested total bed rest after surgery. However, **current** practice is to have patients walk as soon as possible after an operation.

_a_ *Current* means   a. up-to-date.   b. little known.   c. older.

3 **deprive**
(dĭ-prīv′)
– verb

- Isaac's mother **deprives** him of his allowance when he doesn't do his household jobs.
- Dad complains that his low-fat, low-calorie diet **deprives** him of everything he enjoys eating.

_a_ *Deprive of* means   a. to keep from.   b. to offer to.   c. to protect from.

4 **hesitate**
(hĕz′ĭ-tāt′)
– verb

- I **hesitated** so long about buying the car that someone else bought it first.
- Rodrigo **hesitated** to ask Julie to marry him. He wasn't sure he was ready to get married.

_b_ *Hesitate* means   a. to act quickly.   b. to be undecided.   c. to be pleased.

5 **maintain**
(mān-tān′)
– verb

- When driving, it's important to **maintain** a safe distance between your car and the car ahead of you.
- My brother must have excellent study skills. He was able to **maintain** a B average throughout college while holding a full-time job.

_a_ *Maintain* means   a. to keep up.   b. to give up.   c. to pass up.

6 **minimum**
(mĭn′ə-məm)
– adjective

- The **minimum** number of people allowed for each bus tour is eight. If fewer people sign up, the trip will be canceled.
- What's the **minimum** price you'll take for your car? I can't afford to pay much.

_c_ *Minimum* means   a. oldest.   b. biggest.   c. lowest.

7 objection
(əb-jĕk′shən)
– *noun*

- Luz had a strong **objection** to the wallpaper her husband picked out for their living room. "It looks like a doctor's waiting room," she complained.
- Granddad had a strong **objection** to boys wearing long hair. Once when my father refused to get a haircut, Granddad cut his hair while he was asleep.

c Objection means   a. interest in.   b. memory of.   c. dislike of.

8 originate
(ə-rĭj′ə-nāt′)
– *verb*

- The ice-cream cone **originated** at the 1904 World's Fair in St. Louis. An ice-cream seller ran out of cups, so he wrapped a waffle around the ice cream and sold it that way.
- Many people believe that baseball **originated** in Cooperstown, New York, in 1839. However, it must have started earlier, since the sport was mentioned in English publications as early as 1744.

b Originate means   a. to continue.   b. to begin.   c. to delay.

9 penalize
(pē′nə-līz′)
– *verb*

- Whenever my parents heard I had been kept after school, they would **penalize** me again at home.
- The judge decided to **penalize** the young thief with one hundred hours of volunteer work.

c Penalize means   a. to depend upon.   b. to answer.   c. to punish.

10 reliable
(rĭ-lī′ə-bəl)
– *adjective*

- Joe Sherman is a **reliable** mechanic. You can count on him to tell you the truth and to fix whatever is wrong with your car.
- It's important to me to have a **reliable** baby sitter. I would be very worried if I left my baby with someone I couldn't depend on to do a careful job.

b Reliable means   a. modern.   b. able to be trusted.   c. not expensive.

Matching Words with Definitions

Following are definitions of the ten words. **Print** each word next to its definition. If you look closely at each word in context, you will be able to figure out its meaning.

1.	*objection*	A dislike; feeling of being against something; disapproval
2.	*hesitate*	To stop because of not being able to decide; put off acting because of feeling unsure
3.	*deprive*	To take away from; keep from having or enjoying
4.	*minimum*	Smallest in size or amount that is allowed or possible; least
5.	*maintain*	To continue; carry on; keep in existence
6.	*current*	Modern; existing now; in general use or practice today
7.	*originate*	To come into being; start
8.	*penalize*	To punish; cause to suffer for doing something wrong
9.	*advise*	To give advice to; recommend
10.	*reliable*	Able to be depended upon; trustworthy

CAUTION: Do not go any further until you are sure the above answers are correct. Then you can use the definitions to help you in the following practices. Your goal is eventually to know the words well enough so that you don't need to check the definitions at all.

➤ *Check 1*

Using the answer line, complete each item below with the correct word from the box.

a. **advise**	b. **current**	c. **deprive**	d. **hesitate**	e. **maintain**
f. **minimum**	g. **objection**	h. **originate**	i. **penalize**	j. **reliable**

_____reliable_____ 1. A worker who is honest and does his job carefully would be called a ___ worker.

_____advise_____ 2. My aunt is not a good patient. She rarely does what her doctor ___s her to do.

_____minimum_____ 3. The opposite of the highest salary the company allows would be its ___ salary.

_____penalize_____ 4. It used to be more common for teachers to ___ students by hitting them.

_____originate_____ 5. We can say that the place where a river starts is where it ___s.

_____current_____ 6. We might refer to styles that are widely worn today as ___ fashions.

_____deprive_____ 7. Prisons ___ people of much of their freedom.

_____hesitate_____ 8. I ___ to work more than ten hours a week this semester. I have such difficult classes that I may need more time than usual for studying.

_____objection_____ 9. I have an ___ to that comedian because his jokes often hurt other people.

_____maintain_____ 10. You must keep up a B average to keep your football uniform. In other words, if you don't ___ good grades, you're off the team.

NOTE: Now check your answers to these questions by turning to page 249. Going over the answers carefully will help you prepare for the remaining practices, for which answers are not given.

➤ *Check 2*

Using the answer lines, complete each item below with **two** words from the box.

_____penalize_____
_____deprive_____ 1–2. The best way to ___ Eric when he does something bad is to ___ him of his bicycle for a day.

_____minimum_____
_____reliable_____ 3–4. The girls accepted jobs that paid the ___ wage, hoping that they would get raises once they proved they were ___ workers.

_____objection_____
_____maintain_____ 5–6. My doctor has an ___ to "crash diets." Although they cause a quick reduction° in weight, they do not help the dieter ___ that new, lower weight.

_____current_____
_____advise_____ 7–8. Keisha likes her hair cut in the most ___ style. Her hairdresser ___s her about the newest fashionable looks.

_____originate_____
_____hesitate_____ 9–10. The fox terrier is a dog that ___d in England, where fox hunting was popular. It was valued there by hunters because it would not ___ to run into a fox's tunnel and drive the animal out.

➤ *Related Words*

Once you learn a new word, you can more easily understand many related words. Below are ten words related to the core words of this chapter. Use their definitions to help you write in the word that best completes each item.

a. **maintenance**, *noun*	The work of keeping something in good condition
b. **minimize**, *verb*	To reduce as much as possible
c. **originally**, *adverb*	In the beginning
d. **recur**, *verb*	To happen or appear again
e. **rely**, *verb*	To depend

_____ *recur* _____ 1. While most dreams appear only once, some do ___. For example, one young girl dreamed over and over that she was trying to run from danger, but her shoes were slippery.

_____ *maintenance* _____ 2. Proper ___ of a car involves regularly changing the oil and the sparkplugs.

_____ *minimize* _____ 3. To ___ the damage from a burn, put the burned area in cold water as soon as possible.

_____ *originally* _____ 4. It's hard to believe these shoes were ___ white—now they are gray with dirt.

_____ *rely* _____ 5. Richard shouldn't ___ on his mother so much—he even takes his laundry home for her to wash.

f. **adviser**, *noun*	Someone who gives advice or suggestions
g. **currently**, *adverb*	Now; at the present time
h. **hesitant**, *adjective*	Slow to act; not coming to a decision
i. **object**, *verb*	To speak out against
j. **penalty**, *noun*	A punishment

_____ *hesitant* _____ 6. Since the child was faced with thirty flavors of ice cream, it was not surprising that he was ___ about which one to choose.

_____ *currently* _____ 7. I am ___ enrolled as a full-time student, so I can work only at a part-time job.

_____ *object* _____ 8. So many people ___ed to the idea of a giant weekend rock concert in town that the idea was given up.

_____ *penalty* _____ 9. The soccer player touched the ball with her hands; as a ___, the other team got a free goal kick.

_____ *adviser* _____ 10. As I looked for an ___ to help me make a difficult decision, I thought about several people whom I like and respect.

➤ *Word Work*

A. Write each word next to the examples that best match it.

a. **advise**	b. **hesitate**	c. **originate**
d. **penalize**	e. **reliable**	

penalize   1. Send a murderer to prison.
Keep a teenager from a party because of poor behavior.
Tell a wild four-year-old to go to her room.

reliable   2. A car that always starts
A friend who is there when you need her
A bus that is never late

advise   3. Tell a good friend to stay in school.
Suggest to your sister that she should develop her musical talent.
Encourage an elderly person to get a pet.

hesitate   4. Being unable to decide whether to ask Gil to the dance
Stopping because of being uncertain about which way to go
Delaying the purchase of a new car because of doubt about paying so much

originate   5. Friday gets its name from "Freya," the name of a Norse goddess.
Ice-cream sundaes get their name because they were first sold only on Sundays.
Floating Ivory soap was invented accidentally when a soap-mixing machine was left on too long.

B. In the space provided, write the letter of the choice that best completes each item.

b   6. You are likely to have an **objection** to something
      a. helpful.   b. harmful.   c. recent.

c   7. To **maintain** good health, you should
      a. start smoking.   b. shop.   c. exercise.

a   8. **Current** movies are
      a. playing now.   b. old classics.   c. comedies.

c   9. Raised in an orphanage, the child was **deprived** of
      a. regular meals.   b. clothing and shelter.   c. a mother and father.

b   10. To buy clothing at the **minimum** cost, go to
      a. department stores.   b. garage sales.   c. France.

➣ *Word Parts*

A. The suffixes *-ance* and *-ence* often mean "the act, state, or quality of."

Examples: *maintain* — to keep in existence   *patient* — willing to put up with something
maintenance — the act of keeping   *patience* — the quality of being patient
in existence

On each answer line, write the word from the box that means the same as the *italicized* words.

a. **avoidance**	b. **excellence**	c. **dependence**
d. **interference°**	e. **maintenance**	

_____interference_____ 1. "I know you mean well," the woman said to her mother. "But I'm 25 now, and your *act of interfering* in how I do my job is not helpful."

_____dependence_____ 2. My father's *state of depending* on caffeine is not healthy for him.

_____excellence_____ 3. Takeo aims for *the quality of being excellent* in everything he does.

_____maintenance_____ 4. The *act of maintaining* of good grades requires a lot of willpower.

_____avoidance_____ 5. Anna's *act of avoiding* milk is easily explained—she is allergic to it.

B. The prefix *in -* often means "not," which can change words to their opposites.

Examples: *direct* — in a straight line   *humane°* — kind
indirect — not in a straight line   *inhumane* — not kind

On each answer line, write the word from the box that best completes the item.

f. **incapable**	g. **inconvenient**	h. **indistinct°**
i. **inexpensive**	j. **inhumane**	

_____indistinct_____ 6. The fog was so thick that the road signs were ___, and I could barely see them.

_____inconvenient_____ 7. I wish there were a grocery store nearby—it is ___ to have to drive all the way across town.

_____inhumane_____ 8. Treatment of elderly patients is sometimes ___. Some have been tied down to their chairs and ignored.

_____incapable_____ 9. The firefighters rescued all the people, but they were ___ of saving the building.

_____inexpensive_____ 10. Since we are on a budget, we buy ___ furniture at flea markets. In comparison° with our friends' new furniture, the old pieces we buy are often of better quality.

➣ *Final Check*

Read the passages carefully. Then fill in each blank with the word that best fits the context.

A. Toasters

a. **current**	b. **maintain**	c. **minimum**
d. **originate**	e. **reliable**	

Although the practice of eating toasted bread (1)_____*originate*_____d about 4600 years ago, the pop-up electric toaster was not invented until 1919. These early pop-up toasters were not very (2)_____*reliable*_____—they broke down often. Also, they weren't able to (3)_____*maintain*_____ an even temperature but grew hotter and hotter with each piece of bread toasted. Some poor-quality machines even popped the toast all the way across the room. Over the years, toasters have certainly improved. (4)_____*Current*_____ ones give us a (5)_____*minimum*_____ of problems with repairs and temperature control.

B. A Mean Man

f. **advise**	g. **deprive**	h. **hesitate**
i. **objection**	j. **penalize**	

Mr. Barker says that he has no (6)_____*objection*_____ to kids—as long as they don't come into his yard, as long as they don't (7)_____*deprive*_____ him of peace and quiet, and as long as they don't grow up to be teenagers.

Neighborhood kids say he's the meanest man they ever met. Who can blame them? If he sees them choosing up sides for a ball game in the street, for example, he doesn't (8)_____*hesitate*_____ a minute. He runs right to his window and yells, "You can't do that in front of MY house!" The kids are afraid of him, but they yell back that the street belongs to everybody. "Well, I (9)_____*advise*_____ you to watch your step!" he replies. "If any of you kids break my window or step on my flowers, you will be (10)_____*penalize*_____d." Then he slams his window shut. Maybe a hard life has made Mr. Barker the way he is, but it's hard to have warm feelings for someone so obnoxious°.

➤ *Questions for Discussion*

1. Does someone you know have a nickname? How did that nickname **originate**?

2. Whom do you think of as a **reliable** person in your life? Whom do you think of as not reliable? Explain your answers.

3. Name one **current** song, movie, or TV show that you enjoy. Then explain why you like it.

4. What do you think should be the **minimum** legal age for people to buy alcohol? To vote? To serve in the military?

5. Is there a time when it was clear to you that a friend was making a mistake? Did you try to **advise** the friend to do things differently, or did you **hesitate** to interfere? Tell about what your friend was doing and what you did, if anything.

➤ *Ideas for Writing*

1. Write a paper about what you think are some proper ways to **penalize** children when they misbehave. For example, do you think it is ever right to punish a child by spanking? Or do you think a better punishment is to **deprive** children of something they want?

2. What is one thing you especially dislike about the school you attend? Write about your **objection**, explaining what it is is based on. End your paper by telling what you would **advise** the people who run the school to do about that problem.

Check Your Performance   **CHAPTER 6**

Activity	Number Right	Points	Total
Check 2	_____	× 10 =	_____
Related Words	_____	× 10 =	_____
Word Work	_____	× 10 =	_____
Word Parts	_____	× 10 =	_____
Final Check	_____	× 10 =	_____

Enter your scores above and in the vocabulary performance chart on the inside back cover of the book.

CHAPTER

7

abrupt	eager
astonish	endure
classify	exclaim
complex	horizontal
consent	recollect

Ten Words in Context

In the space provided, write the letter of the meaning closest to that of each **boldfaced** word. Use the context of the sentences to help you figure out each word's meaning.

1 abrupt
(ə-brŭpt′)
– *adjective*

- Seat belts in cars protect passengers from injuries caused by **abrupt** stops.
- An **abrupt** burst of laughter during the church service surprised everyone.

_c_ *Abrupt* means   a. silent.   b. simple.   c. not expected.

2 astonish
(ə-stŏn′ĭsh)
– *verb*

- A magician **astonished** the audience by making seemingly impossible things happen.
- The announcement that the factory was closing forever **astonished** the employees, who had not known their jobs were in danger.

_c_ *Astonish* means   a. to delay.   b. to encourage.   c. to surprise.

3 classify
(klăs′ə-fī′)
– *verb*

- The stamp collector **classified** her stamps by countries—she put all the stamps from France together, all the stamps from Spain together, and so on.
- I was surprised to learn that the sea horse is **classified** by scientists as a fish.

_b_ *Classify* means   a. to lose.   b. to group.   c. to remember.

4 complex
(kəm-plĕks′)
– *adjective*

- Because income tax forms are so **complex**, many people hire professionals to prepare their tax returns.
- Our family is rather **complex**—it includes many second marriages and stepfamilies. At family reunions we spend a lot of time trying to figure out how we are all related.

_a_ *Complex* means   a. hard to understand.   b. helpful.   c. small.

5 consent
(kən-sĕnt′)
– *verb*

- Only applicants who **consented** to a drug test were considered for the job.
- Enrique proposed to Anna by putting up a billboard saying, "Will you marry me?" She **consented** with her own sign that said, "Of course I will."

_a_ *Consent* means   a. to say yes.   b. to listen.   c. to disagree.

6 eager
(ē′gər)
– *adjective*

- I am always **eager** to read the latest murder story by my favorite mystery writer.
- Our dog is **eager** to greet us when we come home. She jumps up on us and begins licking our hands before the door is even shut.

_c_ *Eager* means   a. bored.   b. patient.   c. happily excited.

7 endure
(ĕn-dŏŏr′)
– *verb*

- We'll have to **endure** a few more weeks of cold, gray winter before spring arrives.
- Until someone finds a cure for the common cold, there's not much to do but **endure** the runny noses and sneezes.

__c__ *Endure* means   a. to enjoy.   b. to organize.   c. to live with unwillingly.

8 exclaim
(ĭk-sklām′)
– *verb*

- "Wow!" "Ooooh!" "Aaah!" the crowd **exclaimed** as the colorful fireworks burst in the sky.
- When a cardinal landed on the bird feeder, the little girl **exclaimed**, "Look! A red blue jay!"

__c__ *Exclaim* means   a. to remember.   b. to complain.   c. to call out.

9 horizontal
(hŏr′ĭ-zŏn′tl)
– *adjective*

- The surgery left a **horizontal** scar that runs from one side of my stomach to the other.
- **Horizontal** stripes on clothing generally make the wearer look wider.

__c__ *Horizontal* means   a. dirty.   b. little.   c. running from side to side.

10 recollect
(rĕk′ə-lĕkt′)
– *verb*

- Can you **recollect** much about being in first grade?
- I couldn't **recollect** my sister's phone number, so I had to call the phone company's information number.

__b__ *Recollect* means   a. to agree with.   b. to remember.   c. to arrange.

Matching Words with Definitions

Following are definitions of the ten words. **Print** each word next to its definition. If you look closely at each word in context, you will be able to figure out its meaning.

1. _____horizontal_____   Lying flat; lying or extending from side to side (as opposed to going up and down)

2. _____endure_____   To put up with; bear patiently

3. _____eager_____   Looking forward to with great interest or desire

4. _____complex_____   Not simple; not easy to understand or figure out

5. _____consent_____   To agree to something

6. _____exclaim_____   To speak or cry out suddenly, as from strong feelings or surprise

7. _____classify_____   To arrange or organize into groups or types; place in a category°

8. _____recollect_____   To remember; bring an image or idea back to mind

9. _____astonish_____   To surprise greatly; amaze

10. _____abrupt_____   Sudden and unexpected

CAUTION: Do not go any further until you are sure the above answers are correct. Then you can use the definitions to help you in the following practices. Your goal is eventually to know the words well enough so that you don't need to check the definitions at all.

➤ *Check 1*

Using the answer line, complete each item below with the correct word from the box.

a. **abrupt**	b. **astonish**	c. **classify**	d. **complex**	e. **consent**
f. **eager**	g. **endure**	h. **exclaim**	i. **horizontal**	j. **recollect**

endure   1. Sometimes I think I can't ___ one more day of winter, but I know I have to put up with it until spring.

classify   2. Did you know that scientists ___ the whale as a mammal? Most people think of it as a fish.

recollect   3. Although I remember little about first grade, I ___ my year in third grade very clearly.

astonish   4. The great magician Houdini would ___ audiences by escaping from chains, locked trunks, and even sealed coffins.

exclaim   5. The day after Jackie had her waist-length hair cut short, nearly everyone she met ___ed, "Oh! Your hair!"

abrupt   6. A car would probably come to an ___ stop if a dog ran out in front of it.

eager   7. Knowing that she had done well on every test, Phyllis was ___ to see her final grade for the course.

complex   8. Why must our tax forms be so ___? Why can't the government make them easier to understand?

horizontal   9. It's true that ___ stripes on clothing make you look wider, and stripes that go up and down make you look taller.

consent   10. If you won the lottery, would you ___ to having your name and picture printed in the newspaper?

NOTE: Now check your answers to these questions by turning to page 249. Going over the answers carefully will help you prepare for the remaining practices, for which answers are not given.

➤ *Check 2*

Using the answer lines, complete each item below with **two** words from the box.

abrupt   1–2. In early spring, ___ changes in the weather can ___ everyone. It may
astonish   be mild and sunny in the morning, then snowing by bedtime.

consent   3–4. I didn't want to have dental surgery, but I decided to ___ to it rather
endure   than ___ my toothache any longer. I just want the pain to cease°.

recollect   5–6. I am thinking of buying Felix a striped T-shirt for his birthday, but I
horizontal   can't ___ if he likes to wear ___ stripes or stripes that go up and down.

classify   7–8. Scientists ___ animals in a ___ system of groupings, using features
complex   such as being warm- or cold-blooded and having feathers or scales.

eager   9–10. My kids are not exactly ___ to go to school; when I wake them every
exclaim   morning, they ___, "Oh, no! Isn't it Saturday yet?"

➤ *Related Words*

Once you learn a new word, you can more easily understand many related words. Below are ten words related to the core words of this chapter. Use their definitions to help you write in the word that best completes each item.

a. **eagerly**, *adverb*	With excitement and impatience
b. **eagerness**, *noun*	An impatient desire for something
c. **exclamation**, *noun*	A cry or shout of excitement or strong feeling
d. **horizon**, *noun*	The level line where earth (or water) and sky seem to meet
e. **recollection**, *noun*	A memory

_____*recollection*_____ 1. Ramon fell off his bicycle and was knocked out; later he had no ___ of the accident—he couldn't remember it at all.

_____*eagerly*_____ 2. Sitting on the front steps, I waited ___ for the mail to arrive; I was expecting a letter from my boyfriend.

_____*eagerness*_____ 3. My little daughter was too excited on Christmas morning—in her ___ to see her presents, she tumbled down the stairs.

_____*horizon*_____ 4. In the movie, the shipwrecked sailors constantly watched for a rescue ship on the ___.

_____*exclamation*_____ 5. When their rescuers finally appeared, the sailors shouted out a one-word ___: "Saved!"

f. **abruptly**, *adverb*	Suddenly; unexpectedly
g. **astonishment**, *noun*	Great surprise or amazement
h. **classification**, *noun*	A group or division
i. **complexity**, *noun*	The quality of being detailed and hard to understand
j. **endurance**, *noun*	The ability to bear a hardship

_____*endurance*_____ 6. Distance runners need to have not only strength and speed, but also ___, to keep on going with pain and thirst for so many miles.

_____*classification*_____ 7. Tomatoes belong to the ___ of fruits, not the category° of vegetables.

_____*complexity*_____ 8. The ___ of the subject makes my chemistry course difficult, but it is also very interesting. Since I want to maintain° a good grade-point average, I'll have to study hard.

_____*abruptly*_____ 9. Heidi's boyfriend took her by surprise when he ___ asked her to marry him.

_____*astonishment*_____ 10. When Heidi told us about the engagement, she said, "Imagine my ___! He always said he wasn't the marrying kind."

➤ *Word Work*

A. In the space provided, write the letter of the word that most closely relates to the situation in each item.

_b_   1. At one point on the highway, there are eight lanes of traffic, three different levels, and about twenty signs with arrows pointing every which way.

    a. eager   b. complex   c. consent

_a_   2. Len's leaving his job was very sudden; one day he just marched in and said, "I quit."

    a. abrupt   b. horizontal   c. classify

_c_   3. The trees that had fallen during the storm lay flat on the ground.

    a. recollect   b. consent   c. horizontal

_a_   4. When the doors of the store opened on the day of the big sale, shoppers rushed in, excited about finding the best bargains.

    a. eager   b. horizontal   c. consent

_c_   5. The boys sort the coins they've saved into separate piles: pennies here, nickels there, dimes next, and then quarters.

    a. endure   b. exclaim   c. classify

B. In the space provided, write the letter of the choice that best completes each item.

_b_   6. Thelma **recollects** her neighbor's kindness. She

    a. is disappointed   b. knows her neighbor   c. doubts that her neighbor
        in her neighbor.   can be kind.   can be kind.

_c_   7. You are likely to **exclaim** a

    a. list.   b. stamp collection.   c. statement of surprise.

_b_   8. The rich heroine in the story announces that she wants to marry a poor woodcutter. Her father tells her, "I will never **consent** to such a marriage!" Her father felt that the woodcutter would be

    a. a good match for his daughter.   b. a poor match for his daughter.

_b_   9. When my best friend told me that he and his wife were divorcing, I was **astonished**. Obviously, I

    a. had expected the   b. had not expected   c. was not very interested.
        divorce for a long time.   it to happen.

_a_ 10. It is difficult to **endure**

    a. a terrible headache.   b. a good dinner.   c. a sunny day.

➤ *Synonyms and Antonyms*

A. Synonyms. Write the letter of the word or phrase that most nearly means the **same** as each boldfaced word.

_c_ 1. **abrupt**

      a. expected   b. delayed

      c. sudden   d. polite

_d_ 2. **astonish**

      a. borrow   b. request

      c. allow   d. surprise

_d_ 3. **classify**

      a. set aside for later   b. have no use for

      c. decide the value   d. organize into groups

_a_ 4. **endure**

      a. bear up under   b. remember

      c. agree   d. deny

_b_ 5. **exclaim**

      a. tell   b. call out

      c. notice   d. bear

B. Antonyms. Write the letter of the word or phrase that most nearly means the **opposite** of each boldfaced word.

_a_ 6. **complex**

      a. simple   b. true

      c. interesting   d. wise

_b_ 7. **consent**

      a. try   b. disagree

      c. begin   d. practice

_d_ 8. **eager**

      a. unsteady   b. perfect

      c. expected   d. not interested

_c_ 9. **horizontal**

      a. in a circle   b. lying at a slant

      c. straight up and down   d. outside

_a_ 10. **recollect**

      a. forget   b. forgive

      c. plan   d. wonder

➤ *Final Check*

Read the passages carefully. Then fill in each blank with the word that best fits the context.

A. A Special Memory

a. **astonish**	b. **consent**	c. **eager**
d. **horizontal**	e. **recollect**	

Tony and I often did things without asking our mom to (1)_____*consent*_____ to our activities—because she probably wouldn't. Besides, we loved secret projects. One summer we built a treehouse hidden among some tall trees on Mr. Leary's lot. The window was crooked, and the floor wasn't exactly (2)_____*horizontal*_____, although the tilt wasn't too bad. We took Mom's ladder to use as our stairs and decorated the place with an old rug and some pillows.

One day we heard Mom yelling up to us, "So that's where my ladder went!" Then she told us that Mr. Leary had called to say that the treehouse had to come down. "You could fall and get hurt," she explained, "and he doesn't want to get sued—and he's right. That treehouse is dangerous. I advise° you to come down from there right now."

But that night, (3)_____*eager*_____ to spend one last hour there, Tony and I sneaked out and headed for the treehouse. As we got near it, we were (4)_____*astonish*_____ed to see a candle glowing in the crooked window, so we climbed up very quietly and peeked in. I can still (5)_____*recollect*_____ the scene clearly. There was Mom, sitting on one of our pillows, smiling. Next to her were a pitcher of lemonade and three glasses. "It's about time you got here," she said. "What took you so long?"

B. Watch Your Manners!

f. **abrupt**	g. **classify**	h. **complex**
i. **endure**	j. **exclaim**	

Most of us think we know how to be polite. But some things that Americans (6)_____*classify*_____ as good manners may seem rude in other parts of the world. Every culture has its own (7)_____*complex*_____ set of rules about what is and isn't acceptable.

For example, an American who went to a birthday party in Japan brought the fun to an (8)_____*abrupt*_____ end by giving a clock as a present. In Japan, giving anyone a clock is a way of saying "I hope your time is running out"—in other words, "I hope you die soon." Also, Americans in China are seen as bad-tempered when they (9)_____*exclaim*_____ something loudly, out of excitement or to make a point. In China, a loud voice is a sign of strong anger.

Of course, foreign visitors to the United States can also misunderstand our ways. For instance, one Arab who was a guest at a banquet in Washington later complained, "I didn't get a thing to eat." It turned out he had said, "No, thank you," each time he was offered food. In his country, it was good manners to refuse food several times before accepting it. His American hosts didn't know that, so they just let the poor fellow (10)_____*endure*_____ his hunger.

➤ *Questions for Discussion*

1. Scientists think there may once have been some kind of life on Mars—not little green men, but simple life forms. If this turns out to be true, would it **astonish** you? Why or why not?

2. Which do you find harder to **endure**: a heat wave in the summer or bitter cold in the winter? What do you like to do to help you deal with the discomfort?

3. Can you think of an **abrupt** event you have experienced, that is, something that happened suddenly and without warning? It might have been something important, like the end of a relationship, or something minor, like a sudden rainstorm. Tell what it was like.

4. What things in your life would you **classify** as too **complex**? Can you think of any ways you might try to make the things in this group simpler?

5. Did you ever **exclaim** something without meaning to—in class, for instance, or on a bus, or at a movie? Can you **recollect** how it happened? Can you remember how you felt and what happened afterwards?

➤ *Ideas for Writing*

1. Write about a time when, as a child or later, you were **eager** to do something, but your parents wouldn't **consent**. Try to explain both points of view, yours and theirs. How do you feel now about what happened?

2. **Classifying** items helps to show the similarities and differences between them. Write a paper in which you classify something into two or three groups. Explain the features of each group and how each member of the group fits in. For instance, you might divide your classes into those in which the teacher lectures and those that require students to participate actively.

Check Your Performance   **CHAPTER 7**

Activity	Number Right	Points	Total
Check 2	_____	× 10 =	_____
Related Words	_____	× 10 =	_____
Word Work	_____	× 10 =	_____
Synonyms and Antonyms	_____	× 10 =	_____
Final Check	_____	× 10 =	_____

Enter your scores above and in the vocabulary performance chart on the inside back cover of the book.

adequate	potential
appeal	respond
awkward	vanish
customary	variety
establish	wholesome

Ten Words in Context

In the space provided, write the letter of the meaning closest to that of each **boldfaced** word. Use the context of the sentences to help you figure out each word's meaning.

1 adequate
(ăd′ĭ-kwĭt)
– *adjective*

- When I didn't have time to wash the windows, I hired a neighbor's child to do it. He did an **adequate** job—not perfect, but good enough.
- Open sandals are not **adequate** footwear for factory work. You should wear heavy shoes to protect your feet.

_a_ *Adequate* means   a. OK.   b. poor.   c. popular.

2 appeal
(ə-pēl′)
– *verb*

- Every year, Jerry Lewis goes on TV to **appeal** to viewers for money to help people with the illness muscular dystrophy.
- When police can't solve a crime, they sometimes **appeal** to the public for help.

_c_ *Appeal* means   a. to answer.   b. to run.   c. to make a request.

3 awkward
(ôk′wərd)
– *adjective*

- When I was 13, I was very **awkward**. My feet seemed too big, and I was always tripping over things.
- Rico is such an **awkward** dancer that he constantly steps on his partner's feet.

_b_ *Awkward* means   a. not strong.   b. not graceful.   c. kind.

4 customary
(kŭs′tə-měr′ē)
– *adjective*

- In some towns, it's **customary** for the "Welcome Wagon" to visit newcomers and tell them about the town.
- Americans usually eat their big meal in the evening. In Ireland, however, it is **customary** to eat a big dinner in the afternoon and a light meal at night.

_b_ *Customary* means   a. not polite.   b. normal.   c. rare.

5 establish
(ĭ-stăb′lĭsh)
– *verb*

- The first lending library was **established** in Scotland in 1725.
- The first movie theater in the United States was **established** in New Orleans in 1896.

_c_ *Establish* means   a. to leave.   b. to stop.   c. to start.

6 potential
(pə-tĕn′shəl)
– *noun*

- My grandmother had the **potential** to be a great teacher, but she couldn't afford to go to college.
- Everyone agrees that Carlos has the **potential** of being a major league baseball player. To become that good, he must continue to work hard.

_c_ *Potential* means   a. request.   b. memory.   c. ability.

7 respond
(rĭ'spŏnd')
– *verb*

- You asked me a question, so why don't you stop talking for a minute so that I can **respond**?
- The group of men whistled and called out to Kim as she walked by, but she didn't **respond** at all. She simply kept walking.

_a_ *Respond* means   a. to reply.   b. to repeat.   c. to leave.

8 vanish
(văn'ĭsh)
– *verb*

- The magician made the rabbit **vanish** by slipping it under a secret door.
- You gave a stranger $500 in cash to paint your house? How do you know he won't **vanish** with the money?

_c_ *Vanish* means   a. to answer.   b. to begin.   c. to go out of sight.

9 variety
(və-rī'ə-tē)
– *noun*

- In the spring, the woods contain a **variety** of wildflowers, including bluebells, daffodils, and violets.
- Instead of being a **variety** of colors, all of Gale's clothes were lavender or purple.

_a_ *Variety* means   a. mixture.   b. absence.   c. shade.

10 wholesome
(hōl'səm)
– *adjective*

- Ken used to spend hours in a smoky video arcade where drug dealers hung out, but now he prefers more **wholesome** activities, like sports and music.
- We now know smoking is not **wholesome**, but early cigarette ads claimed physical and mental benefits for smokers.

_c_ *Wholesome* means   a. obvious.   b. expensive.   c. healthy.

Matching Words with Definitions

Following are definitions of the ten words. **Print** each word next to its definition. If you look closely at each word in context, you will be able to figure out its meaning.

1. _____establish_____   To bring into being; set up
2. _____appeal_____   To make an important request (to someone for something)
3. _____variety_____   A number of different kinds; assortment
4. _____wholesome_____   Tending to improve the character, the mind, or the body
5. _____respond_____   To answer, either by word or by action
6. _____adequate_____   Good enough (to meet the need)
7. _____customary_____   Usual; commonly done
8. _____vanish_____   To disappear from sight
9. _____awkward_____   Clumsy; not graceful
10. _____potential_____   A natural ability that may or may not develop; possibility

CAUTION: Do not go any further until you are sure the above answers are correct. Then you can use the definitions to help you in the following practices. Your goal is eventually to know the words well enough so that you don't need to check the definitions at all.

➣ *Check 1*

Using the answer line, complete each item below with the correct word from the box.

a. **adequate**	b. **appeal**	c. **awkward**	d. **customary**	e. **establish**
f. **potential**	g. **respond**	h. **vanish**	i. **variety**	j. **wholesome**

potential   1. An acorn has the ___ to be an oak tree.

vanish   2. I looked everywhere for my car keys, but they seem to have ___ed into thin air.

variety   3. Rodney has worked in a ___ of positions, including trucker, carpenter, and rancher.

appeal   4. The signs the children put up on telephone poles ___ed to people to help find their lost cat.

wholesome   5. Starting a day with exercise is more ___ than starting the day with a cigarette.

adequate   6. I'd love a huge apartment, but this small one is ___; it serves my needs.

establish   7. The American Girl Scouts were ___ed in 1912.

customary   8. People's habits can be referred to as their ___ behavior.

respond   9. When asked a question, we usually ___, even if it's only to say, "I don't know."

awkward   10. On land, crocodiles seem slow and ___, but once in the water they are fast and graceful swimmers.

NOTE: Now check your answers to these questions by turning to page 249. Going over the answers carefully will help you prepare for the remaining practices, for which answers are not given.

➣ *Check 2*

Using the answer lines, complete each item below with **two** words from the box.

establish
wholesome   1–2. Parents were happy when the Youth Club was ___ed in town because it gave their kids a ___ place to go, have fun, and meet their friends.

variety
adequate   3–4. The ___ of fruits and vegetables at Fresh Foods is ___, but not as good as the selection at Grocery Giant.

appeal
potential   5–6. A talent agent ___ed to Christi's parents to let her appear in commercials. He thought Christi had the ___ of being a very good model and making a lot of money. However, her parents had an objection° to letting a ten-year-old work.

vanish
respond   7–8. In my dream, an old woman says, "Hurry! Come with me!" But I never go with her—she ___es before I have a chance to ___.

customary
awkward   9–10. It is ___ for people to bow to one another in Japan. When Fred visited that country he bowed too, even though he felt ___ doing it.

➤ *Related Words*

Once you learn a new word, you can more easily understand many related words. Below are ten words related to the core words of this chapter. Use their definitions to help you write in the word that best completes each item.

a. **customarily**, *adverb*	Usually
b. **establishment**, *noun*	A business
c. **response**, *noun*	An answer
d. **unwholesome**, *adjective*	Having a bad effect on health or character
e. **various**, *adjective*	Several; of different kinds

_____establishment_____ 1. One of the oldest ___s in the city is the Red Lion Inn, which was built in 1835.

_____unwholesome_____ 2. Letty's parents are afraid that her older boyfriend, who has been in trouble with the law, is an ___ influence on her.

_____response_____ 3. When we asked the crying child what was the matter, her only ___ was to cry louder.

_____customarily_____ 4. Quaker religious services ___ take place in silence.

_____various_____ 5. We tried ___ ways to get rid of the mice in our house, including traps, poison, and a cat.

f. **responsive**, *adjective*	Reacting in a positive way
g. **custom**, *noun*	A habit
h. **inadequate**, *adjective*	Not good enough
i. **potentially**, *adverb*	Possibly; able to happen
j. **re-establish**, *verb*	To set up again

_____inadequate_____ 6. It is natural to feel ___ on the first days of a new job—there is so much to learn!

_____responsive_____ 7. The teacher was not ___ to the students' suggestion that the test be canceled.

_____potentially_____ 8. A loaded gun in the same house with curious children creates a ___ deadly situation—an accident could easily happen.

_____custom_____ 9. It is my grandfather's ___ to walk three miles each morning before breakfast.

_____re-establish_____ 10. After years of being out of touch, Dad and his brother have ___ed their friendship.

➤ *Word Work*

A. Write each word next to the examples that best match it.

a. **appeal**	b. **awkward**	c. **customary**
d. **variety**	e. **wholesome**	

_____customary_____ 1. Ice cream and cake at a birthday party
Saying "Bless you" when someone sneezes
Saying "Hello" when answering the phone

_____appeal_____ 2. Ask people to become blood donors for the Red Cross.
Seek new volunteers for the public library.
Call upon the public to provide tips to help the police solve a crime.

_____wholesome_____ 3. A teen dance that is alcohol- and smoke-free
A bowl of shredded-wheat cereal, topped with sliced banana and skim milk
A morally uplifting movie

_____awkward_____ 4. Bumping into someone in the doorway
Tripping over your shoelace
Spilling your coffee

_____variety_____ 5. Dogs: German shepherds, cocker spaniels, Italian bulldogs
Ice cream: Strawberry, peach, butter pecan
Art supplies: Crayons, markers, oil paints, watercolors

B. In the space provided, write the letter of the word that most closely relates to the situation in each item.

_a_ 6. The Spanish-speaking students are going to set up their own Latino Club.

    a. establish   b. vanish   c. variety

_b_ 7. The wading pool is big enough for the children to splash around and cool off, even if they can't really swim in it.

    a. vanish   b. adequate   c. respond

_c_ 8. After watching Pablo play basketball with his friends, the coach said, "You ought to try out for the team. I think you could become a terrific player."

    a. variety   b. awkward   c. potential

_a_ 9. Jen taught her dog to obey whenever he hears her say "Sit!"

    a. respond   b. various   c. vanish

_b_ 10. The famous pilot Amelia Earhart took off on a round-the-world flight in the summer of 1937 and was never seen again.

    a. appealed   b. vanished   c. established

➤ *Word Parts*

A. The prefix *re-* often mean "again."

> ***Examples:*** *utilize°* — to make use of
> *reutilize* — to make use of again

On each answer line, write the word from the box that best completes the item.

a. **reanalyze°**	b. **re-establish**	c. **reheat**
d. **relearn**	e. **reutilize°**	

_____reheat_____ 1. When I get home late from work, I usually find some leftovers that I can ___ for dinner.

_____relearn_____ 2. It is easier to ___ something you once knew and forgot than to learn something for the first time.

_____relocate_____ 3. Mr. Amin did not give up when a highway was built where his store had once been. He decided to ___ his business in another part of town.

_____reanalyze_____ 4. After finishing a difficult math problem, I often ___ it, just to be sure I have the correct answer.

_____reutilize_____ 5. After I empty plastic bags from the supermarket, I ___ them. I may use them as storage bags or even bring them back to the supermarket to use there again.

B. The prefix *un-* often means "not." It can change words to their opposites.

> ***Examples:*** *intentional°* — done on purpose   *stable* — steady
> *unintentional* — not done on purpose; done by accident   *unstable°* — not steady

On each answer line, write the word from the box that best completes the item.

f. **unintentional°**	g. **uninterested**	h. **unlucky**
i. **unstable°**	j. **unwholesome**	

_____uninterested_____ 6. Most dogs are ___ in vegetables.

_____unwholesome_____ 7. Many people eat an ___ diet, filled with fried foods, fatty meats, and sugar, and lacking in vegetables and grains.

_____unintentional_____ 8. "Oh, I'm sorry," said the man who bumped into me. "That was ___."

_____unlucky_____ 9. So many people believe that the number thirteen is ___ that some hotels won't give a room that number.

_____unstable_____ 10. Our strangely shaped dining-room chairs are so ___ that several people have fallen out of them.

➤ *Final Check*

Read the passages carefully. Then fill in each blank with the word that best fits the context.

A. Big Brothers and Sisters

a. **appeal**	b. **establish**	c. **potential**
d. **variety**	e. **wholesome**	

This week, the local Big Brother/Big Sister Agency (1)_____*appeal*_____ed to the community for volunteers. The organization is looking for men and women who are willing to (2)_____*establish*_____ a new friendship with a young boy or girl from a single-parent home. The only thing required for becoming a volunteer is the desire to become friends with the children, to help them to stay in school, and to choose (3)_____*wholesome*_____ activities that will keep them out of trouble. Volunteers can do a (4)_____*variety*_____ of things with their little "brothers" or "sisters," such as taking them to the park or going out to eat. Whatever activities they choose, volunteers will play an important part in the children's lives, helping them to build their (5)_____*potential*_____ to live full lives and become good citizens.

B. Kevin's First Date

f. **adequate**	g. **awkward**	h. **customary**
i. **respond**	j. **vanish**	

If you ask Kevin what the most embarrasing time of his life was, he will surely tell you about his first date, for a ninth-grade dance. He was so afraid of rejection° when he asked the girl to go with him that he almost didn't notice when she consented° to be his date.

The day of the dance was no better. Between the time he rang her doorbell and the time her father answered, he forgot his date's name—completely. He mumbled something about school (he did remember the school's name), and the girl's father let him in. The man then shot some questions at Kevin, to make sure he was an (6)_____*adequate*_____ date for his darling daughter. Kevin could barely (7)_____*respond*_____ to the questions because his nervous thirteen-year-old voice squeaked and cracked so much.

Since it was (8)_____*customary*_____ for boys to bring flowers on this special occasion, Kevin had done so. But when his date came down the stairs in a thin-strapped pink dress and he opened the florist's box, he became even more nervous. Inside was an excessively° large flower in a bright orange color that didn't go at all with the pink dress. As he pinned the giant blossom onto the gown, he made an (9)_____*awkward*_____ movement, stuck his finger, and bled—on the dress. The girl was so astonished° that her mouth fell open. He wanted to (10)_____*vanish*_____ from the face of the earth and never be seen again. He even considered transferring to another school. As it was, he developed such a poor attitude° about dating that he didn't ask another girl out for the next two years.

➤ *Questions for Discussion*

1. Have you and your parents ever disagreed about whether or not a person was a **wholesome** influence in your life? How did you see that person, and how did that differ from the way your parents saw him or her?

2. What holiday is celebrated in a big way in your family? What are some of the **customary** ways in which you celebrate that holiday each year?

3. If a genie offered you just one wish, how would you **respond**?

4. Think of a younger person you know who has the **potential** to develop a particular talent. Who is the person, and what is his or her special ability? How do you think he or she can develop that ability?

5. Do people on the street ever **appeal** to you for money? Does this make you feel **awkward**? What do you do when that happens?

➤ *Ideas for Writing*

1. Most students have had the experience of thinking that they were doing an **adequate** job in a certain class, but having a teacher or parent think they weren't working up to their **potential**. Write about a time that has happened to you. How did you **respond** to the person who encouraged you to do better?

2. What are some **wholesome** activities that you enjoy? How do you feel that they improve your mind, body, or character? Write about a **variety** of such activities and how they affect you.

Check Your Performance			CHAPTER 8
Activity	*Number Right*	*Points*	*Total*
Check 2	_____	× 10 =	_____
Related Words	_____	× 10 =	_____
Word Work	_____	× 10 =	_____
Word Parts	_____	× 10 =	_____
Final Check	_____	× 10 =	_____

Enter your scores above and in the vocabulary performance chart on the inside back cover of the book.

CHAPTER 9

brutal	interpret
discipline	propose
eliminate	resort
emphasis	ultimate
furthermore	vague

Ten Words in Context

In the space provided, write the letter of the meaning closest to that of each **boldfaced** word. Use the context of the sentences to help you figure out each word's meaning.

1 brutal
(broot′l)
– *adjective*

- Brenda's first husband was **brutal**. When he beat her for the third time, she finally left him.
- Troy's mother never hit him, but she was **brutal**. Her cruel words were more painful than any beating could have been.

_c_ *Brutal* means   a. youthful.   b. hardly ever seen.   c. mean.

2 discipline
(dĭs′ə-plĭn)
– *verb*

- The ballplayer was put out of the game for hitting an umpire. He was also **disciplined** with a $2,000 fine.
- José wanted to teach his children to be nonviolent, so he **disciplined** them in gentle ways, such as sending them to their rooms for some quiet "time out."

_a_ *Discipline* means   a. to punish.   b. to leave.   c. to turn to for help.

3 eliminate
(ĭ-lĭm′ə-nāt′)
– *verb*

- If you hang up clothes right after the dryer stops, you can **eliminate** the need to iron many items.
- Because my father has high blood pressure, he's supposed to **eliminate** salt from his diet.

_b_ *Eliminate* means   a. to add to.   b. to remove.   c. to repeat.

4 emphasis
(ĕm′fə-sĭs)
– *noun*

- Brad's father placed a lot of **emphasis** on doing well in sports but gave little attention to doing well in school.
- In my Spanish class, too much **emphasis** was given to reading and not enough to speaking.

_c_ *Emphasis* means   a. delay.   b. addition.   c. importance.

5 furthermore
(fûr′thər-môr′)
– *adverb*

- "I don't believe your story about a flat tire," said Hal's boss. "And **furthermore**, I haven't believed any of your other excuses for being late."
- The Bulls will win because they are a talented team. **Furthermore**, they are coached well.

_c_ *Furthermore* means   a. instead.   b. later.   c. also.

6 interpret
(ĭn-tûr′prĭt)
– *verb*

- After Ray had a dental x-ray, the dentist sat down with him to **interpret** it.
- How should I **interpret** the fact that, although we were friendly yesterday, Jean refused to speak to me today?

_a_ *Interpret* means   a. to explain.   b. to suggest.   c. to discover.

7 propose
(prə-pōz′)
– *verb*

- Our little brother **proposed** buying our parents a puppy for Christmas, but instead we gave them a coffee grinder.
- Rafael was obviously too tired to study, so his mother **proposed** that he take a nap and get back to work later.

_c_ *Propose* means   a. to predict.   b. to remember.   c. to suggest.

8 resort
(rĭ-zôrt′)
– *verb*

- Once my friend was so low on money that he **resorted** to selling his blood to a blood bank.
- Although school was hard for me, I never **resorted** to cheating.

_c_ *Resort to* means   a. to explain.   b. to forget about.   c. to turn to.

9 ultimate
(ŭl′tə-mĭt)
– *adjective*

- Although her husband had affairs before, Suzanne felt his love affair with her own sister was the **ultimate** stab in the back.
- Saying they learned a lot in class is the **ultimate** compliment students can pay a teacher.

_a_ *Ultimate* means   a. greatest.   b. most interesting.   c. unknown.

10 vague
(vāg)
– *adjective*

- On the essay test, give detailed answers, not **vague** ones.
- Ben had only a **vague** idea of what yeast was. He knew it was used to make beer and bread, but he wasn't sure what it did.

_a_ *Vague* means   a. general.   b. curious.   c. wrong.

Matching Words with Definitions

Following are definitions of the ten words. **Print** each word next to its definition. If you look closely at each word in context, you will be able to figure out its meaning.

1. _vague_ — Not clear; not exact; not definite
2. _propose_ — To put forward for thinking over or accepting; suggest (an idea)
3. _discipline_ — To punish; cause to suffer for doing something wrong
4. _resort_ — To turn or go (to) for help; make use of for aid
5. _brutal_ — Cruel; heartless
6. _emphasis_ — Special attention; importance given to something
7. _furthermore_ — In addition; besides
8. _eliminate_ — To get rid of; do away with
9. _interpret_ — To explain the meaning of; make sense of
10. _ultimate_ — Greatest; highest possible

CAUTION: Do not go any further until you are sure the above answers are correct. Then you can use the definitions to help you in the following practices. Your goal is eventually to know the words well enough so that you don't need to check the definitions at all.

➤ *Check 1*

Using the answer line, complete each item below with the correct word from the box.

a. **brutal**	b. **discipline**	c. **eliminate**	d. **emphasis**	e. **furthermore**
f. **interpret**	g. **propose**	h. **resort**	i. **ultimate**	j. **vague**

discipline	1. Ms. Ramirez took her son's bike away for a week to ___ him after he lied to her.
ultimate	2. Your ___ goal is the highest one you hope to reach.
resort	3. If you were low on cash, would you ___ to selling your blood?
vague	4. When I ask my children where they're going, I don't accept ___ answers. I want to know exactly where they'll be.
interpret	5. Since I didn't understand the results of my blood test, the doctor ___ed it for me.
propose	6. We encourage our children to ___ weekend activities in which the whole family can participate.
eliminate	7. People take aspirin to ___ headaches.
furthermore	8. One way to introduce an additional point is with the word "___."
emphasis	9. Your boss will put the greatest ___ on the project he or she considers most important.
brutal	10. Someone without mercy can be ___.

NOTE: Now check your answers to these questions by turning to page 249. Going over the answers carefully will help you prepare for the remaining practices, for which answers are not given.

➤ *Check 2*

Using the answer lines, complete each item below with **two** words from the box.

vague _furthermore_	1–2. "Your answers were too ___," said the teacher. "You should have made them more clear by adding details. ___, you skipped several questions."
discipline _resort_	3–4. Even though there are plenty of gentle ways to ___ a child, many parents are quick to ___ to spanking when a child behaves badly. Many parents need to learn how to penalize° their children in positive ways.
ultimate _eliminate_	5–6. Liz has cut down her smoking to only three cigarettes a day, but her ___ goal is to ___ smoking from her life.
emphasis _interpret_	7–8. Chu's parents had never seen an American-style report card before, so when Chu's teacher met with them, her ___ was on helping them ___ what it said.
propose _brutal_	9–10. Gail ___d that we go to the movies instead of attending a boxing match because she feels that boxing is a ___ sport.

➢ *Related Words*

Once you learn a new word, you can more easily understand many related words. Below are ten words related to the core words of this chapter. Use their definitions to help you write in the word that best completes each item.

a. **brutality**, *noun*	Cruelty
b. **emphasize**, *verb*	To give special force to; stress
c. **interpreter**, *noun*	Someone who translates one language into another
d. **ultimately**, *adverb*	In the end; finally
e. **vagueness**, *noun*	The condition of not being clear

_____emphasize_____ 1. The instructions in this beginners' cookbook ___ measuring ingredients carefully.

_____brutality_____ 2. The Humane° Society came to check on Mr. Speck when neighbors reported his ___ to his dogs.

_____ultimately_____ 3. Marcos worked hard as a roofer for ten years, saved his money, and ___ started his own roofing business.

_____interpreter_____ 4. Because Julie speaks English and Vietnamese equally well, she often serves as an ___ for her parents and customers in their restaurant.

_____vagueness_____ 5. The memory of an event when I was three years old has the ___ of a hardly remembered dream.

a. **brute**, *noun*	A cruel person
b. **disciplinary**, *adjective*	Having to do with teaching a lesson or punishing
c. **elimination**, *noun*	The getting rid of something
d. **proposal**, *noun*	An idea; suggestion
e. **vaguely**, *adverb*	Not clearly

_____proposal_____ 6. No one liked Dad's ___ that we spend our vacation at home painting the house.

_____disciplinary_____ 7. The vice-principal at our school is in charge of ___ matters, such as deciding if a student should be suspended.

_____brute_____ 8. The police chief said, "We will find the ___s who beat this poor teenager to death."

_____elimination_____ 9. The Salk vaccine, developed in the 1950s, led to the ___ of polio in many parts of the world.

_____vaguely_____ 10. Sidney looks like his brother only ___. They're about the same size, and there is something similar about their mouths and eyes.

➤ *Word Work*

A. In the space provided, write the letter of the word that most closely relates to the situation in each item.

_c_ 1. When I asked a passerby for directions to the post office, she pointed somewhere behind me and said, "It's over there a couple of blocks."

    a. brutal   b. discipline   c. vague

_b_ 2. I hired an accountant to explain my tax forms to me.

    a. discipline   b. interpret   c. propose

_b_ 3. A citizens' group will present their idea for a community playground to the town council.

    a. emphasis   b. propose   c. eliminate

_c_ 4. The group of teenagers surrounded the sleeping street person and then began to kick him with their heavy boots.

    a. furthermore   b. interpret   c. brutal

_a_ 5. Because she came in so late last night, Sharon isn't allowed to go out in the evening for two weeks.

    a. discipline   b. eliminate   c. resort

B. In the space provided, write the letter of the choice that best completes each item.

_c_ 6. The **ultimate** power in the kingdom belongs to

    a. the weak.   b. the poor.   c. the king.

_b_ 7. To give **emphasis** to their words, people often

    a. stutter.   b. speak more loudly.   c. are cruel.

_c_ 8. The word **furthermore** can be useful when you want to

    a. repeat yourself.   b. change your mind.   c. add a point to what you've already said.

_c_ 9. Politicians sometimes say they want to **eliminate**

    a. voters.   b. schools.   c. hunger.

_a_ 10. If you **resort** to the personal ads for dates, you probably believe that the ads are

    a. helpful.   b. harmful.   c. useless.

➤ *Synonyms and Antonyms*

A. Synonyms. Write the letter of the word or phrase that most nearly means the **same** as each boldfaced word.

___d___ 1. **emphasis**

    a. flavor   b. memory

    c. laughter   d. importance

___c___ 2. **furthermore**

    a. on the other hand   b. for instance

    c. also   d. instead

___d___ 3. **interpret**

    a. punish   b. memorize

    c. resist   d. explain

___a___ 4. **propose**

    a. suggest   b. deny

    c. lie   d. pretend

___a___ 5. **resort to**

    a. turn to   b. avoid

    c. suggest   d. talk about

B. Antonyms. Write the letter of the word or phrase that most nearly means the **opposite** of each boldfaced word.

___b___ 6. **brutal**

    a. firm   b. kindly

    c. quiet   d. small

___c___ 7. **discipline**

    a. greet   b. interrupt

    c. reward   d. drop

___d___ 8. **eliminate**

    a. ignore   b. hang around

    c. refuse   d. add

___a___ 9. **ultimate**

    a. least possible   b. most difficult

    c. clear   d. medium

___b___ 10. **vague**

    a. needed   b. exact

    c. trusted   d. loud

➤ *Final Check*

Read the passages carefully. Then fill in each blank with the word that best fits the context.

A. Differences in a Gym Program

a. **emphasis**	b. **interpret**	c. **propose**
d. **ultimate**	e. **vague**	

Last spring, some parents spoke to the school board about the gym program at Walnut Street School. The parents protested the difference in programs offered to boys and girls. The boys were taught a variety° of active sports and given good equipment. They had the chance to join several teams. For girls, however, the (1)_____*emphasis*_____ in gym was on dancing and exercise. They had no teams and little equipment.

Why were there such big differences between the two programs? The school district's rules about physical education were (2)_____*vague*_____. Since they didn't say exactly what should be taught, each school (3)_____*interpret*_____ed the rules in its own way.

The parents (4)_____*propose*_____d allowing both boys and girls to use all the gym equipment at the school. And they appealed° to the school board for some sports teams to be organized for the girls. They pointed out that girls have as much potential° in sports and as much need for physical fitness as boys do. Their (5) _____*ultimate*_____ goal was to give all the children an equal gym experience.

B. Teaching a Lesson

f. **brutal**	g. **discipline**	h. **eliminate**
i. **furthermore**	j. **resort**	

One reason that parents may have to (6)_____*discipline*_____ children is to (7)_____*eliminate*_____ behaviors that are rude or hurtful. Unfortunately, some parents use (8)_____*brutal*_____ punishments to teach their children to be good. But cruel treatment only serves to demonstrate° to children that it is acceptable for them to (9)_____*resort*_____ to hitting and punching when they need to solve a problem. (10)_____*Furthermore*_____, children who are hit too often and too hard are deprived° of a feeling of safety. They grow up expecting that the whole world will be cruel to them, and thus, they often become cruel to others.

➤ *Questions for Discussion*

1. When have you witnessed someone acting in a **brutal** fashion? What did the person do? How did you feel about what was happening?

2. Think about some of the major problems of our society, such as drug abuse, unemployment, poverty, hunger, and crime. Which problem do you think it is most important to **eliminate**? Why did you choose the one you did?

3. What are some of your earliest, most **vague** memories?

4. What is one change that you would like to **propose** in how your workplace or household is run?

5. What, for you, would be the **ultimate** vacation? Where would you go, and what would you do?

➤ *Ideas for Writing*

1. Write a paper describing a change you would like to **propose** in how your workplace or household is run. Describe in detail—not **vaguely**—how your suggestion would work.

2. TV, movies, and magazines are constantly giving us messages about fashion, body image, and other things having to do with outward appearance. Do you think there is too much **emphasis** on "looking good" in society today? Write a paper that explains your feelings about this constant flow of messages and its effect on young people. How do you think people **interpret** these messages? Do they realize that outward appearance is just one part of life, or does appearance become the **ultimate** part of life?

Check Your Performance			CHAPTER 9
Activity	*Number Right*	*Points*	*Total*
Check 2	_____	× 10 =	_____
Related Words	_____	× 10 =	_____
Word Work	_____	× 10 =	_____
Synonyms and Antonyms	_____	× 10 =	_____
Final Check	_____	× 10 =	_____

Enter your scores above and in the vocabulary performance chart on the inside back cover of the book.

CHAPTER

10

accustomed	occur
anticipate	reluctant
linger	revise
miserable	specific
misinterpret	version

Ten Words in Context

In the space provided, write the letter of the meaning closest to that of each **boldfaced** word. Use the context of the sentences to help you figure out each word's meaning.

1 **accustomed**
(ə-kŭs′təmd)
– *adjective*

- Although my grandfather was **accustomed** to sucking a sugar cube while he drank tea, the sugar never seemed to harm his teeth.
- After years of living in sunny Puerto Rico, Alma had trouble becoming **accustomed** to the snowy Minnesota weather.

__c__ *Accustomed* means   a. uncomfortable with.   b. shocked by.   c. used to.

2 **anticipate**
(ăn-tĭs′ə-pāt′)
– *verb*

- Lee **anticipated** heavy traffic this morning, so he left for the airport an hour early.
- Because I **anticipated** a snowstorm, I bought extra groceries in case I couldn't get to the store for several days.

__c__ *Anticipate* means   a. to doubt.   b. to enjoy.   c. to think likely to happen.

3 **linger**
(lĭng′gər)
– *verb*

- My husband has difficulty leaving any social event. He likes to **linger** by the door, chatting on and on with our hosts.
- After the bowling matches are over, we usually **linger** for a while to talk to our friends on the other teams.

__b__ *Linger* means   a. to stare.   b. to stay.   c. to expect.

4 **miserable**
(mĭz′ər-ə-bəl)
– *adjective*

- The Farrells were **miserable** on their camping trip because the green flies wouldn't stop biting them for a minute.
- Gino is sure to be **miserable** during the allergy season if he doesn't get shots.

__a__ *Miserable* means   a. uncomfortable.   b. not proper.   c. rested.

5 **misinterpret**
(mĭs′ĭn-tûr′prĭt)
– *verb*

- When I invited my new neighbor to dinner, she **misinterpreted** my neighborliness as romantic interest.
- It's clear that Jay **misinterpreted** his wife's request. He brought her flowers for a vase instead of flour for a cake.

__c__ *Misinterpret* means   a. to want.   b. to cause.   c. to understand wrongly.

6 **occur**
(ə-kûr′)
– *verb*

- A robbery **occurred** at the restaurant just minutes after we left.
- The first moonwalk **occurred** on July 20th, 1969, after Neil Armstrong stepped on the moon and said, "That's one small step for a man, one giant leap for mankind."

__c__ *Occur* means   a. to find.   b. to disappear.   c. to happen.

90

7 reluctant
(rĭ-lŭk′tənt)
– *adjective*

- Since I'm **reluctant** to have people know my phone number, I keep it unlisted.
- Although the lawyer was **reluctant** to tell his client such disappointing news, he had no choice but to do so.

_b_ *Reluctant* means   a. known.   b. unwilling.   c. excited.

8 revise
(rĭ-vīz′)
– *verb*

- Don't just write a paper out once and hand it in. It's important to **revise** what you write until your paper is in good shape.
- Recent price increases for lumber have made it necessary for carpenters to **revise** their construction charges.

_b_ *Revise* means   a. to remember.   b. to make changes in.   c. to read again.

9 specific
(spĭ-sĭf′ĭk)
– *adjective*

- Gina said that she and Howard had some sort of quarrel, but she didn't give me any **specific** information.
- I give very **specific** instructions to new baby sitters so they'll understand exactly what I want done. I even show exactly how to diaper and feed my son.

_c_ *Specific* means   a. hard to believe.   b. hurried.   c. detailed.

10 version
(vûr′zhən)
– *noun*

- The play *West Side Story* is a modern musical **version** of Shakespeare's *Romeo and Juliet*.
- There have been at least six movies about Frankenstein's monster, but the best is still the 1931 **version**, with Boris Karloff.

_a_ *Version* means   a. retelling.   b. suggestion.   c. correction.

Matching Words with Definitions

Following are definitions of the ten words. **Print** each word next to its definition. If you look closely at each word in context, you will be able to figure out its meaning.

1. _____accustomed_____   In the habit of; used to

2. _____reluctant_____   Unwilling; wanting not to do something

3. _____specific_____   Definite; exact

4. _____linger_____   To delay leaving; remain, especially as if unwilling to leave

5. _____miserable_____   Very unhappy or uncomfortable

6. _____anticipate_____   To expect; foresee

7. _____misinterpret_____   To understand incorrectly

8. _____version_____   A story told in a different form or with a different point of view

9. _____occur_____   To happen; take place

10. _____revise_____   To change in order to improve or to include new information

CAUTION: Do not go any further until you are sure the above answers are correct. Then you can use the definitions to help you in the following practices. Your goal is eventually to know the words well enough so that you don't need to check the definitions at all.

➤ *Check 1*

Using the answer line, complete each item below with the correct word from the box.

a. **accustomed**	b. **anticipate**	c. **linger**	d. **miserable**	e. **misinterpret**
f. **occur**	g. **reluctant**	h. **revise**	i. **specific**	j. **version**

linger   1. Could you ___ for a few minutes after the meeting so I can talk privately to you?

anticipate   2. I ___ about forty guests at our New Year's Eve party, but I'm preparing food for fifty, just in case.

occur   3. It's about time the city put up a stop sign at that corner—an accident ___s there every month or two.

reluctant   4. Although the apartment met our needs, we were ___ to sign a long-term lease.

version   5. Dina wrote a ___ of *Romeo and Juliet* that has a happy ending.

specific   6. Because Clark's directions were so ___, I found his new home without difficulty.

miserable   7. After our cat was run over by a car, my son felt ___ for weeks.

accustomed   8. For someone brought up in a warm climate, it may take time to become ___ to cold weather.

misinterpret   9. Another word for "misunderstand" is "___."

revise   10. Before we present our play to the third-grade class, we will ___ it so it is easier for young children to understand.

NOTE: Now check your answers to these questions by turning to page 249. Going over the answers carefully will help you prepare for the remaining practices, for which answers are not given.

➤ *Check 2*

Using the answer lines, complete each item below with **two** words from the box.

accustomed
misinterpret   1–2. When I was in Mexico, I became ___ to having people ___ what I said because I speak Spanish so poorly.

anticipate
linger   3–4. I ___d having an boring afternoon at work, so I ___ed in the restaurant to make lunch last as long as possible. I was not at all eager° to return to the office.

specific
version   5–6. My son asked for *The Wizard of Oz* for his birthday, but he wasn't ___ about whether he wanted the book or the musical film ___.

miserable
occur   7–8. No one hates arguments more than Martin—he becomes ___ whenever they ___. Unfortunately, in his household, disputes° are abundant°.

reluctant
revise   9–10. I am ___ to show you my story until I've had a chance to ___ it. It really needs considerable° changing before it will be good enough for anyone to read.

➤ *Related Words*

Once you learn a new word, you can more easily understand many related words. Below are ten words related to the core words of this chapter. Use their definitions to help you write in the word that best completes each item.

a. **accustom**, *verb*	To get used to
b. **anticipation**, *noun*	The act of looking forward to something
c. **interpret°**, *verb*	To explain the meaning (of something)
d. **misery**, *noun*	Great unhappiness
e. **revision**, *noun*	An improved form of an earlier work

_____ *misery* _____ 1. It is sad to think of how much ___ wars have caused.

_____ *anticipation* _____ 2. The dog's ___ of going for a walk was clear—he sat by the door with a leash in his mouth.

_____ *interpret* _____ 3. I didn't understand what my blood-pressure numbers meant, so I asked the nurse to ___ them for me.

_____ *accustom* _____ 4. In his job as a security guard, James had to ___ himself to staying awake all night.

_____ *revision* _____ 5. My writing teacher kept asking me to improve my paper. She finally accepted the third ___.

f. **interpretation**, *noun*	An explanation of the meaning or importance of something
g. **lingering**, *adjective*	Remaining; not leaving
h. **occurrence**, *noun*	An event; something that happened
i. **reluctance**, *noun*	The state of being unwilling to do something
j. **specify**, *verb*	To state exactly or in detail

_____ *specify* _____ 6. In the personal ads, people looking for dates ___ their work, hobbies, and favorite activities.

_____ *occurrence* _____ 7. There was a strange ___ at school today involving two students, a banana peel, and a can of red paint.

_____ *reluctance* _____ 8. I understand Dad's ___ to ride roller coasters—I don't like to ride on them, either.

_____ *interpretation* _____ 9. When Jack didn't show up at Emma's party, Emma's ___ was that he didn't want to run into his former girlfriend there.

_____ *lingering* _____ 10. The room was empty when I arrived, but the ___ smell of perfume told me that a woman had just left.

➤ *Word Work*

A. In the space provided, write the letter of the word that most closely relates to the situation in each item.

_b_ 1. A strange and wonderful event always happens to me in January.

      a. lingers   b. occurs   c. miserable

_c_ 2. A friend says, "Catch you later," but you think he says, "Let's buy a gator."

      a. anticipate   b. linger   c. misinterpret

_a_ 3. Earthquake survivors huddle in the rain, with their houses destroyed and nowhere to go.

      a. miserable   b. revise   c. specific

_c_ 4. You know you should visit Great-Uncle Lem over the holidays, but he makes you watch hours of his boring home movies and you really don't want to go.

      a. accustomed   b. version   c. reluctant

_b_ 5. After the students read the novel *The Grapes of Wrath*, they watched the movie of the same name.

      a. linger   b. version   c. reluctant

B. In the space provided, write the letter of the choice that best completes each item.

_b_ 6. Today you are likely to **anticipate**

      a. your birthday party last year.
      b. a phone call your friend promised to make.
      c. an argument you had yesterday.

_b_ 7. The person who is most likely to **linger** is

      a. a friend who is in a rush.
      b. a guest at a luncheon.
      c. a person about to get off a bus.

_b_ 8. A student might **revise** a paper that

      a. seems perfect.
      b. is too long.
      c. has been handed in to the teacher.

_c_ 9. A **specific** description of a cold would be

      a. "I feel sick."
      b. "I have congestion."
      c. "I have fever, a stuffy nose, and a sore throat."

_a_ 10. Most people are **accustomed** to

      a. their jobs.   b. the future.   c. life at the South Pole.

➤ *Analogies*

Each item below starts with a pair of words in CAPITAL LETTERS. For each item, figure out the relationship between these two words. Then decide which of the choices (*a*, *b*, *c*, or *d*) expresses a similar relationship. Write the letter of your choice on the answer line. (All the repeated words in these items are from this unit.)

_a_ 1. RELUCTANT : WILLING ::

    a. brutal : kind   b. rapid : fast

    c. anger : argument   d. shy : quiet

_c_ 2. MISERABLE : HAPPY ::

    a. awkward° : clumsy   b. bright : shining

    c. current° : old-fashioned   d. famous : brave

_c_ 3. LINGER : REMAIN ::

    a. purposely : accidentally   b. complex° : simple

    c. fix : repair   d. wait : depart

_d_ 4. ANTICIPATE : EXPECT ::

    a. recollect° : forget   b. cause : effect

    c. explain: understand   d. smash : break

_b_ 5. SPECIFIC : GENERAL ::

    a. unfamiliar : nervous   b. eager° : unwilling

    c. shy : quiet   d. bees : honey

_b_ 6. OCCUR : HAPPEN ::

    a. run : walk   b. vanish° : disappear

    c. shout : whisper   d. vague° : specific°

_d_ 7. REVISE : SENTENCE ::

    a. discipline° : punishment   b. write : print

    c. sing: book   d. propose° : suggestion

_d_ 8. OBJECTION° : APPROVAL ::

    a. doctor : illness   b. night : moon

    c. emphasis : importance   d. argument : agreement

_a_ 9. MISINTERPRET : MISUNDERSTAND ::

    a. penalize° : punish   b. expect : surprise

    c. agree : disagree   d. discipline° : reward

_b_ 10. RECOLLECT° : EVENT ::

    a. question : answer   b. interpret° : message

    c. walk : exercise   d. establish° : destroy

➤ *Final Check*

Read the passages carefully. Then fill in each blank with the word that best fits the context.

A. Knowing How to Argue

a. **linger**	b. **misinterpret**	c. **occur**
d. **reluctant**	e. **specific**	

Ron and Marlene have a great marriage, and I think one reason is that they know how to argue. Many couples think arguing is bad, but I think they (1)___*misinterpret*___ what arguing really is. It can be a good way to settle problems. When couples are (2)___*reluctant*___ to argue, they may not solve their problems, and their angry feelings can (3)___*linger*___ for a long time. Ron and Marlene don't hesitate° to argue and get it over with. What's good about the way they argue is that they talk only about the (4)___*specific*___ thing that made them angry. For example, if Marlene is angry that Ron isn't doing his share of the housework, that is all she talks about. She doesn't throw in, "And furthermore°—that new friend of yours from work is a jerk!" Knowing Ron and Marlene has taught me that arguments (5)___*occur*___ in even the best marriages, and that they can make a good relationship stronger.

B. A Change of School, A Change of Heart

f. **accustomed**	g. **anticipate**	h. **miserable**
i. **revise**	j. **version**	

Matt and his family were moving, and Matt hated the whole idea. He had lived in Centerville his entire life and gone to school with the same group of friends. He had (6)___*anticipate*___d graduating from Centerville High School and going to Centerville Community College. Now he was going to have to (7)___*revise*___ his whole plan for the future, and he didn't like it a bit. "How can I ever become (8)___*accustomed*___ to a new school?" he asked his parents. "Everyone will already know each other. I'll have no friends."

At first, it seemed that Matt was right. At his new high school, he walked around alone, not smiling or talking to anyone. Finally a friendly teacher advised° him to improve his attitude°. "I know you're feeling lonely and (9)___*miserable*___," he said. "But you look as though you hate this school and everyone in it. If you'll look a little friendlier, you will find new friends here." Matt decided to try. He began to talk to his classmates and take part in class. He even helped write a funny (10)___*version*___ of "Cinderella" that his Spanish class performed for the rest of the school. By New Year, Matt was able to tell his parents that he was starting to feel at home in his new school.

➤ *Questions for Discussion*

1. Describe something that happens regularly—perhaps every day, or every week, or every year—that you **anticipate** with pleasure. What makes you look forward to it?

2. Has a friend ever asked you for a favor that you were **reluctant** to do? Describe what he or she asked for and why you did not want to say yes. Did you end up doing what your friend asked you to do?

3. Have you ever read something and then seen a television or movie **version** of the same story? Which did you prefer? Why?

4. Tell about a time when someone **misinterpreted** something you did or said. What did you mean? What did the person think you meant?

5. What are some reasons why a student might **linger** after school instead of going straight home?

➤ *Ideas for Writing*

1. Write about something that **occurred** that made you feel **miserable**. What happened? Why did you feel so bad about it? Did you ever become **accustomed** to what happened, or does it still bother you?

2. Write a paper about the best or worst job you ever had. Provide plenty of **specific** details that make very clear to the reader just why the job was a good one or a bad one. **Revise** the paper at least once, adding even more details when you do so.

Check Your Performance			**CHAPTER 10**
Activity	*Number Right*	*Points*	*Total*
Check 2	_____	× 10 =	_____
Related Words	_____	× 10 =	_____
Word Work	_____	× 10 =	_____
Analogies	_____	× 10 =	_____
Final Check	_____	× 10 =	_____

Enter your scores above and in the vocabulary performance chart on the inside back cover of the book.

UNIT TWO: *Review*

The box at the right lists twenty-five words from Unit Two. Using the clues at the bottom of the page, fill in these words to complete the puzzle that follows.

The grid (filled answers):

1 Across: DEPRIVE
4 Across: ULTIMATE
7 Across: ASTONISH
10 Across: RESORT
12 Across: EAGER
14 Across: BRUTAL
17 Across: ELIMINATE
21 Across: CURRENT
23 Across: AWKWARD
24 Across: ESTABLISH
25 Across: RELIABLE

2 Down: VANISH
3 Down: VARIETY
5 Down: ENDURE
6 Down: CONSENT
8 Down: SPECIFIC
9 Down: REVISE
11 Down: OCCUR
13 Down: OBJECTION
15 Down: ADVISE
16 Down: MISERABLE
18 Down: LINGER
19 Down: ABRUPT
20 Down: POTENTIAL
22 Down: VAGUE

Word box:

abrupt
advise
astonish
awkward
brutal
consent
current
deprive
eager
eliminate
endure
establish
linger
miserable
objection
occur
potential
reliable
resort
revise
specific
ultimate
vague
vanish
variety

ACROSS

1. To take away from; keep from having or enjoying
4. Greatest; highest possible
7. To surprise greatly; amaze
10. To turn or go (to) for help; make use of for aid
12. Looking forward to with great interest or desire
14. Cruel; heartless
17. To get rid of; do away with
21. Modern; existing now; in general use or practice today
23. Clumsy; not graceful
24. To bring into being; set up
25. Able to be depended upon

DOWN

2. To disappear from sight
3. A number of different kinds; assortment
5. To put up with; bear impatiently
6. To agree to something
8. Definite; exact
9. To change in order to improve or to include new information
11. To happen; take place
13. A dislike; feeling of being against something
15. To give advice to; recommend
16. Very unhappy or uncomfortable
18. To delay leaving; remain
19. Sudden and unexpected
20. A natural ability that may or may not develop; possibility
22. Not clear; not exact; not definite

UNIT TWO: Test 1

PART A
Choose the word that best completes each item and write it in the space provided.

___penalize___   1. My parents used to ___ me for misbehaving at the supper table by making me sit on the stairs, where I could hear the conversation but not take part in it.

     a. interpret   b. penalize   c. revise   d. originate

___originated___   2. It has been said that the practice of drinking tea ___ in China thousands of years ago when some tea leaves accidently blew into a pot of boiling water.

     a. originated   b. misinterpreted   c. vanished   d. recollected

___minimum___   3. That restaurant doesn't accept reservations for small groups. The ___ number of people in your party must be five.

     a. vague   b. complex   c. current   d. minimum

___hesitates___   4. A beginning typist ___ often, while an experienced typist hits the keys rapidly.

     a. advises   b. hesitates   c. occurs   d. endures

___advise___   5. My sister-in-law knows a lot about cars, so I've asked her to ___ me as I decide which one to buy.

     a. cry out   b. deprive   c. recollect   d. advise

___maintain___   6. I try to ___ my friendship with Sarah, but it's difficult to keep a relationship going when we're separated by so many miles.

     a. maintain   b. revise   c. respond   d. deprive

___current___   7. It used to be taught in schools that George Washington cut down a cherry tree with an ax and then confessed the deed to his father. However, ___ thinking is that the story was invented after Washington died.

     a. horizontal   b. reluctant   c. current   d. vague

___objection___   8. Garlic is delicious, but many people have an ___ to the way it makes one's breath smell.

     a. objection   b. potential   c. version   d. variety

___deprives___   9. When Mona's children behave badly, she does not spank them; instead, she ___ them of something they enjoy, such as their bicycles or roller skates.

     a. resorts   b. endures   c. proposes   d. deprives

___reliable___   10. Although my car is old, it is still ___; it gets me to work every day.

     a. abrupt   b. reliable   c. miserable   d. ultimate

(Continues on next page)

    horizontal   11. We stared at the long brownish ___ thing floating in the river, wondering if it was a log or an alligator.

         a. horizontal   b. accustomed   c. adequate   d. wholesome

    proposed   12. At the town meeting, several people had ideas about what to do with the empty supermarket building. One woman ___ that it be turned into a skating rink.

         a. vanished   b. resorted   c. endured   d. proposed

    wholesome   13. Playing outdoors for hours is more ___ than watching TV for hours.

         a. reluctant   b. awkward   c. eager   d. wholesome

PART B
Write **C** if the italicized word is used **correctly**. Write **I** if the word is used **incorrectly**.

  I   14. "To *misinterpret* my instructions," said the teacher, "listen carefully."

  I   15. The famous ballet dancer is *awkward*; he moves so lightly his feet seem to never touch the ground.

  C   16. It was *customary* for people to smile at each other in Laura's small town. Although she now lives in a large city, she still smiles at every stranger that she passes.

  C   17. I think it is *brutal* to keep chickens in crowded conditions and then cut off their beaks to keep them from pecking one another.

  I   18. If you want to gain weight, you can *eliminate* more calories in your diet by adding nuts and olive oil to your meals.

  C   19. I'm so *accustomed* to living near the fire department that whenever a siren goes off, I hardly notice.

  I   20. The angry diner called the restaurant manager and complained that her meal had been cold, *adequate*, and too expensive.

  I   21. Many people in town were angry when the beautiful old courthouse was *established* in order to make room for an ugly, new shopping center.

  C   22. The directions Kim gave me to the new apartment were so *vague* that I got very mixed up on my way there.

  C   23. Because her husband was sick and couldn't work, Corinne *appealed* to their landlady for extra time to pay the rent.

  I   24. The *ultimate* job in a successful business career might be running errands in a large office.

  C   25. Our store is well thought of because we put an *emphasis* on pleasing customers rather than on making as many sales as possible in a day.

Score   (Number correct) _____ × 4 = _____%

Enter your score above and in the vocabulary performance chart on the inside back cover of the book.

UNIT TWO: Test 2

PART A
Complete each item with a word from the box. Use each word once.

a. **abrupt**	b. **anticipate**	c. **classify**	d. **consent**	e. **discipline**
f. **exclaim**	g. **potential**	h. **recollect**	i. **resort**	j. **revise**
k. **specific**	l. **vanish**	m. **variety**		

_____ *potential* _____ 1. Every time Robert takes a girl out, he thinks about whether she has the ___ to be a good wife.

_____ *vanish* _____ 2. Wouldn't it be wonderful if dirt ___ed as easily and completely in real life as it does in the soap ads?

_____ *variety* _____ 3. The Four Corners of the World Restaurant offers dishes from a ___ of countries, including France, Vietnam, Ethiopia, and Brazil.

_____ *discipline* _____ 4. To ___ him for writing on the wall of a school bathroom, the principal made Matt paint every bathroom on that floor.

_____ *resort* _____ 5. Although Ed has a hot temper, I don't think he would ever ___ to violence.

_____ *anticipate* _____ 6. Because we had ___d eight people for dinner, we were surprised when twelve showed up.

_____ *revise* _____ 7. Ronald always shows his short stories to his wife and then ___s them after listening to her comments.

_____ *specific* _____ 8. When you write out the directions for me, please include the ___ streets I have to turn on.

_____ *abrupt* _____ 9. The picnic came to an ___ end when a sudden thunderstorm seemed to come out of nowhere.

_____ *classify* _____ 10. In high school, students often ___ one another as belonging to an in-group or an out-group.

_____ *consent* _____ 11. "I will ___ to your getting a puppy," Mrs. Anders told her children, "*if* you promise that you will take care of walking, feeding, brushing, and housetraining it."

_____ *exclaim* _____ 12. Sandra didn't want to hurt her boyfriend's feelings when she unwrapped the ugly orange sweater he had bought her, so she ___ed, "Wow, it's so colorful!"

_____ *recollect* _____ 13. I was so tired last night that although I ___ talking with John, I can't remember what either of us said. *(Continues on next page)*

PART B
Write **C** if the italicized word is used **correctly**. Write **I** if the word is used **incorrectly**.

_C_ 14. When the man shook hands with the child and said, "How do you do?" the child *responded*, "How do I do what?"

_I_ 15. Bart was sad when his best friend moved *furthermore* from his house.

_C_ 16. It was fun to go to my first soccer game with Franco. He knows the sport so well that he could *interpret* everything that was going on for me.

_I_ 17. Rico didn't seem to enjoy the party—he *lingered* before most of the other guests had even shown up.

_I_ 18. The students were *miserable* when their teacher said, "It's such a beautiful day—let's forget about the math test and go outside to play softball."

_C_ 19. Christmas and New Year's Eve are two holidays that *occur* in December.

_I_ 20. Naturally, most people are *reluctant* to win an all-expenses-paid vacation.

_C_ 21. Which *version* of *The Wizard of Oz* did you like better, the movie with Judy Garland or the one with Diana Ross?

_I_ 22. The speaker *astonished* the audience by opening his speech with, "Good evening, and thank you all for coming."

_C_ 23. Because the novel is so *complex*, it begins with a chart that lists all the characters and shows how they are related to one another.

_C_ 24. To get through exam week, I had to *endure* several nights without much sleep.

_C_ 25. After hiking for miles with nothing to eat, the friends were *eager* for dinner.

Score   (Number correct) _____ × 4 = _____%

Enter your score above and in the vocabulary performance chart on the inside back cover of the book.

UNIT TWO: Test 3

PART A: Synonyms

In the space provided, write the letter of the choice that is most nearly the **same** in meaning as the **boldfaced** word.

_a_ 1. **advise**   **a)** give advice to   **b)** expect   **c)** praise   **d)** forget

_d_ 2. **anticipate**   **a)** put up with   **b)** remember   **c)** dislike   **d)** expect

_a_ 3. **appeal**   **a)** ask   **b)** add to   **c)** disappear   **d)** explain

_b_ 4. **astonish**   **a)** continue   **b)** surprise   **c)** refuse   **d)** begin

_b_ 5. **classify**   **a)** make clear   **b)** arrange by type   **c)** begin   **d)** put up with

_c_ 6. **deprive**   **a)** suggest   **b)** turn to   **c)** take from   **d)** forget

_a_ 7. **discipline**   **a)** punish   **b)** raise up   **c)** continue   **d)** happen

_b_ 8. **eliminate**   **a)** add to   **b)** get rid of   **c)** disappear   **d)** make more difficult

_b_ 9. **emphasis**   **a)** least   **b)** importance   **c)** retelling   **d)** possibility

_c_ 10. **endure**   **a)** punish   **b)** demand   **c)** put up with   **d)** explain

_b_ 11. **establish**   **a)** remain   **b)** start   **c)** turn to   **d)** suggest

_c_ 12. **furthermore**   **a)** instead   **b)** later   **c)** in addition   **d)** by the way

_a_ 13. **interpret**   **a)** explain   **b)** depend on   **c)** suggest   **d)** change

_b_ 14. **maintain**   **a)** begin   **b)** continue   **c)** give up on   **d)** cry out

_a_ 15. **misinterpret**   **a)** understand wrongly   **b)** argue   **c)** depend on   **d)** surprise

_c_ 16. **occur**   **a)** begin   **b)** put off   **c)** take place   **d)** remember

_c_ 17. **potential**   **a)** memory   **b)** feeling   **c)** possibility   **d)** number

_d_ 18. **propose**   **a)** wait   **b)** make worse   **c)** agree   **d)** suggest

_a_ 19. **resort to**   **a)** turn to   **b)** give away   **c)** accept as true   **d)** refuse

_b_ 20. **respond**   **a)** disappear   **b)** answer   **c)** surprise   **d)** remember

_d_ 21. **revise**   **a)** throw out   **b)** remain   **c)** agree   **d)** change

_c_ 22. **specific**   **a)** common   **b)** least   **c)** exact   **d)** important

_c_ 23. **ultimate**   **a)** least   **b)** most strange   **c)** greatest   **d)** newest

_d_ 24. **variety**   **a)** value   **b)** reason   **c)** few   **d)** several different kinds

_a_ 25. **version**   **a)** retelling   **b)** dislike   **c)** assortment   **d)** penalty

(Continues on next page)

PART B: Antonyms
In the space provided, write the letter of the choice that is most nearly **opposite** in meaning to the **boldfaced** word.

_a_ 26. **abrupt**   **a)** slow   **b)** willing   **c)** secret   **d)** scary

_c_ 27. **accustomed**   **a)** not exact   **b)** not similar to   **c)** not used to   **d)** not needed

_b_ 28. **adequate**   **a)** willing   **b)** not enough   **c)** not dependable   **d)** unhappy

_d_ 29. **awkward**   **a)** up and down   **b)** polite   **c)** complicated   **d)** graceful

_c_ 30. **brutal**   **a)** well-known   **b)** shaky   **c)** gentle   **d)** dark

_b_ 31. **complex**   **a)** cheerful   **b)** simple   **c)** lucky   **d)** natural

_d_ 32. **consent**   **a)** surprise   **b)** reward   **c)** appear   **d)** refuse

_b_ 33. **current**   **a)** wise   **b)** old-fashioned   **c)** unusual   **d)** common

_d_ 34. **customary**   **a)** willing   **b)** most   **c)** clear   **d)** unusual

_a_ 35. **eager**   **a)** not interested   **b)** not believing   **c)** ready   **d)** clear

_d_ 36. **exclaim**   **a)** refuse   **b)** forget   **c)** allow   **d)** whisper

_c_ 37. **hesitate**   **a)** ignore   **b)** suggest   **c)** rush ahead   **d)** reward

_b_ 38. **horizontal**   **a)** careless   **b)** up and down   **c)** dark   **d)** square

_d_ 39. **linger**   **a)** appear   **b)** insult   **c)** forget   **d)** hurry away

_d_ 40. **minimum**   **a)** unhealthy   **b)** loud   **c)** painful   **d)** most

_b_ 41. **miserable**   **a)** hard to understand   **b)** happy   **c)** willing   **d)** clear

_a_ 42. **objection**   **a)** approval   **b)** joke   **c)** win   **d)** loss

_a_ 43. **originate**   **a)** end   **b)** explain   **c)** leave   **d)** expect

_b_ 44. **penalize**   **a)** hurry   **b)** reward   **c)** give   **d)** appear

_d_ 45. **recollect**   **a)** answer   **b)** ask   **c)** know   **d)** forget

_d_ 46. **reliable**   **a)** not known   **b)** not enough   **c)** not usual   **d)** not dependable

_c_ 47. **reluctant**   **a)** surprised   **b)** least   **c)** willing   **d)** careless

_c_ 48. **vague**   **a)** lowest   **b)** not clumsy   **c)** clear   **d)** not exact

_c_ 49. **vanish**   **a)** expect   **b)** keep   **c)** appear   **d)** wait

_a_ 50. **wholesome**   **a)** unhealthy   **b)** simple   **c)** useful   **d)** old-fashioned

---

Score   (Number correct) _____ × 2 = _____%

Enter your score above and in the vocabulary performance chart on the inside back cover of the book.

Unit Three

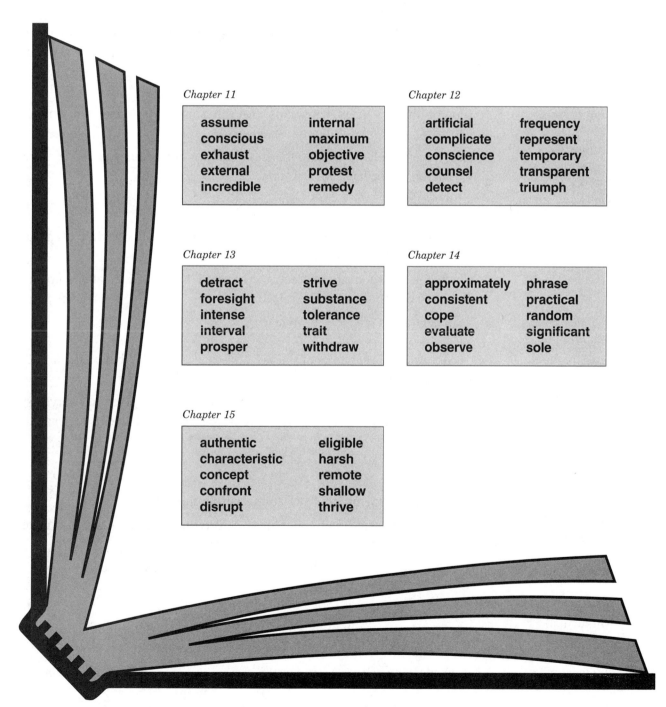

Chapter 11

assume	internal
conscious	maximum
exhaust	objective
external	protest
incredible	remedy

Chapter 12

artificial	frequency
complicate	represent
conscience	temporary
counsel	transparent
detect	triumph

Chapter 13

detract	strive
foresight	substance
intense	tolerance
interval	trait
prosper	withdraw

Chapter 14

approximately	phrase
consistent	practical
cope	random
evaluate	significant
observe	sole

Chapter 15

authentic	eligible
characteristic	harsh
concept	remote
confront	shallow
disrupt	thrive

assume	internal
conscious	maximum
exhaust	objective
external	protest
incredible	remedy

Ten Words in Context

In the space provided, write the letter of the meaning closest to that of each **boldfaced** word. Use the context of the sentences to help you figure out each word's meaning.

1 **assume**
(ə-sōom′)
– *verb*

- I **assumed** he was telling the truth, but he wasn't.
- We **assumed** the sun would shine during the outdoor wedding—what a mistake! When it comes to weather, one must not take anything for granted.

_c_ *Assume* means   a. to fear.   b. to forget.   c. to believe.

2 **conscious**
(kŏn′shəs)
– *adjective*

- I don't think Jim is **conscious** that he sometimes seems very rude. Otherwise, he wouldn't be so ill-mannered.
- As Arlene gave her speech to the class, she was **conscious** that people were whispering in the back of the room.

_b_ *Conscious* means   a. pleased.   b. aware.   c. relieved.

3 **exhaust**
(ĭg-zôst′)
– *verb*

- The twelve-hour drive **exhausted** me so much that I couldn't even eat dinner before I went to bed.
- Chopping firewood all afternoon **exhausted** Ken. In fact, afterward, he collapsed on the sofa and fell asleep.

_c_ *Exhaust* means   a. to delay.   b. to teach.   c. to tire.

4 **external**
(ĭk-stûr′nəl)
– *adjective*

- The **external** appearances of the two houses were similar, but on the inside, the homes differed quite a bit.
- When my grandmother first came to America, she was given her very first orange. Since no one had told her to remove its **external** layer, she began to eat the peel.

_c_ *External* means   a. final.   b. new.   c. outer.

5 **incredible**
(ĭn-krĕd′ə-bəl)
– *adjective*

- The moon landing of 1969 was an **incredible** achievement.
- It's **incredible** that a cat could survive forty-three days locked in a crate without food and water, and yet it has happened.

_b_ *Incredible* means   a. expected.   b. hard to believe.   c. correct.

6 **internal**
(ĭn-tûr′nəl)
– *adjective*

- The sofa's covering is torn, but its **internal** condition is fine.
- The car looks terrific, so you'd never guess that some of its **internal** parts—the motor, brakes, and heater—need major repair.

_a_ *Internal* means   a. inside.   b. hard.   c. light in weight.

7 maximum
(măk′sə-məm)
– *adjective*

• The sign told the **maximum** weight the elevator could safely carry.

• Three hundred miles per hour is the **maximum** speed for this airplane; it can go no faster.

_a_ *Maximum* means   a. greatest.   b. worst.   c. longest.

8 objective
(əb-jĕk′tĭv)
– *noun*

• The **objective** of the workshop on time management is to teach people to get the most done in the least amount of time.

• Chris and Tomas realized they could not be business partners. Chris's **objective** was to make a lot of money, while Tomas's was to help people in the community.

_b_ *Objective* means   a. cost.   b. goal.   c. excuse.

9 protest
(prə-tĕst′)
– *verb*

• When a man was discovered beating his dogs, an animal-rights group **protested**.

• "Stop it," Billy's mother **protested**. "You can't pour blue food coloring into the mashed potatoes."

_c_ *Protest* means   a. to ask.   b. to suggest.   c. to complain.

10 remedy
(rĕm′ĭ-dē)
– *noun*

• Grandma's **remedy** for a cold was to wear garlic around her neck. It never cured her cold, but at least no one came close enough to her to catch it.

• There's no quick **remedy** for a broken heart; only time will heal it.

_b_ *Remedy* means   a. memory.   b. treatment.   b. main cause.

Matching Words with Definitions

Following are definitions of the ten words. **Print** each word next to its definition. If you look closely at each word in context, you will be able to figure out its meaning.

1. _____remedy_____   A cure; something that heals

2. _____incredible_____   Unbelievable; amazing; extraordinary

3. _____conscious_____   Aware (of something); noticing (that something is or was happening or existing)

4. _____external_____   Outer; located outside

5. _____protest_____   To complain; express dissatisfaction

6. _____objective_____   A purpose; goal

7. _____assume_____   To suppose to be true; take for granted

8. _____exhaust_____   To tire greatly

9. _____internal_____   Inner; located inside

10. _____maximum_____   Most; highest; largest possible

CAUTION: Do not go any further until you are sure the above answers are correct. Then you can use the definitions to help you in the following practices. Your goal is eventually to know the words well enough so that you don't need to check the definitions at all.

➤ *Check 1*

Using the answer line, complete each item below with the correct word from the box.

a. **assume**	b. **conscious**	c. **exhaust**	d. **external**	e. **incredible**
f. **internal**	g. **maximum**	h. **objective**	i. **protest**	j. **remedy**

internal	1. The ___ part of a banana is its sweet, creamy flesh.
external	2. The ___ part of a banana is its peel.
maximum	3. The ___ speed allowed here is sixty-five miles an hour.
remedy	4. Do you think there will ever be a ___ for the common cold?
incredible	5. The Grand Canyon is the most ___ sight I've ever seen. It's so huge that it's hard to believe even when you're standing right there looking at it.
conscious	6. As Shelly tried to study, she became ___ of a loud "drip, drip" from the kitchen faucet.
objective	7. My sister's ___ is to be a fashion designer.
protest	8. If you don't like a company's policy, why not ___? For example, you could write a strong letter of complaint.
assume	9. Rather than ___ it would not rain on our outdoor wedding, we rented a large tent, just in case.
exhaust	10. Mental work can ___ someone as much as physical work.

NOTE: Now check your answers to these questions by turning to page 250. Going over the answers carefully will help you prepare for the remaining practices, for which answers are not given.

➤ *Check 2*

Using the answer lines, complete each item below with **two** words from the box.

protest / *exhaust*	1–2. "You walk too fast!" Linda ___ed to her long-legged brother. "You'll ___ me before we go two blocks!"
external / *internal*	3–4. Although the accident victim had only a few ___ bruises, he had serious ___ injuries, including damage to his kidneys.
incredible / *remedy*	5–6. It's ___ that penicillin, a ___ for various infections, was discovered by accident after some mold grew in a laboratory dish.
assume / *conscious*	7–8. I had ___d that my coworkers enjoyed the music in our office, but they said they were not even ___ of it. However, once when the music ceased°, everyone suddenly became very aware of the silence.
objective / *maximum*	9–10. Jill's ___ for the summer is to earn the ___ amount of money possible, so she has two jobs. What a contrast° between her and her brother! He's putting in the minimum° number of hours allowed where he works and going to the beach as much as possible.

➤ *Related Words*

Once you learn a new word, you can more easily understand many related words. Below are ten words related to the core words of this chapter. Use their definitions to help you write in the word that best completes each item.

a. **consciousness**, *noun*	The state of being awake
b. **internally**, *adverb*	Beneath the surface; on the inside
c. **protester**, *noun*	Someone who speaks out against something
d. **remedial**, *adjective*	Meant to improve one's skills or knowledge
e. **self-conscious**, *adjective*	Uncomfortably aware of one's behavior or appearance

_____remedial_____ 1. Carlo's grades have gone up in every subject since he took a ___ reading course.

_____consciousness_____ 2. I fell down the front steps, knocked my head, and lost ___; when I woke up, I was back in my house.

_____internally_____ 3. Although Marie managed to act pleasant during the party, ___ she was extremely angry. Her boyfriend had gotten drunk and was quite obnoxious°.

_____protester_____ 4. A meeting about abortion, sex education in schools, or another topic that lots of people disagree about is sure to attract some ___s. Most people are not neutral° about such widely discussed topics—they have strong feelings one way or the other.

_____self-conscious_____ 5. When Rodney first moved from Georgia to New York City, he felt ___ about his Southern accent. At times he was even reluctant° to speak.

f. **assumption**, *noun*	A belief; something that is considered to be true
g. **credible**, *adjective*	Believeable
h. **creed**, *noun*	A formal statement of religious beliefs
i. **exhaustion**, *noun*	A state of being extremely tired
j. **maximize**, *verb*	To make as great as possible

_____assumption_____ 6. For many centuries, it was a common ___ that the Earth was flat.

_____maximize_____ 7. Gina ___s the buying power of her dollars by shopping for good bargains.

_____credible_____ 8. I'm not accustomed° to giving money to people on the street, but sometimes it's hard to turn down a person whose hard-luck story seems ___.

_____creed_____ 9. When I first went to my friend's church, she explained to me her religion's ___.

_____exhaustion_____ 10. After he'd battled a blaze for nearly twenty-four hours, the firefighter's ___ was so great that he fell asleep without even taking off his boots.

➤ *Word Work*

A. Write each word next to the examples that best match it.

a. **assume**	b. **external**	c. **incredible**
d. **protest**	e. **remedy**	

___*external*___ 1. Orange peel
Book covers
Gift wrapping

___*remedy*___ 2. Swallowing sugar to get rid of hiccups
Holding ice on a bruise to reduce swelling and pain
Taking antibiotics to clear up an ear infection

___*incredible*___ 3. The actual invention in 1956 of diapers for birds!
Glass and brick being made from the same main ingredient: sand!
The U.S. Army training bats to drop bombs during World War II!

___*assume*___ 4. That most people in your class are right-handed
That there are lots of people named Smith in your local phone book
That your friends like pizza with sausage more than pizza with a peculiar° topping such as anchovies

___*protest*___ 5. Writing letters to the White House about taxes being too high
Demanding that a nuclear-power plant be shut down
Marching in front of a courthouse with signs saying we should eliminate° the death penalty

B. In the space provided, write the letter of the choice that best completes each item.

__c__ 6. Susan's **objective** is

a. that college tuition is too high.   b. failing math last semester.   c. to graduate from college with a degree in accounting.

__c__ 7. Because the accident victim suffered **internal** bleeding, he

a. was bleeding a great deal.   b. was bleeding a little.   c. didn't realize that he was bleeding.

__b__ 8. A person who is **exhausted** might want to

a. go to a party.   b. take a nap.   c. get a job.

__a__ 9. You will usually be fully **conscious** of

a. a loud noise nearby.   b. your own breathing.   c. a small event taking place one hundred miles away.

__c__ 10. The sign on the carnival ride says, **"Maximum** weight for riders is 80 pounds." This means that adults

a. are the only ones allowed on the ride.   b. must go with children on the ride.   c. are usually not allowed on the ride.

➤ *Word Parts*

A. The prefix *self-* often means "oneself."

Examples: *defense* — protection   *conscious* — aware
              self-defense — protection of oneself   *self-conscious* — uncomfortably aware of
                                                           oneself

On each answer line, write the word from the box that means the same as the *italicized* words.

a. **self-centered**	b. **self-conscious**	c. **self-control**
d. **self-critical°**	e. **self-educated**	

_____self-critical_____ 1. Corey is so *critical of oneself*. He must have a low opinion of himself.

_____self-control_____ 2. It takes *control of oneself* not to eat too many fresh, warm chocolate-chip cookies.

_____self-centered_____ 3. That writer is so *centered on himself!* After talking about himself for an hour, he said, "But enough about me. What do you think of my writing?"

_____self-conscious_____ 4. Irene felt uncomfortably *conscious of herself* because of her new hair color, so she was relieved when most people didn't even notice it.

_____self-educated_____ 5. My grandfather was a *educated by oneself* man; although he didn't even attend high school, he learned a great deal on his own.

B. The suffix *-ness* means "the quality or state of."

Examples: *wholesome°* — tending to improve the character, mind, or body
              wholesomeness — the quality of tending to improve the character, mind, or body

Examples: *conscious* — aware
              consciousness — the state of being aware

On each answer line, write the word from the box that best completes the item.

f. **awkwardness°**	g. **consciousness**	h. **eagerness°**
i. **usefulness**	j. **vagueness°**	

_____eagerness_____ 6. With great ___, the family stood in line to enter Disneyland.

_____consciousness_____ 7. The accident victim lost ___ and did not wake up for several days.

_____awkwardness_____ 8. Because they are growing so rapidly, many teenagers go through a period of ___ when it seems they are forever tripping over their own feet.

_____usefulness_____ 9. This camping knife is really wonderful for its _____. It provides a screwdriver, toothpick, bottle-opener, magnifying glass, and tweezers.

_____vagueness_____ 10. The ___ of the instructions for putting this storage box together is driving me crazy. They are so unclear that I don't even know which side is up.

➤ *Final Check*

Read the passages carefully. Then fill in each blank with the word that best fits the context.

A. Coming Out of a Coma

a. **exhaust**	b. **external**	c. **incredible**
d. **internal**	e. **remedy**	

"Hi, Mom," Francis said. The effort of speaking (1)_____*exhaust*_____ed him, and he closed his eyes again.

To his mother, these were the best words she had ever heard. The idea that her son was speaking again, after ten weeks in a coma, was (2)_____*incredible*_____. He had been gone from this world for so long that it seemed he'd never return. Those ten weeks had been difficult to endure°. Whenever Ms. King had visited Francis at the hospital, he had been completely still. There were no (3)_____*external*_____ signs that he was thinking or feeling anything. He was, as the doctors put it, "a vegetable." But Ms. King maintained° the hope that he still had some (4)_____*internal*_____ life. Could he, perhaps, hear her words? Could he feel her hand squeezing his? She tried to reach him in any way she could during her daily visits.

Now, although Ms. King knew there was no quick (5)_____*remedy*_____ for her son's serious injuries, the simple words "Hi, Mom" gave her hope that he could, someday, live a full life again.

B. The Office Doughnut Contest

f. **assume**	g. **conscious**	h. **maximum**
i. **objective**	j. **protest**	

"Are you telling me there are no doughnuts left? I don't believe it!" Joan said. "How could a huge supply of doughnuts be gone already?"

"I don't know how," Fran responded°. "I just know none are left."

"When I brought three dozen doughnuts in this morning, I (6)_____*assume*_____d I'd get to eat at least one," Joan said. "After all, the (7)_____*maximum*_____ number of people who ever work in this place is ten. Today, Sue isn't even here. It's hard to believe that the other eight of you could eat thirty-six doughnuts in less than three hours. I even expected to have surplus° doughnuts for tomorrow."

Then Fran and Joan became (8)_____*conscious*_____ of laughing in the office next door. When they looked in, the fate of the missing doughnuts became evident°. Three grown men were tossing doughnuts across the room. Their (9)_____*objective*_____ was to throw the doughnuts onto the pencils held up by three other grown men.

"I don't believe you guys!" Joan (10)_____*protest*_____ed. "Just you wait. Next time it's my turn to bring in the doughnuts, I'll bring in cream- and jelly-filled doughnuts, and we'll see how you play your little game then."

➤ *Questions for Discussion*

1. Describe a time when something **incredible** but true happened to you. Or tell of a time when something hard to believe happened to someone you know.

2. What is one **objective** you hope to achieve within the next year? How do you plan to reach that goal?

3. What do you think should be the **maximum** number of students in a sixth-grade class? A high-school writing class? A college lecture class?

4. Most families have a few of their own **remedies** for minor illnesses or injuries. Tell about some ways your family deals with bruises, sickness, or maybe even hurt feelings. Are these remedies applied **internally** or **externally**? How do they work?

5. When have you **assumed** that something was true and then found out that you were mistaken? For example, you might have assumed that two people were related and later found out they weren't, or you may have believed that someone agreed with you on some point and then found out he or she did not.

➤ *Ideas for Writing*

1. Describe a job you have done that **exhausted** you. What did you do? How did you feel?

2. Write about a time when you **protested** against something you thought was wrong or unfair. How did you become **conscious** of the situation? What was your **objective** in making your opinion known?

Check Your Performance			**CHAPTER 11**
Activity	*Number Right*	*Points*	*Total*
Check 2	_____	× 10 =	_____
Related Words	_____	× 10 =	_____
Word Work	_____	× 10 =	_____
Word Parts	_____	× 10 =	_____
Final Check	_____	× 10 =	_____

Enter your scores above and in the vocabulary performance chart on the inside back cover of the book.

artificial	frequency
complicate	represent
conscience	temporary
counsel	transparent
detect	triumph

Ten Words in Context

In the space provided, write the letter of the meaning closest to that of each **boldfaced** word. Use the context of the sentences to help you figure out each word's meaning.

1 **artificial**
(är′tə-fĭsh′əl)
– *adjective*

- My uncle, who lost his left arm in an accident, was recently fitted for an **artificial** arm.
- **Artificial** flowers made of paper or silk last for years.

_b_ *Artificial* means   a. short-term.   b. made by humans.   c. heavy.

2 **complicate**
(kŏm′plə-kāt′)
– *verb*

- Cooking for a crowd is difficult enough, so I don't **complicate** the job with fancy dishes. I keep the food simple.
- Don't **complicate** the game with too many rules.

_a_ *Complicate* means   a. to make difficult.   b. to find.   c. to remember.

3 **conscience**
(kŏn′shəns)
– *noun*

- After Lena stole the compact disk, her **conscience** bothered her so much that she couldn't enjoy listening to the music.
- It's strange but true that some criminals don't have a **conscience**. They really don't believe that it is wrong to cheat, steal, or even kill.

_c_ *Conscience* means   a. budget.   b. plan of action.   c. moral sense.

4 **counsel**
(koun′səl)
– *verb*

- My basketball coach **counseled** me to work at the shoe store fewer hours each week to gain more time to study.
- I **counseled** Angela to break up with her violent boyfriend.

_c_ *Counsel* means   a. to allow.   b. to join.   c. to suggest to.

5 **detect**
(dĭ-tĕkt′)
– *verb*

- If you **detect** a gas leak, leave immediately and call for help.
- Rachel never actually says that she dislikes Ron, but I **detect** a tone of dislike in her voice.

_b_ *Detect* means   a. to control.   b. to notice.   c. to want.

6 **frequency**
(frē′quən-sē)
– *noun*

- Luis and Adam used to visit each other once or twice a week, but since Adam got married, the **frequency** of their visits has gone down.
- I don't like to watch movies on TV because the **frequency** of ads is so great. I prefer to rent movies and see them without all the interruptions.

_a_ *Frequency* means   a. rate.   b. cost.   c. action.

7 represent
(rĕp′rĭ-zĕnt′)
– *verb*

- Will you speak for yourself in court, or will a lawyer **represent** you?
- Loretta will **represent** her class at the Student Council meetings.

_c_ *Represent* means   a. to leave.   b. to hire.   c. to speak for.

8 temporary
(tĕm′pə-rĕr′ē)
– *adjective*

- Mimi used a **temporary** green hair dye just for St. Patrick's Day.
- A **temporary** worker will be hired to fill in for Kwan until she recovers from her injury.

_b_ *Temporary* means   a. large.   b. short-term.   c. false.

9 transparent
(trăns-pâr′ənt)
– *adjective*

- At first, I thought the glass in the door was **transparent** and that I was seeing someone on the other side. But when I got closer, I realized that it was a mirror and I was looking at myself.
- **Transparent** wrap allows you to see what's inside a container.

_a_ *Transparent* means   a. able to be seen through.   b. old.   c. thick.

10 triumph
(trī′əmf)
– *noun*

- Our football team's **triumph** over the state's first-place team was the reason for a huge party.
- My brother's good teachers, his understanding parents, and his own hard work all led to his **triumph** over a learning disability.

_c_ *Triumph* means   a. loss.   b. meeting.   c. win.

Matching Words with Definitions

Following are definitions of the ten words. **Print** each word next to its definition. If you look closely at each word in context, you will be able to figure out its meaning.

1. _____transparent_____   Allowing light to pass through so that objects on the other side can be seen

2. _____counsel_____   To give advice or guidance to; advise°

3. _____frequency_____   How often something happens

4. _____detect_____   To notice; discover that something exists or is present

5. _____triumph_____   An outstanding or very satisfying success; victory

6. _____conscience_____   A sense of what is right or wrong in one's behavior

7. _____represent_____   To act or speak for

8. _____complicate_____   To make difficult by adding or involving many parts or details; make complex°

9. _____temporary_____   Lasting or serving for a limited time only; not permanent

10. _____artificial_____   Made to imitate something natural

CAUTION: Do not go any further until you are sure the above answers are correct. Then you can use the definitions to help you in the following practices. Your goal is eventually to know the words well enough so that you don't need to check the definitions at all.

➤ *Check 1*

Using the answer line, complete each item below with the correct word from the box.

a. **artificial**	b. **complicate**	c. **conscience**	d. **counsel**	e. **detect**
f. **frequency**	g. **represent**	h. **temporary**	i. **transparent**	j. **triumph**

_____ *triumph* _____ 1. Beating the first-place team was a greater ___ for the players than winning over the last-place team.

_____ *artificial* _____ 2. That horror movie must have used gallons of ___ blood.

_____ *counsel* _____ 3. How many hours a week would you ___ a student to work?

_____ *frequency* _____ 4. The ___ of our company newsletter is about once a month.

_____ *complicate* _____ 5. If you ___ a job, you make it harder to do.

_____ *conscience* _____ 6. A person who is cruel must not have much of a ___.

_____ *temporary* _____ 7. Substitute teachers get ___ assignments, often for only a day or two at a time.

_____ *represent* _____ 8. Elected officials are supposed to ___ the voters.

_____ *transparent* _____ 9. In the winter, we put sheets of ___ plastic over our windows to help keep out the cold.

_____ *detect* _____ 10. Although Norah has lived in New York for years, I can still ___ a slight Southern accent in her voice.

NOTE: Now check your answers to these questions by turning to page 250. Going over the answers carefully will help you prepare for the remaining practices, for which answers are not given.

➤ *Check 2*

Using the answer lines, complete each item below with **two** words from the box.

_____ *frequency* _____
_____ *counsel* _____ 1–2. To reduce the ___ of infections, people should be ___ed to wash their hands often and well. They should also be advised° to keep counters and cutting boards free of bacteria.

_____ *conscience* _____
_____ *artificial* _____ 3–4. If your ___ won't allow you to wear real fur, choose ___ fur instead. Fake fur looks great and feels good, too!

_____ *triumph* _____
_____ *temporary* _____ 5–6. I lost ten pounds last year. That was a great victory, but my ___ was only ___. I've gained every ounce of it back.

_____ *transparent* _____
_____ *detect* _____ 7–8. The eyes are sometimes called "the windows of the soul," as if they were ___ and one could ___ a person's soul by looking into them.

_____ *represent* _____
_____ *complicate* _____ 9–10. The Block Association worked well when it ___ed only the residents of our street, but it has ___d matters by trying to speak for other parts of the neighborhood as well.

➤ *Related Words*

Once you learn a new word, you can more easily understand many related words. Below are ten words related to the core words of this chapter. Use their definitions to help you write in the word that best completes each item.

a. **artificially**, *adverb*	Unnaturally
b. **complication**, *noun*	An added detail that causes confusion or difficulty
c. **conscientious**, *adjective*	Careful about following one's sense of right and wrong
d. **transparency**, *noun*	A picture viewed by shining light through it
e. **triumphant**, *adjective*	Winning

complication   1. If you ask me, planning a birthday party is difficult enough; trying to make it a surprise party is an unnecessary ___.

artificially   2. My nephew's favorite watermelon bubble gum is ___ colored and flavored—it looks like a neon sign and tastes like nothing on Earth, least of all watermelon.

triumphant   3. When their team scored the winning touchdown, the ___ players hugged each other and jumped up and down. The other team, feeling miserable°, walked away with their heads down.

transparency   4. Professor Ives illustrated her lecture by using an overhead ___ of some important charts.

conscientious   5. Raul is a ___ parent—he works hard at being a good father and takes his responsibilities very seriously. He is a good example to his children and never disciplines° them with violence.

f. **counselor**, *noun*	A person in the profession of giving advice or guidance
g. **detective**, *noun*	Someone whose job is to find the information needed to solve crimes
h. **frequent**, *adjective*	Appearing often; regular
i. **representative**, *noun*	A person who speaks for someone else
j. **temporarily**, *adverb*	For a short time; not permanently

temporarily   6. When their homes were damaged by a flood, many families were housed ___ at a local army base.

counselor   7. My wife and I are considering divorce, but we've decided to see a marriage ___ and try to find a way to stay together.

detective   8. The most famous ___ in the world is Sherlock Holmes. He solves murder cases by noticing small but important details. He is also able to analyze° events and come to brilliant conclusions.

representative   9. If you feel strongly about a public issue, don't hesitate° to write to your ___ in Congress; remember that he or she was elected to speak for you.

frequent   10. Airlines offer special discounts to "___ fliers," people who travel often.

➤ *Word Work*

A. Write each word next to the examples that best match it.

a. **artificial**	b. **detect**	c. **frequency**
d. **temporary**	e. **triumph**	

_____*artificial*_____   1. Plastic grass
Wax fruit
A glass eye

_____*triumph*_____   2. A neighborhood basketball team wins the city championship.
Your kids get all A's on their report cards.
You finally succeed in quitting smoking.

_____*detect*_____   3. Spot a child's chocolate fingerprints on a candy dish.
Discover a thief's footprints.
Notice fear in someone's voice.

_____*frequency*_____   4. Mail delivery: once a day, six days a week
Flu shots: once a year
The Main Street bus: every half hour

_____*temporary*_____   5. Campers' tents set up on the shore of a lake
A place you live in until your new home is ready
Extra salespeople hired for the holiday season

B. In the space provided, write the letter of the choice that best completes each item.

_b_   6. A **transparent** dome on a stadium lets in

a. rain.   b. sunlight.   c. air.

_a_   7. The school would **complicate** students' lives if it

a. changed the whole   b. reduced tuition.   c. installed a coffee machine
class schedule at midterm.   at the library.

_b_   8. Because of your **conscience**, you might

a. buy silk flowers.   b. apologize to your brother   c. forget to pay back
for yelling at him.   a loan.

_b_   9. You might **represent**

a. a hot summer's day.   b. your neighborhood   c. a good book.
in the city council.

_c_   10. If you wanted to **counsel** friends who seemed to be drinking too much, you would

a. mind your own   b. avoid any contact   c. talk to them about the
business and say nothing.   with them.   dangers of their behavior.

➤ *Synonyms and Antonyms*

A. **Synonyms**. Write the letter of the word or phrase that most nearly means the **same** as each boldfaced word.

_c_ 1. **conscience**

    a. rate   b. talent

    c. moral sense   d. victory

_c_ 2. **counsel**

    a. win   b. make difficult

    c. give advice to   d. imitate

_d_ 3. **detect**

    a. act for   b. ignore

    c. disapprove   d. notice

_a_ 4. **frequency**

    a. how often something happens   b. allowing light to pass through

    c. difficulty   d. short time

_c_ 5. **represent**

    a. imitate   b. discover

    c. speak for   d. succeed

B. **Antonyms**. Write the letter of the word or phrase that most nearly means the **opposite** of each boldfaced word.

_c_ 6. **artificial**

    a. new   b. easy

    c. natural   d. old

_b_ 7. **complicate**

    a. lose   b. make easier

    c. ignore   d. pay attention to

_d_ 8. **temporary**

    a. easy   b. light-blocking

    c. important   d. lasting forever

_a_ 9. **transparent**

    a. blocking out light   b. natural

    c. easy   d. long-lasting

_b_ 10. **triumph**

    a. darkness   b. loss

    c. success   d. game

➤ *Final Check*

Read the passages carefully. Then fill in each blank with the word that best fits the context.

A. The People's Choice

a. **conscience**	b. **frequency**	c. **represent**
d. **temporary**	e. **triumph**	

Suppose you are a candidate running for public office—and you win. What a (1)_____*triumph*_____! But now consider this: What is the best way to (2)_____*represent*_____ those who voted for you? How do you know what "the people" want? Sometimes the great (3)_____*frequency*_____ of letters and phone calls makes you think you know what all the people want. Think again! For most people, interest in what their elected officials are doing is only (4)_____*temporary*_____; you will never hear from many of them again. Also, of course, the voters who don't write or call may feel differently from those who do. All right, then, you say, I'll just act according to my own (5)_____*conscience*_____ and do what I think is right. Not so fast! Remember that you're supposed to be "the people's choice." So what should you do? If you know the answer to that question, I propose° that you call the politicians in Washington immediately. They've been looking for the answer for over two hundred years.

B. The Christmas Wars

f. **artificial**	g. **complicate**	h. **counsel**
i. **detect**	j. **transparent**	

Christmastime is supposed to be peaceful, but in some families it renews old battles. One is the dispute° between those who like a sweet-smelling, natural Christmas tree and those who prefer a shiny (6)_____*artificial*_____ tree, with no pine needles to mess up the floor. Another common battle goes on between parents, who seek the best places to hide the gifts until the big day, and children, who search tirelessly to (7)_____*detect*_____ clues about where those hiding places are. No matter what efforts a parent may make to (8)_____*complicate*_____ the search by shoving the gifts inside luggage or under three layers of linens, kids soon find them.

Then, of course, because the boxes and packages are not (9)_____*transparent*_____, the kids have to resort° to opening a corner of the wrapping. Or they try to determine° what's inside by shaking, bouncing, and rattling the box. Sooner or later, they make enough noise to catch an adult's attention. At this point the kids come out from behind the furnace or under the bed, trying very hard to look innocent. The parents get mad, the kids are in tears—Merry Christmas, everyone! It's hard to know how to (10)_____*counsel*_____ parents in this situation. Would the best advice be to ask Grandpa or Grandma to take the kids for a month or so?

➤ *Questions for Discussion*

1. Why do fans have a sense of **triumph** when their team wins? After all, the fans didn't do any of the playing; they only watched and cheered. Can you explain their reaction?

2. How would you **counsel** a teenager who wanted to drop out of school? Can you think of anything special to say about this—something that doesn't just repeat the advice that kids usually hear?

3. People tend to think that anything "**artificial**" is worse than something "natural." Can you think of an opposite example: a human-made product that is better than the natural thing?

4. When someone is lying to you, do you think you can usually **detect** it? If so, how? If not, why not?

5. **Transparent** objects have various advantages. One obvious benefit, for example, is letting more light into a room. What are some other ways in which something transparent can be useful?

➤ *Ideas for Writing*

1. Henry David Thoreau wrote, "Our life is frittered away by detail. . . . Simpify, simplify." Write about some ways you might make your own life simpler by getting rid of activities that **complicate** it, or at least by reducing their **frequency**.

2. Write about a time you had to do something difficult because your **conscience** demanded that you do it. For instance, you may have had to say no to a friend in order to avoid doing something you felt was wrong. Explain the situation and the choices you faced; then tell what you finally decided to do and why.

Check Your Performance   **CHAPTER 12**

Activity	Number Right	Points	Total
Check 2	_____	× 10 =	_____
Related Words	_____	× 10 =	_____
Word Work	_____	× 10 =	_____
Synonyms and Antonyms	_____	× 10 =	_____
Final Check	_____	× 10 =	_____

Enter your scores above and in the vocabulary performance chart on the inside back cover of the book.

detract	strive
foresight	substance
intense	tolerance
interval	trait
prosper	withdraw

Ten Words in Context

In the space provided, write the letter of the meaning closest to that of each **boldfaced** word. Use the context of the sentences to help you figure out each word's meaning.

1 detract
(dĭ-trăkt′)
– *verb*

- A headache can **detract** from even the most enjoyable experience.
- Eating with someone who slurps can **detract** from the pleasure of a good meal.

c *Detract* means   a. to grow.   b. to pass.   c. to take away.

2 foresight
(fôr′sīt′)
– *noun*

- Jen had the **foresight** to apply to several colleges, knowing that she might not get into the one she wanted most.
- People who are always late show a lack of **foresight**.

a *Foresight* means   a. wise planning.   b. courage.   c. strength.

3 intense
(ĭn-těns′)
– *adjective*

- After hours in the blazing sun, the hikers felt **intense** thirst.
- Dad went to the emergency room because of **intense** pain in his lower back.

a *Intense* means   a. very great.   b. unimportant.   c. imaginary.

4 interval
(ĭn′tər-vəl)
– *noun*

- The **interval** between Christmas and New Year's Day is only a week.
- There was an **interval** of several hours between the births of the twins—in fact, they were born on separate days.

c *Interval* means   a. happiness.   b. difference in importance.   c. space.

5 prosper
(prŏs′pər)
– *verb*

- The company is so strong that it is expected to **prosper** even though similar companies are going out of business.
- Somone who always jumps from job to job is not likely to **prosper**.

b *Prosper* means   a. to believe.   b. to do well.   c. to take back.

6 strive
(strīv)
– *verb*

- Many people **strive** to become movie stars, but few succeed.
- Every year, many mountain climbers **strive** to reach the top of Mount Everest.

c *Strive* means   a. to make a mistake.   b. to make a discovery.   c. to make an effort.

7 **substance**
(sŭb'stəns)
– *noun*

- Snails leave a trail of a shiny **substance** everywhere they crawl.
- Gold is such a soft **substance** that it can be pounded into a very thin sheet.

_a_ *Substance* means   a. material.   b. light.   c. force.

8 **tolerance**
(tŏl'ər-əns)
– *noun*

- The **tolerance** of our neighbors is obvious when you see children of different races playing together at their house.
- Because of the Johnsons' **tolerance**, their son-in-law's different religion is not a problem for the family.

_b_ *Tolerance* means   a. planning.   b. respect for others.   c. financial success.

9 **trait**
(trāt)
– *noun*

- My friend's nicest **trait** is her ability to laugh at herself.
- My worst **trait** is always worrying about what people think of me.

_a_ *Trait* means   a. personal quality.   b. goal.   c. preparation.

10 **withdraw**
(wĭth-drô')
– *verb*

- When I realized I was working Thursday, I had to **withdraw** my offer to baby-sit for my sister's kids.
- "Please **withdraw** your fingers from my shoulder," the woman said to her coworker. "And keep your hands to yourself."

_c_ *Withdraw* means   a. give.   b. find.   c. take back.

Matching Words with Definitions

Following are definitions of the ten words. **Print** each word next to its definition. If you look closely at each word in context, you will be able to figure out its meaning.

1. _____*trait*_____ A quality or feature, as of personality, for which a person is known

2. _____*tolerance*_____ Respect for the differing views, practices, and characteristics of others; freedom from prejudice

3. _____*detract*_____ To take away something desirable (from); reduce the quality or value of

4. _____*withdraw*_____ To take back (something or a statement); remove

5. _____*intense*_____ Extreme in strength or degree; very strong

6. _____*foresight*_____ Care in planning or preparing for the future

7. _____*interval*_____ The period of time between two events

8. _____*strive*_____ To try hard

9. _____*prosper*_____ To succeed, especially financially

10. _____*substance*_____ Physical material; matter of a particular type

CAUTION: Do not go any further until you are sure the above answers are correct. Then you can use the definitions to help you in the following practices. Your goal is eventually to know the words well enough so that you don't need to check the definitions at all.

➤ *Check 1*

Using the answer line, complete each item below with the correct word from the box.

a. **detract**	b. **foresight**	c. **intense**	d. **interval**	e. **prosper**
f. **strive**	g. **substance**	h. **tolerance**	i. **trait**	j. **withdraw**

_____*withdraw*_____ 1. I wished I could ___ my angry words, but it was too late.

_____*detract*_____ 2. That ugly vacant lot ___s from the beauty of the neighborhood.

_____*strive*_____ 3. Shelby ___s to do well in all her classes.

_____*trait*_____ 4. Patience is an important ___ for a preschool teacher.

_____*foresight*_____ 5. Budgeting requires the ___ to think of future expenses.

_____*tolerance*_____ 6. Martin Luther King taught that all people should be viewed with ___, no matter what their race or religious beliefs.

_____*intense*_____ 7. Barbara practices swimming for many hours each day, driven by her ___ desire to compete in the Olympics.

_____*interval*_____ 8. There's an ___ of an hour between two of my classes today.

_____*substance*_____ 9. The man was arrested after police saw him sell someone a white ___ in a plastic bag.

_____*prosper*_____ 10. At first, the Savings Mart didn't do well, but after it lowered its prices and increased its advertising, the store began to ___.

NOTE: Now check your answers to these questions by turning to page 250. Going over the answers carefully will help you prepare for the remaining practices, for which answers are not given.

➤ *Check 2*

Using the answer lines, complete each item below with **two** words from the box.

_____*trait*_____
_____*tolerance*_____ 1–2. One of Paul's unpleasant ___s is that he has very little ___ for anyone who disagrees with his opinions.

_____*prosper*_____
_____*strive*_____ 3–4. People who ___ tend to be individuals who ___ to do their jobs well, spend less than they earn, and save for the future.

_____*interval*_____
_____*detract*_____ 5–6. I like to watch a movie without interruption. Even the short ___ of a TV ad ___s from my enjoyment.

_____*intense*_____
_____*foresight*_____ 7–8. After we drove to the beach and ran out into the ___ sunshine of midday, we realized that none of us had had the ___ to bring along sunblock lotion.

_____*withdraw*_____
_____*substance*_____ 9–10. The principal made two people ___ from school last term for being addicted to some ___—for one it was alcohol, and for the other it was cocaine. They were counseled° to get professional help.

➤ *Related Words*

Once you learn a new word, you can more easily understand many related words. Below are ten words related to the core words of this chapter. Use their definitions to help you write in the word that best completes each item.

a. **detractor**, *noun*	A critic; one who points out the bad points of something
b. **intensify**, *verb*	To make something stronger or more powerful
c. **intent**, *adjective*	Having the mind firmly set on a purpose
d. **prosperity**, *noun*	Financial success
e. **tolerant**, *adjective*	Willing to bear patiently (something not especially liked)

_____tolerant_____ 1. Jane was ___ of her daughter's having many pets until the girl brought home a giant spider. Then Jane finally said no.

_____intensify_____ 2. If you give the dog food at the table, he won't stop begging—in fact, he will linger° at the table and ___ his begging.

_____detractor_____ 3. Most people in the audience liked the school board's plan, but one ___ kept pointing out things that he thought were wrong with the plan.

_____prosperity_____ 4. People who are born into a life of ___ may find it hard to understand the problems of the poor.

_____intent_____ 5. Since she was in second grade, Lisa had been ___ upon becoming an airline pilot.

f. **insight**, *noun*	Understanding
g. **intensity**, *noun*	Great power
h. **prosperous**, *adjective*	Successful; well-off
i. **substantial**, *adjective*	Solidly built; not fragile°
j. **tolerate**, *verb*	To put up with; bear

_____prosperous_____ 6. Levi Strauss was a poor tailor until he became ___ by making and selling "Levi's" jeans.

_____insight_____ 7. Peter is a good counselor because he has so much ___ into why people do the things they do.

_____tolerate_____ 8. I'd like to hear my favorite band in concert, but I don't think I could ___ the crowds of people there.

_____intensity_____ 9. The ___ of his hunger made it impossible for Bart to think of anything but food. He was conscious° of only his growling stomach.

_____substantial_____ 10. In the children's story "The Three Little Pigs," the lazy pigs build houses of sticks and straw that are easy to destroy. But the hardworking pig wants to inhabit° a strong house, so he builds a ___ house of bricks.

➤ *Word Work*

A. In the space provided, write the letter of the word that most closely relates to the situation in each item.

___a___ 1. When my mother travels on a plane, she keeps her pills in her purse, in case the airline loses her luggage.

      a. foresight   b. intense   c. tolerance

___a___ 2. People who were in on the "ground floor" of the personal computer industry became extremely wealthy.

      a. prosper   b. withdraw   c. detract

___c___ 3. Of the children in our family, my sister is known as the funny one, my brother is the hard-working one, and I am the athletic one.

      a. substance   b. interval   c. trait

___c___ 4. Kwan spent a lot of time worrying during the five days between her job interview and the day she learned she was hired.

      a. withdraw   b. substance   c. interval

___b___ 5. What is that blob of glowing green stuff on the kitchen table?

      a. tolerance   b. substance   c. trait

B. In the space provided, write the letter of the choice that best completes each item.

___c___ 6. People who have an **intense** need to win
      a. don't care much if they win or not.
      b. are not aware of wanting to win.
      c. want very badly to win.

___a___ 7. A sign of Rob's **tolerance** is that
      a. he has friends of many different races and religions.
      b. he studies very hard.
      c. he wears expensive clothes.

___c___ 8. Something that would probably **detract** from your enjoyment of a party would be
      a. the host playing your favorite music.
      b. having a great conversation with someone you met there.
      c. someone loudly telling an embarrassing story about you.

___b___ 9. If you and a friend have an argument and you **strive** to understand her point of view, you
      a. don't care what she thinks.
      b. really want to understand her.
      c. know that she is right and you are wrong.

___b___ 10. You might **withdraw** a compliment to someone if
      a. you admire that person greatly.
      b. you become angry at that person.
      c. you never did say anything nice to that person.

➤ *Word Parts*

A. The suffix *-ous* means "full of" or "having much."

> ***Examples:*** *fury* — violent anger   *prosper* — to succeed financially
> *furious* — full of violent anger   *prosperous* — having much financial success

On each answer line, write the word from the box that best completes the item.

a. **envious**	b. **famous**	c. **furious**
d. **joyous**	e. **prosperous**	

_____*famous*_____ 1. Elvis Presley is still very well known; in fact, he may be more ___ today than he was when he was alive.

_____*furious*_____ 2. During her latest fight with her boyfriend, Jill was so ___ that she threw a book at him.

_____*prosperous*_____ 3. Not many people "get rich quick" by winning the lottery; most of us have to work long and hard to become ___.

_____*joyous*_____ 4. The wedding of my eighty-year-old grandmother was a ___ occasion for the family.

_____*envious*_____ 5. It is hard not to feel ___ of Paul, who seems to have everything good in life: a great marriage, a wonderful job, terrific kids, and lots of friends.

B. The suffix *-al* often means "the act of."

> ***Examples:*** *deny* — to say that something is not true
> *denial* — the act of saying that something is not true
>
> *refuse* — to say "no" to doing or giving or accepting something
> *refusal* — the act of saying "no" to something

On each answer line, write the word from the box that best completes the item.

f. **approval**	g. **betrayal°**	h. **denial**
i. **survival**	j. **withdrawal**	

_____*withdrawal*_____ 6. The ___ of one thousand dollars from the man's bank account was unusual. He usually took out only fifty dollars or so.

_____*betrayal*_____ 7. Giving secret information to an enemy is a ___ of one's country.

_____*survival*_____ 8. My mother strongly believes in the soul's ___ after death, but my father believes there is nothing after death.

_____*denial*_____ 9. Mark's ___ that he had eaten the cookies surprised me because I noticed Oreo crumbs all over his bed.

_____*approval*_____ 10. We can't leave work early without our boss's ___.

➤ *Final Check*

Read the passages carefully. Then fill in each blank with the word that best fits the context.

A. What's Your Type?

a. **intense**	b. **prosper**	c. **strive**
d. **tolerance**	e. **trait**	

If being stuck behind a slow-moving car drives you nuts or if you are often impatient with a friend's progress in completing a task, you may be what researchers classify° as a Type A personality. A (1)_____*trait*_____ shared by Type A people is the desire to make effective use of time. They (2)_____*strive*_____ to accomplish more in an hour than other people do in a day. A typical example of Type A behavior is the man who built a desk onto the front of his exercise bike. Sitting in front of the TV set, he could exercise, watch football, and pay bills all at the same time. Type A's often have little (3)_____*tolerance*_____ for the calmer Type B people, who Type A's feel waste a lot of time. Naturally, Type A people often (4)_____*prosper*_____ financially, driven as they are to achieve the maximum° success at whatever they do. However, they also suffer from heart disease more often than the more relaxed Type B's. It seems that the Type A's (5)_____*intense*_____ need for success creates a lot of tension, which causes damage to the body.

B. What a Circus!

f. **detract**	g. **foresight**	h. **interval**
i. **substance**	j. **withdraw**	

I didn't actually volunteer to go to the circus. I was sort of volunteered. My son Tommy was going with his first-grade class, and he told his teacher to sign me up. When I saw how eager° he was for me to accompany° his class, I couldn't (6)_____*withdraw*_____ the offer.

So there I was, along with a handful of other parents and ninety excited six- and seven-year-olds. I don't really recollect° a great deal of the circus. What I do remember is the purple (7)_____*substance*_____ that someone spilled on my sneaker, because it never washed off. I remember a lot about the inside of the bathroom, because I took so many children there. I remember washing cotton candy off a lot of faces, since I had the (8)_____*foresight*_____ to bring a box of baby wipes along. And I remember the boy who exclaimed°, "Oh, no!" and hid his face in my lap when an acrobat took a scary walk across a high horizontal° wire.

But nothing could (9)_____*detract*_____ from the fun those kids had. To them, every act was a wonder. Even when the juggler dropped three of his four bowling pins, the kids thought he was great. Just watching all the activity exhausted° the children. In the brief (10)_____*interval*_____ between our boarding the bus to go home and Tommy's falling asleep, he told me, "That was the bestest circus ever. You were really lucky to get to come along." Looking back at it all, I think I was, too.

➤ *Questions for Discussion*

1. Do you know someone in your community who has **prospered** more than most of the people around him or her? How did this person manage to succeed? Do you think this success was a matter of luck or ability, or both?

2. Think of a time in your past when you had to **strive** to achieve something difficult. What were you trying to do, and why did you succeed or fail?

3. Describe a time in your life when you demonstrated **tolerance** for another person's opinions or behavior. In what way were that person's thoughts or actions different from what you were accustomed° to? How did you show your acceptance?

4 Think of a close friend or family member and describe several of that person's **traits**. Which of those qualities have influenced you the most?

5. Some people like waiting for something nice to happen. They are able to enjoy the **interval** between deciding to do something—for instance, buying some new clothes—and actually doing it. Others hate to wait. As soon as they decide to buy something new, they want to be at the mall doing it. What kind of person are you? Can you patiently look ahead to a nice event? Or does waiting **detract** from your enjoyment of the experience?

➤ *Ideas for Writing*

1. Write about a time when you experienced a very **intense** emotion—joy, sadness, hatred, rage, embarrassment, or something else. What produced such a strong feeling in you?

2. Think of a situation in your life in which you wish you had shown more **foresight**. Describe what happened. Then explain how things might have turned out differently if you had planned ahead better. Or, instead, tell about a time when you were very glad that you did have foresight.

Check Your Performance			CHAPTER 13
Activity	*Number Right*	*Points*	*Total*
Check 2	_____	× 10 =	_____
Related Words	_____	× 10 =	_____
Word Work	_____	× 10 =	_____
Word Parts	_____	× 10 =	_____
Final Check	_____	× 10 =	_____

Enter your scores above and in the vocabulary performance chart on the inside back cover of the book.

approximately	phrase
consistent	practical
cope	random
evaluate	significant
observe	sole

Ten Words in Context

In the space provided, write the letter of the meaning closest to that of each **boldfaced** word. Use the context of the sentences to help you figure out each word's meaning.

1 approximately
(ə-prŏk′sə-mĭt-lē)
– *adverb*

- A month is **approximately** thirty days long.
- The suspect in the murder case is a dark-haired white woman who is **approximately** forty years old.

_c_ *Approximately* means   a. certainly.   b. never.   c. about.

2 consistent
(kən-sĭs′tənt)
– *adjective*

- To be rated number one in tennis, a player must be a **consistent** winner, not a winner now and then.
- I would rather work for someone with a **consistent** manner than someone full of praise one day and screaming insults the next.

_a_ *Consistent* means   a. steady.   b. early.   c. surprising.

3 cope
(kōp)
– *verb*

- The death of a beloved pet is hard to **cope** with.
- I read an interesting article on how to **cope** with difficult people.

_c_ *Cope with* means   a. to value.   b. to predict.   c. to handle.

4 evaluate
(ĭ-văl′yoo-āt′)
– *verb*

- I need to **evaluate** both job offers before I decide which to accept.
- Several long-distance phone companies make the same promises, so it is hard to **evaluate** which is best.

_b_ *Evaluate* means   a. to ignore.   b. to judge.   c. to remember.

5 observe
(əb-zûrv′)
– *verb*

- Medical students are allowed to **observe** surgeons at work.
- The children lay on the ground to **observe** some ants building an anthill.

_a_ *Observe* means   a. to see.   b. to think about.   c. to control.

6 phrase
(frāz)
– *noun*

- The **phrase** "at this point in time" can be reduced to a single word: *now.*
- The **phrase** "Tom, Dick or Harry" means "any member of the general public."

_b_ *Phrase* means   a. puzzle.   b. word group.   c. answer.

7 **practical**
(prăk′tĭ-kəl)
– *adjective*

- Mom puts old socks to **practical** use as dust rags.
- The two single friends realized it would be **practical** to move in together and split the rent.

_c_ *Practical* means   a. done for practice.   b. expensive.   c. sensible.

8 **random**
(răn′dəm)
– *adjective*

- We studied two paintings in art class. One was a clearly organized arrangement of black and white dots; the other seemed to be a **random** collection of spots and streaks of brilliant color.
- The movement of clouds may seem to be **random**, but scientists know that there is a pattern to how they move.

_a_ *Random* means   a. without order.   b. rare.   c. useful.

9 **significant**
(sĭg-nĭf′ĭ-kənt)
– *adjective*

- My factory job was hard but worthwhile because I earned a **significant** part of my college expenses.
- Doctors have found that a good attitude can play a **significant** role in helping people recover from diseases.

_b_ *Significant* means   a. busy.   b. large.   c. easy.

10 **sole**
(sōl)
– *adjective*

- After her husband died, the woman was the **sole** support of a large family.
- The **sole** reason my cousin ever calls me is to ask for money.

_a_ *Sole* means   a. only.   b. friendly.   c. early.

Matching Words with Definitions

Following are definitions of the ten words. **Print** each word next to its definition. If you look closely at each word in context, you will be able to figure out its meaning.

1. _____ *significant* _____   Quite large in amount or quantity; important in amount
2. _____ *approximately* _____   Almost, but not exactly; more or less
3. _____ *random* _____   Not having a plan, purpose, or pattern; chance
4. _____ *evaluate* _____   To decide on the value of (something)
5. _____ *cope* _____   To deal with difficulties; handle
6. _____ *sole* _____   Only; being the only one
7. _____ *practical* _____   Useful and sensible
8. _____ *observe* _____   To watch with attention
9. _____ *consistent* _____   Steady; regular
10. _____ *phrase* _____   A group of words with a meaning; an expression

CAUTION: Do not go any further until you are sure the above answers are correct. Then you can use the definitions to help you in the following practices. Your goal is eventually to know the words well enough so that you don't need to check the definitions at all.

➤ *Check 1*

Using the answer line, complete each item below with the correct word from the box.

a. **approximately**	b. **consistent**	c. **cope**	d. **evaluate**	e. **observe**
f. **phrase**	g. **practical**	h. **random**	i. **significant**	j. **sole**

_____ *consistent* _____   1. Rhonda is a ___ student, bringing home B's regularly.

_____ *significant* _____   2. The Murphys have so many pets that they spend a ___ amount of their grocery money to feed them.

_____ *evaluate* _____   3. The course on "Smart Shopping" teaches people how to ___ the worth of products and services.

_____ *observe* _____   4. To learn to make lasagna, I ____d my mother making it.

_____ *random* _____   5. I like to take ___ walks, without any plan in mind.

_____ *cope* _____   6. My friends helped me ___ with my father's death.

_____ *phrase* _____   7. People just learning English are often puzzled by ___s such as "on the up-and-up" and "You don't say!"

_____ *sole* _____   8. I barely know my neighbor—the ___ conversation we ever have is saying "Good morning" to each other.

_____ *practical* _____   9. White furniture is not ___ for a family with little kids who wear dirty shoes and spill Kool-Aid.

_____ *approximately* _____ 10. "I'd like you to cut off this much," Eileen told her hairdresser, indicating° ___ two inches.

NOTE: Now check your answers to these questions by turning to page 250. Going over the answers carefully will help you prepare for the remaining practices, for which answers are not given.

➤ *Check 2*

Using the answer lines, complete each item below with **two** words from the box.

_____ *practical* _____
_____ *cope* _____   1–2. Dave found an inexpensive, ___ way to ___ with his problem of mice in his house—he got a cat.

_____ *approximately* _____
_____ *significant* _____   3–4. Pizza is Little Italy's best seller, bringing in ___ 30 percent of the profits, a very ___ part of the restaurant's income.

_____ *evaluate* _____
_____ *observe* _____   5–6. The best way to ___ a college and decide if it is right for you is to visit it and ___ classes and other activities there.

_____ *phrase* _____
_____ *random* _____   7–8. The ___ "a chance meeting" refers to a ___ meeting—in other words, one that happens accidentally.

_____ *sole* _____
_____ *consistent* _____   9–10. The ___ exercise I get is walking—nothing else. But I am ___ about it—I do it every day. I prefer solitary° walks so that I don't have to talk to anyone.

➤ *Related Words*

Once you learn a new word, you can more easily understand many related words. Below are ten words related to the core words of this chapter. Use their definitions to help you write in the word that best completes each item.

a. **evaluation**, *noun*	A judgment of the value or quality of something
b. **impractical**, *adjective*	Not sensible; not useful
c. **inconsistent**, *adjective*	Not steady; changing; not dependable
d. **observant**, *adjective*	Watchful; paying careful attention
e. **at random**, *adverb*	Without a plan or purpose

__at random__ 1. Waiting to see the dentist, Loni picked up a magazine ___, not even noticing its title.

__inconsistent__ 2. We have an ___ supply of hot water—sometimes there is plenty; at other times, there's not enough for even one shower.

__evaluation__ 3. The restaurant closed down abruptly° after a bad ___ by the health department.

__observant__ 4. If you were more ___, you would have noticed that we have been driving in a circle for a considerable° amount of time.

__impractical__ 5. I rarely buy clothing in ___ fabrics that I can't stick in the washing machine or that require ironing. I don't want to complicate° my housework any more than necessary.

f. **insignificant**, *adjective*	Small in size or amount
g. **observation**, *noun*	The careful watching of someone or something
h. **observatory**, *noun*	A building that houses telescopes for the study of the stars
i. **rephrase**, *verb*	To say again, but in a different way
j. **significance**, *noun*	Importance

__observation__ 6. The detectives' ___ of the house led them to believe that there was an illegal gambling operation going on inside.

__observatory__ 7. Last Saturday, science students went on a field trip to an ___, where they were able to look at the planets and even watch a meteor shower.

__rephrase__ 8. Santiago asked Abby, "Will you marry me?" Then, before she could answer, he said, "Let me ___ that—will you marry me in two years when I get my degree?"

__significance__ 9. The invention of the printing press was of great ___ because it made books available to people who could not afford hand-copied ones.

__insignificant__ 10. I was astonished° to see a woman at the supermarket drop a quarter and not pick it up. She must have thought it was an ___ amount of money.

➤ *Word Work*

A. In the space provided, write the letter of the word that most closely relates to the situation in each item.

| a. **consistent** | b. **evaluate** | c. **phrase** |
| d. **random** | e. **significant** | |

_____*evaluate*_____ 1. We will grade the history projects for originality, neatness, and accuracy.

_____*consistent*_____ 2. Kyle is never late for work—he walks in that door at 8:50 every morning, just like clockwork.

_____*significant*_____ 3. You may think my earnings from baby-sitting are small, but they are an important part of my budget—they paid for all my books this semester.

_____*random*_____ 4. The visitors to the city just wandered up and down the streets, stopping to look at anything that caught their eye.

_____*phrase*_____ 5. The line "Make my day!" was made popular by Clint Eastwood.

B. Write each word next to the examples that best match it.

| f. **approximately** | g. **cope** | h. **observe** |
| i. **practical** | j. **sole** | |

_____*practical*_____ 6. Buying milk for the family instead of a cola drink
Patching old jeans instead of throwing them out
Getting enough sleep before an important test

_____*approximately*_____ 7. A distance of around two miles between the cousins' houses
About 150 people at the meeting
A cost of close to ninety cents a pint for strawberries this summer

_____*observe*_____ 8. A teacher watches the class taking a test.
Cats stare out the window at birds on a feeder.
Police officers sit in their car and watch for speeding cars.

_____*cope*_____ 9. Having a flat tire and then putting on a new one
Losing a job and then signing up for a class to learn new job skills
Feeling lonely and joining a social club

_____*sole*_____ 10. Just one person living on the island
One egg left in the refrigerator
A boy with no brothers or sisters

➤ *Synonyms and Antonyms*

A. Synonyms. Write the letter of the word or phrase that most nearly means the **same** as each boldfaced word.

_b_   1. **cope**

        a. compete with   b. manage

        c. quarrel   d. agree

_a_   2. **evaluate**

        a. judge   b. pay for

        c. see   d. borrow

_c_   3. **observe**

        a. set a goal   b. perform

        c. watch   d. handle

_d_   4. **phrase**

        a. a practice   b. something useful

        c. a plan   d. a group of words

_b_   5. **sole**

        a. important   b. only

        c. sensible   d. unplanned

B. Antonyms. Write the letter of the word or phrase that most nearly means the **opposite** of each boldfaced word.

_b_   6. **approximately**

        a. well-known   b. exactly

        c. not clear   d. often

_d_   7. **consistent**

        a. having a plan   b. not close

        c. valuable   d. not regular

_a_   8. **practical**

        a. useless   b. valuable

        c. attractive   d. common

_d_   9. **random**

        a. not steady   b. interesting

        c. unknown   d. planned

_d_ 10. **significant**

        a. wrong   b. unclear

        c. dull   d. small in amount

➤ *Final Check*

Read the passages carefully. Then fill in each blank with the word that best fits the context.

A. Practicing Kindness

a. **consistent**	b. **evaluate**	c. **observe**
d. **phrase**	e. **random**	

Maybe you're heard the (1)_____*phrase*_____ or seen it printed on a bumper sticker. It encourages people to do kind things for no particular reason, with no particular plan. It goes like this: "Practice (2)_____*random*_____ acts of kindness and senseless beauty." I don't know where it originated° or who said it first. But I have seen people putting the idea into practice. I've (3)_____*observe*_____d people putting quarters into parking meters so that a stranger's car wouldn't be ticketed. I've heard of someone paying a family's bill in a restaurant, then leaving before the family found out. I know a man who is (4)_____*consistent*_____ in not letting a day go by without giving someone a sincere compliment.

Why do these people bother? They probably don't stop to (5)_____*evaluate*_____ their actions or objectives°. But if they did, I assume° they would say something like this: Kindness can be catching, just as cruelty can be. When we do something unexpected and nice for another person, who knows where that act of kindness might end?

B. The Stinking Rose

f. **approximately**	g. **cope**	h. **practical**
i. **significant**	j. **sole**	

Centuries ago in Rome, it was called "stinking rose." It was then used to flavor food and for such (6)_____*practical*_____ purposes as fighting colds. Today we call it garlic, and we too find this wonderful substance° delicious and useful. In fact, in one recent year, Americans bought enough garlic to provide every man, woman, and child with (7)_____*approximately*_____ one and a half pounds of the stuff. It is added to a wide variety° of foods, from appetizers to zucchini—even to chocolate peanut butter cups. The unfortunate thing about garlic is that it produces bad breath. One way to (8)_____*cope*_____ with garlic breath is to chew parsley, an excellent natural breath cleaner. Or eat garlic only with others who are also eating it. Being tasty is not the (9)_____*sole*_____ good thing about garlic—it turns out that the ancient Romans were absolutely right about its having health benefits. A (10)_____*significant*_____ number of studies (about 3,000) have been done of the onionlike plant. They suggest that garlic may strengthen the immune system, fight colds, cause a reduction° in blood pressure, and even help prevent cancer.

➤ *Questions for Discussion*

1. How do you **cope** with tension? Are you someone who deals with pressure well, without becoming overly upset? Or do you "fall apart" emotionally? Describe a tense situation in your life and how you have coped (or are coping) with it.

2. Do you know someone whom you would describe as very **practical**? Do you know someone who is not so practical and often does not consider things realistically? Describe those two people, giving examples of how one is sensible and the other is not so sensible.

3. What is a **phrase** that you associate with a particular person in your life? Did a parent, a grandparent, or a friend have a saying that he or she repeated often? What was that phrase, and when was the person likely to say it?

4. Do you have a **significant** amount of free time in your life or only a small amount of free time? What are some of the things you prefer to do in your free time?

5. While your life may change from day to day, there are some parts of your life that are **consistent**, that you can depend on routinely. For example, you may wake up every day to the sound of your alarm clock, or you may have a relationship that you can always count on. What are some of the consistent things in your life that you like best?

➤ *Ideas for Writing*

1. Think of a time when you just sat back and **observed** something happening, such as the behavior of children in a park or the movements of construction workers. Write a paragraph describing a scene that you observed for a while.

2. Some people believe that everyone has a "perfect match"—that there is one person out there who is the **sole** romantic partner for each of us. Others think that people get together at **random** and that there are a number of people out there who would make a good life partner. Write about whether you believe more in "just one true love" or in "lots of possibilities."

Check Your Performance			**CHAPTER 14**
Activity	*Number Right*	*Points*	*Total*
Check 2	_____	× 10 =	_____
Related Words	_____	× 10 =	_____
Word Work	_____	× 10 =	_____
Synonyms and Antonyms	_____	× 10 =	_____
Final Check	_____	× 10 =	_____

Enter your scores above and in the vocabulary performance chart on the inside back cover of the book.

authentic	eligible
characteristic	harsh
concept	remote
confront	shallow
disrupt	thrive

Ten Words in Context

In the space provided, write the letter of the meaning closest to that of each **boldfaced** word. Use the context of the sentences to help you figure out each word's meaning.

1 authentic
(ô-thĕn′tĭk)
– *adjective*

- Don't be fooled if someone tries to sell you an **authentic** diamond ring for $10.99. The stone in that ring is sure to be fake.
- Several people claim to have saved the little girl from the burning building, so no one knows who is the **authentic** hero.

_c_ *Authentic* means   a. old.   b. qualified.   c. real.

2 characteristic
(kăr′ək-tə-rĭs′tĭk)
– *adjective*

- Leon has his family's **characteristic** warm smile.
- Olive oil, garlic, pasta and cheese are **characteristic** parts of the Italian diet.

_a_ *Characteristic* means   a. usual.   b. convenient.   c. strange.

3 concept
(kŏn′sĕpt′)
– *noun*

- When asked for her **concept** of heaven, the child said, "A room full of toys and chocolate."
- My sister doesn't understand the **concept** of living within a budget.

_a_ *Concept* means   a. idea.   b. worst fear.   c. memory.

4 confront
(kən-frŭnt′)
– *verb*

- The restaurant manager really should **confront** that waiter and complain about his rude behavior.
- The opposing lawyer plans to **confront** the accused man with a surprise piece of evidence.

_b_ *Confront* means   a. to avoid.   b. to face.   c. to prepare.

5 disrupt
(dĭs-rŭpt′)
– *verb*

- "One way to **disrupt** a biology class," my roommate said, "is to turn the frogs loose and let them hop all over the floor."
- Parents who are angry about budget cuts plan to **disrupt** tonight's school board meeting with a noisy demonstration.

_c_ *Disrupt* means   a. to manage.   b. to go to.   c. to upset.

6 eligible
(ĕl′ĭ-jə-bəl)
– *adjective*

- Because of his high grades and his parents' low income, my cousin is **eligible** for some good college scholarships.
- It's not true that any American can become president of the United States. To be **eligible**, you have to be at least thirty-five years old.

_a_ *Eligible* means   a. qualified.   b. known.   c. pleased.

7 harsh
(härsh)
– *adjective*

- The **harsh** ruler decided to punish the entire village for one man's crime.
- The scolding the children received was too **harsh**—they hadn't done anything all that bad.

_b_ *Harsh* means   a. fair.   b. rough.   c. wasteful.

8 remote
(rĭ-mōt′)
– *adjective*

- Humans have explored even the most **remote** parts of the planet, areas deep in forests and beneath the seas.
- Some parts of the park are so **remote** that visitors seldom reach them.

_c_ *Remote* means   a. large.   b. typical.   c. distant.

9 shallow
(shăl′ŏ)
– *adjective*

- The lifeguard at the pool insists that young children stay at the **shallow** end.
- The cake won't rise very high in that **shallow** pan; you'll need a pan with higher sides.

_b_ *Shallow* means   a. real.   b. not deep.   c. very wide.

10 thrive
(thrīv)
– *verb*

- The African violets should **thrive** in that sunny window.
- In the past, many premature babies died, but with modern medical care most of them **thrive** and live normal lives.

_a_ *Thrive* means   a. to do very well.   b. to grow weaker.   c. to need too much care.

Matching Words with Definitions

Following are definitions of the ten words. **Print** each word next to its definition. If you look closely at each word in context, you will be able to figure out its meaning.

1. _____shallow_____ Not deep

2. _____confront_____ To face or oppose boldly

3. _____thrive_____ To grow very well; improve physically

4. _____disrupt_____ To cause disorder or confusion; upset

5. _____eligible_____ Qualified to be chosen; desirable as a candidate

6. _____harsh_____ Unkind or cruel; strict; severe

7. _____remote_____ Far away; out-of-the-way; hidden away

8. _____characteristic_____ Typical of someone or something

9. _____concept_____ A general thought; an idea

10. _____authentic_____ Real; true; actual

CAUTION: Do not go any further until you are sure the above answers are correct. Then you can use the definitions to help you in the following practices. Your goal is eventually to know the words well enough so that you don't need to check the definitions at all.

➤ *Check 1*

Using the answer line, complete each item below with the correct word from the box.

a. **authentic**	b. **characteristic**	c. **concept**	d. **confront**	e. **disrupt**
f. **eligible**	g. **harsh**	h. **remote**	i. **shallow**	j. **thrive**

shallow	1. The creek was so ___ that the water came up only to my ankles.
authentic	2. Some imitation pearl necklaces are so beautiful that only a jeweler can tell the pearls are not ___.
harsh	3. Cindy received ___ treatment from her cruel stepmother.
concept	4. The preschool teacher tries to help her little students understand the ___ of sharing.
disrupt	5. The student assembly was ___ed by a fire drill.
thrive	6. The weak, sickly child began to ___ after doctors corrected her heart problem.
remote	7. Professor Lopez studies little-known plants in ___ parts of our state forests.
confront	8. After a man dropped a bag of trash on the ground, another man picked it up and ___ed him, saying, "I think this is yours. Find a trash can."
eligible	9. Students must have at least a B average to be ___ for any of the school sports teams.
characteristic	10. Fat, fleshy leaves are ___ of cactus plants.

NOTE: Now check your answers to these questions by turning to page 250. Going over the answers carefully will help you prepare for the remaining practices, for which answers are not given.

➤ *Check 2*

Using the answer lines, complete each item below with **two** words from the box.

characteristic *authentic*	1–2. The two rings looked alike to me, but the jeweler said that only one had the colorful sparkle that is ___ of an ___ diamond.
confront *disrupt*	3–4. Tomorrow I will ___ our neighbors and protest° about the way that their unleashed dog ___s the children's backyard games.
harsh *thrive*	5–6. A child who does poorly in school with a ___, bad-tempered teacher might ___ with a teacher who is gentle and caring.
eligible *remote*	7–8. Because she is a biologist, Mia is ___ to be part of a research team that will study turtles on a ___ island.
concept *shallow*	9–10. Because babies can drown in very little water, the ___ that they are safe in a ___ pool is false—a reliable° adult must be watching them every second.

➤ *Related Words*

Once you learn a new word, you can more easily understand many related words. Below are ten words related to the core words of this chapter. Use their definitions to help you write in the word that best completes each item.

a. **character**, *noun*	The moral qualities of a person
b. **confrontation**, *noun*	An angry or threatening meeting
c. **disruptive**, *adjective*	Causing confusion or disturbance
d. **inauthentic**, *adjective*	Not real; fake
e. **ineligible**, *adjective*	Not qualified for a particular purpose

_____*inauthentic*_____ 1. The museum directors were shocked to learn that their most famous painting was ___; it was only a very well-done copy.

_____*character*_____ 2. Jerry wouldn't cheat on a test—his ___ is very good.

_____*confrontation*_____ 3. It can be dangerous to try to break up a ___ between a couple of angry dogs.

_____*disruptive*_____ 4. One ___ child can take up more of a teacher's attention than a whole class of well-behaved children.

_____*ineligible*_____ 5. People who are related to any of the judges are ___ to enter the talent contest.

f. **conceive**, *verb*	To have an idea or opinion
g. **disruption**, *noun*	A disturbance or interruption
h. **eligibility**, *noun*	Qualifications; fitness
i. **harshly**, *adverb*	In a cruel or strict manner
j. **harshness**, *noun*	Strictness; cruelty

_____*disruption*_____ 6. There was an interesting ___ in English class today—someone opened a window, and a sparrow flew in.

_____*eligibility*_____ 7. Sports are supposed to be wholesome° activities, so it was especially sad when two athletes lost their ___ to compete in the Olympics because they failed drug tests.

_____*harshly*_____ 8. "Everyone down on the floor. You too, lady," the bank robber said ___ to the elderly woman.

_____*conceive*_____ 9. Children ___ of their parents as very wise and powerful. However, when they become teenagers, they revise° that view quite a bit.

_____*harshness*_____ 10. Benita loves playing the piano, but she quit taking piano lessons because of the ___ of her teacher's methods. He once made her play the same few notes approximately° twenty-five times in a row.

➤ *Word Work*

A. Write each word by the examples that best match it.

a. authentic	**b. characteristic**	**c. disrupt**
d. harsh	**e. thrive**	

_____*disrupt*_____ 1. A baby cries during a religious service.
A cat runs onto a baseball field in the middle of a game.
A fire drill occurs° in the middle of a class.

_____*authentic*_____ 2. A red stone that has been found to be a ruby
An old desk known to be an antique from the seventeenth century
Cave paintings proven to be the work of Stone Age artists

_____*characteristic*_____ 3. The red color of many barns
The sweet smell of roses
The hot summers of Florida

_____*harsh*_____ 4. A person who whips his dogs
A principal who punishes children by forcing them to skip lunch
A drill sergeant screaming orders at a group of new soldiers

_____*thrive*_____ 5. Betsy settles into her new school quickly, makes friends, and earns good grades.
An orphaned kitten grows strong and healthy drinking formula from a bottle.
A fern hanging in the sunny window grows full and beautiful.

B. In the space provided, write the letter of the word that most closely relates to the situation in each item.

_c_ 6. I plan to walk up to my neighbor and tell him that the junk car on his lawn is an eyesore.

   a. shallow   b. eligible   c. confront

_a_ 7. The idea of infinity—of time and space that have no beginning and no end—is difficult for most people to understand.

   a. concept   b. thrive   c. eligible

_c_ 8. Any child between the ages of 5 and 9 who is a resident of Ohio may enter a drawing in the art contest.

   a. confront   b. disrupt   c. eligible

_b_ 9. The hermit lived many miles from town, in a part of the hills that was hard to reach. He wasn't able to cope° very well with the demands of society.

   a. confront   b. remote   c. thrive

_a_ 10. That box isn't deep enough—don't you have one that is a better size to hold a salad bowl?

   a. shallow   b. authentic   c. harsh

➤ *Analogies*

Each item below starts with a pair of words in CAPITAL LETTERS. For each item, figure out the relationship between these two words. Then decide which of the choices (*a, b, c,* or *d*) expresses a similar relationship. Write the letter of your choice on the answer line. (All the repeated words in these items are from this unit.)

_b_ 1. AUTHENTIC : REAL ::

    a. lost : found

    c. expected : surprising

    b. expensive : high-priced

    d. inner : external

_c_ 2. EXTERNAL° : INTERNAL° ::

    a. outside : weather

    c. intense° : weak

    b. sole° : only

    d. red : bright

_c_ 3. HARSH : KIND ::

    a. late : tardy

    c. permanent : temporary°

    b. helpful : useful

    d. incredible° : amazing

_c_ 4. ORANGE : FRUIT ::

    a. cat : dog

    c. penicillin : remedy°

    b. triumph° : loss

    d. strawberry : cherry

_d_ 5. CONFRONT : AVOID ::

    a. strive° : try

    c. tear : rip

    b. eligible : qualified

    d. prosper° : fail

_c_ 6. SHALLOW : DEEP ::

    a. brief: short

    c. laughing : frowning

    b. disrupt : upset

    d. random° : unplanned

_d_ 7. WINDOW : TRANSPARENT° ::

    a. door : doorknob

    c. car : highway

    b. window : curtain

    d. grass : green

_a_ 8. THRIVE : WEAKEN ::

    a. protest° : approve

    c. protect : guard

    b. smile : grin

    d. observe° : watch

_b_ 9. TRAIT° : PATIENCE ::

    a. promise : withdraw°

    c. banker : money

    b. substance° : clay

    d. kindness : intelligence

_b_ 10. GIVE : GIFT ::

    a. run : walk

    c. concept : idea

    b. detect° : clue

    d. exhaust° : tire

➤ *Final Check*

Read the passages carefully. Then fill in each blank with the word that best fits the context.

A. A Modern Fairy Tale

a. **concept**	b. **confront**	c. **disrupt**
d. **eligible**	e. **harsh**	

Many fairy tales are versions° of the same story: A prince has his pick of all the (1)_____*eligible*_____ women in the kingdom. But the girl he likes best is in big trouble, so the prince bravely rescues her. The girl doesn't do much of anything. She just looks pretty. The stories all end with more or less the same phrase°: "They lived happily ever after."

But one fairy tale, "The Paper Bag Princess," gets rid of the (2)_____*concept*_____ of the brave prince and the helpless girl. In it, Princess Elizabeth is engaged to Prince Ronald. But a dragon (3)_____*disrupt*_____s their plans by burning the castle and capturing Ronald. Elizabeth decides to rescue him. Since all her pretty clothes have been burned up, she puts on a paper bag. She bravely (4)_____*confront*_____s the dragon and tricks him into using up all his strength on silly tasks. Then she goes into the dragon's cave and finds Ronald.

Instead of being grateful, however, Ronald gives Elizabeth a (5)_____*harsh*_____ scolding for being covered with dirt and smoke and for wearing a bag. He tells her to come back when she looks like "a real princess." Elizabeth tells Ronald that though he looks like a real prince, with his fancy clothes and neat hair, he is, in fact, "a bum." The last picture in the book shows Elizabeth dancing happily off into the sunset, with the final line "They didn't get married after all."

B. Wolf Children

f. **authentic**	g. **characteristic**	h. **remote**
i. **shallow**	j. **thrive**	

A tale of children being raised by wolves sounds incredible°. However, though hard to believe, one story about wolf children appears to be (6)_____*authentic*_____. In Singapore during the early 1920s, Reverend J. A. L. Singh heard stories of "man-beasts" that were frightening the people of a (7)_____*remote*_____ jungle village. Along with a group of other men, Singh went in search of that hidden village and the strange creatures.

When Singh uncovered a (8)_____*shallow*_____ hole, he discovered a family of wolves. From within the wolves' den, two pale creatures peeked out. Singh's party killed the adult wolves and dug into the den. There they found two human children curled up with the cubs. The children were captured and brought to the village in bamboo cages.

The children never spoke to other humans; instead, they howled and growled like animals. Their diet was equally wolf-like: they preferred raw meat, mice, and cockroaches. And they had the wolf's (9)_____*characteristic*_____ desire to be active at night, as well as a dislike of the indoors. Sadly, the children did not (10)_____*thrive*_____. Both grew weak and died.

➣ *Questions for Discussion*

1. What qualities are **characteristic** of you? In other words, when your family and friends think about you, what traits° would they say are typical of you, and why?

2 Tell about a time you **confronted** another person about something he or she had done. What were you upset about? How did you express your feelings to that person?

3. Name a **remote** place, a spot hardly anyone else knows about, where you go to relax or study. Tell about that place, including what you like about it.

4. What are some common ways that students **disrupt** classroom activities? What are some of the more unusual classroom disruptions you have seen?

5. Tell about a time that you spoke to someone in a **harsh** way, then wished you had not. Why do you think you spoke so unpleasantly?

➣ *Ideas for Writing*

1. What qualities do you think are **characteristic** of a good friendship? Write a paper explaining your **concept** of friendship.

2. Imagine that you could design your own school—one in which you could truly **thrive**. How would it fill your mental, emotional, and physical needs? What subjects would be taught? How would they be presented? Would the teaching be done in classrooms, or in some other setting? Could just anyone attend your school, or would only certain people be **eligible**? Write a description of what a school designed just for you would be like.

Check Your Performance			CHAPTER 15
Activity	*Number Right*	*Points*	*Total*
Check 2	_____	× 10 =	_____
Related Words	_____	× 10 =	_____
Word Work	_____	× 10 =	_____
Analogies	_____	× 10 =	_____
Final Check	_____	× 10 =	_____

Enter your scores above and in the vocabulary performance chart on the inside back cover of the book.

UNIT THREE: Review

The box at the right lists twenty-five words from Unit Three. Using the clues at the bottom of the page, fill in these words to complete the puzzle that follows.

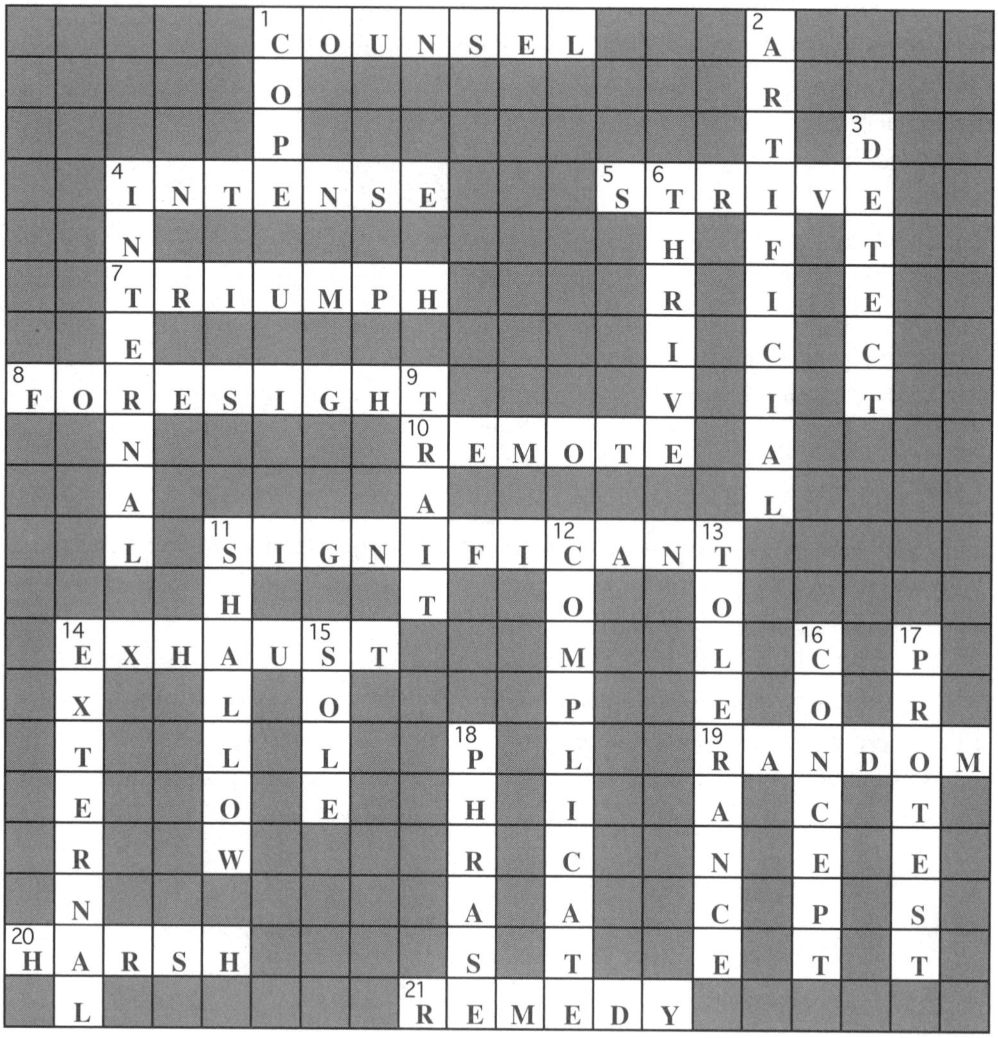

artificial
complicate
concept
cope
counsel
detect
exhaust
external
foresight
harsh
intense
internal
phrase
protest
random
remedy
remote
shallow
significant
sole
strive
thrive
tolerance
trait
triumph

ACROSS

1. To give advice or guidance to
4. Extreme in strength or degree; very strong
5. To try hard
7. An outstanding or very satisfying success; victory
8. Care in planning or preparing for the future
10. Far away; out-of-the-way
11. Quite large in amount or quantity
14. To tire greatly
19. Not having a plan, purpose, or pattern; chance
20. Unkind or cruel; strict; severe
21. A cure; something that heals

DOWN

1. To deal with difficulties
2. Made to imitate something natural
3. To notice; discover that something exists or is present
4. Inner; located inside
6. To grow very well; improve physically
9. A quality or feature, as of personality, for which a person is known
11. Not deep
12. To make difficult by adding or involving many parts or details; make complex
13. Respect for the differing views, practices, and characteristics of others
14. Outer; located outside
15. Only; being the only one
16. A general thought; an idea
17. To complain
18. A group of words with a meaning; an expression

UNIT THREE: Test 1

PART A
Choose the word that best completes each item and write it in the space provided.

triumph   1. Since my math class was very difficult for me, I consider the B I got for the course to be a great ___.

      a. foresight   b. triumph   c. tolerance   d. trait

exhausted   2. When I began exercising I was in such bad shape that walking a mile ___ me, but now I run three miles every day.

      a. observed   b. prospered   c. exhausted   d. protested

counsels   3. It's hard to believe in a doctor who ___ his patients not to smoke, but who smokes himself.

      a. counsels   b. copes with   c. withdraws   d. exhausts

frequency   4. The ___ of Luis's ear infections when he was a little boy was great, but he hasn't had one for years now.

      a. phrase   b. objective   c. frequency   d. conscience

represent   5. "Remember that you ___ all of the people of our city," one man yelled to the mayor, "not just the rich ones."

      a. represent   b. detect   c. protest   d. thrive

temporary   6. It turned out that my son's interest in collecting stamps was only ___. He forgot about it after a couple of months.

      a. temporary   b. intense   c. external   d. transparent

detect   7. If I ___ a hair in my food, then I can't eat another bite of that food, even after I remove the hair.

      a. strive   b. evaluate   c. assume   d. detect

conscience   8. As much as I would love to call in sick to work and go the baseball game, my ___ won't let me.

      a. substance   b. conscience   c. phrase   d. interval

assume   9. Just because Donald is quiet in class, don't ___ that he is stupid.

      a. assume   b. protest   c. disrupt   d. withdraw

conscious   10. As she read in the living room, Anna became ___ of loud voices coming from her parents' room.

      a. appropriate   b. shallow   c. authentic   d. conscious

complicated   11. My daughter invited some friends over for dinner and then ___ my planning by telling me that one is allergic to eggs, another is allergic to milk, and the third is a vegetarian.

      a. prospered   b. complicated   c. thrived   d. detected

(Continues on next page)

_____transparent_____ 12. When they visited the coast, the Martins enjoyed a trip in a glass-bottomed boat. They looked through its ___ bottom and saw many fish and other sea creatures.

      a. transparent   b. random   c. remote   d. harsh

_____artificial_____ 13. The hardware store sells ___ stones made of plastic that you can open and hide a house key in. Then you can hide the key by leaving the "stone" somewhere near your door.

      a. eligible   b. authentic   c. artificial   d. objective

PART B

Write **C** if the italicized word is used **correctly**. Write **I** if the word is used **incorrectly**.

___I___ 14. After using the *external* part of onions and potatoes in a meal, I use the peels to make broth.

___C___ 15. As *incredible* as it seems, the Nile River in Africa has frozen over at least twice.

___I___ 16. The house's *internal* appearance is neat, but inside, it's a real mess.

___C___ 17. The *maximum* legal driving speed in our state is sixty miles an hour.

___I___ 18. My only *objective* to Mimi is that spending time with her is more boring than watching paint dry.

___C___ 19. The play was so bad that we slipped out of the theater during the *interval* between the first and second acts.

___I___ 20. Joan's sickness seemed to be getting better, but over the weekend she had a *remedy* and is now seriously ill.

___I___ 21. The lovely bushes and flowering trees certainly *detract* from the beauty of the neighborhood.

___C___ 22. Knowing that his children often bring home friends after a baseball game, Mr. Hendricks had the *foresight* to make extra hamburgers for dinner.

___C___ 23. The chickens *protest* loudly whenever someone takes their eggs out from under them.

___I___ 24. Many people don't eat much breakfast because their hunger in the morning is *intense*.

___I___ 25. Our boss is so *harsh* that he gives every employee an extra day off on his or her birthday.

Score (Number correct) _____ × 4 = _____%

Enter your score above and in the vocabulary performance chart on the inside back cover of the book.

UNIT THREE: Test 2

PART A

Complete each item with a word from the box. Use each word once.

a. approximately	b. authentic	c. consistent	d. cope	e. disrupt
f. eligible	g. phrase	h. prosper	i. remote	j. shallow
k. substance	l. trait	m. withdraw		

disrupt   1. A swarm of bees ___ed the picnic, sending people running and yelling in every direction.

cope   2. One way to ___ with winter weather is to stay indoors, turn the heat up, play old Beach Boys records, and watch videotapes of Hawaiian hula dancers.

trait   3. When asked what ___ is most important in a boyfriend or girlfriend, many people answer, "A sense of humor."

remote   4. In order to have the peace and quiet he needed to finish his book, the writer moved to a ___ cabin where there were no people, no cars, and not even a telephone.

prosper   5. A lemonade stand would ___ on this corner—hundreds of hot, thirsty people walk by every day.

substance   6. The librarian complained that someone had returned a book with a sticky ___ all over its cover.

authentic   7. If someone tells you he can sell you an ___ diamond bracelet for twenty dollars, don't believe him.

eligible   8. Do you have to be a high-school graduate to be ___ to join the Army?

approximately   9. The car sells for ___ fifteen thousand dollars; the exact price depends on what "extras" you order, such as power windows or a CD player.

consistent   10. I don't think I'd like to live in a place where the weather is so ___ that there is never any change from day to day.

shallow   11. Don't bury those carrot seeds too deep—just dig a ___ hole for each one and cover it with a small amount of soil.

withdraw   12. I had to ___ my offer to buy my friend's old car when I realized I couldn't afford automobile insurance.

phrase   13. My grandfather usually spoke English, but he always greeted friends with the Spanish ___ "Qué pasa?" which means "What's happening?"

(Continues on next page)

PART B

Write **C** if the italicized word is used **correctly**. Write **I** if the word is used **incorrectly**.

_C_ 14. Manuel is a hard-working person who always *strives* to do his best.

_C_ 15. Amanda was the *sole* person at the table who ate meat. Everyone else was a vegetarian.

_C_ 16. After being put in the sun and watered regularly, the once-sickly plant soon *thrived*.

_I_ 17. When I asked the traffic cop directions to the post office, he *evaluated* that it was just down the block.

_I_ 18. Seeing her best friend get off the train, Irene *observed* quickly down the sidewalk to give her a hug.

_I_ 19. My blood pressure is so high that I have scheduled a *random* appointment with my doctor.

_C_ 20. The little girl taught herself the *concept* of "right" and "left" by remembering, "I **write** with my **right** hand."

_I_ 21. The families decided it would be too *practical* to eat in an expensive restaurant.

_I_ 22. I keep a couple of quarters in my pocket for *significant* purchases, such as a pack of gum.

_C_ 23. The letters "ski" are a *characteristic* part of many Polish names, such as Kwilinski and Paderewski.

_I_ 24. Because Linda is so shy, she usually *confronts* people rather than daring to face them and actually talk to them.

_I_ 25. It's plain to see from the way Diane quarrels so often with her friends that she has lots of *tolerance* for other people's opinions.

Score   (Number correct) _____ × 4 = _____ %

Enter your score above and in the vocabulary performance chart on the inside back cover of the book.

UNIT THREE: Test 3

PART A: Synonyms

In the space provided, write the letter of the choice that is most nearly the **same** in meaning as the **boldfaced** word.

_d_ 1. **assume**   **a)** improve   **b)** tire   **c)** manage   **d)** take for granted

_a_ 2. **characteristic**   **a)** typical   **b)** strong   **c)** important   **d)** amazing

_a_ 3. **concept**   **a)** idea   **b)** goal   **c)** period   **d)** knowledge of right and wrong

_c_ 4. **confront**   **a)** interrupt   **b)** take away from   **c)** face boldly   **d)** succeed

_b_ 5. **conscience**   **a)** respect for others   **b)** sense of right and wrong   **c)** feature
          d) how often something happens

_d_ 6. **cope with**   **a)** judge   **b)** remove   **c)** believe   **d)** manage

_a_ 7. **counsel**   **a)** give advice to   **b)** bring together   **c)** send away   **d)** search for

_d_ 8. **detect**   **a)** take from   **b)** speak for   **c)** stop briefly   **d)** discover

_a_ 9. **disrupt**   **a)** upset   **b)** watch   **c)** tire   **d)** complain

_c_ 10. **eligible**   **a)** important   **b)** chosen   **c)** qualified   **d)** amazing

_a_ 11. **evaluate**   **a)** judge   **b)** try   **c)** grow   **d)** take back

_b_ 12. **foresight**   **a)** purpose   **b)** care in planning   **c)** cure   **d)** attention

_d_ 13. **frequency**   **a)** material   **b)** goal   **c)** word group
          d) how often something happens

_a_ 14. **interval**   **a)** time in between   **b)** thought   **c)** system   **d)** word group

_a_ 15. **objective**   **a)** goal   **b)** respect   **c)** cure   **d)** matter

_d_ 16. **observe**   **a)** decide   **b)** succeed   **c)** give advice   **d)** watch

_c_ 17. **phrase**   **a)** period of time   **b)** shape   **c)** word group   **d)** amount

_b_ 18. **remote**   **a)** not usual   **b)** out-of-the-way   **c)** believable
          d) able to be seen through

_a_ 19. **represent**   **a)** speak for   **b)** feel anger against   **c)** make smaller   **d)** send again

_d_ 20. **sole**   **a)** outer   **b)** best   **c)** large   **d)** only

_c_ 21. **substance**   **a)** care   **b)** general thought   **c)** material   **d)** knowledge

_d_ 22. **tolerance**   **a)** win   **b)** possibility   **c)** confusion   **d)** lack of prejudice

_d_ 23. **trait**   **a)** meeting   **b)** story   **c)** plan   **d)** feature

_d_ 24. **transparent**   **a)** fake   **b)** amazing   **c)** proud   **d)** able to be seen through

_b_ 25. **withdraw**   **a)** write down   **b)** take back   **c)** shorten   **d)** watch

(Continues on next page)

151

PART B: Antonyms
In the space provided, write the letter of the choice that is most nearly **opposite** in meaning to the **boldfaced** word.

___c___ 26. **approximately**   a) always   b) useful   c) exactly   d) properly

___d___ 27. **artificial**   a) perfect   b) likeable   c) suitable   d) natural

___d___ 28. **authentic**   a) demanding   b) believable   c) sharp   d) fake

___a___ 29. **complicate**   a) make easy   b) speed up   c) pass over   d) take advice

___d___ 30. **conscious**   a) unqualified   b) unusual   c) unexpected   d) unaware

___b___ 31. **consistent**   a) gentle   b) changing   c) rude   d) weak

___b___ 32. **detract**   a) stay the same   b) add to   c) fail   d) rest

___a___ 33. **exhaust**   a) give energy to   b) explain   c) expect   d) get worse

___c___ 34. **external**   a) useless   b) harmful   c) inner   d) close

___d___ 35. **harsh**   a) planned   b) nearby   c) useful   d) kindly

___c___ 36. **incredible**   a) regular   b) not possible   c) easy to believe
d) disagreeable

___b___ 37. **intense**   a) accidental   b) weak   c) long-lasting   d) helpless

___d___ 38. **internal**   a) real   b) deep   c) honest   d) outer

___a___ 39. **maximum**   a) least possible   b) legal   c) exact   d) able

___a___ 40. **practical**   a) not sensible   b) not inside   c) not easy   d) not possible

___c___ 41. **prosper**   a) make easy   b) face   c) fail   d) help

___b___ 42. **protest**   a) put an end to   b) approve   c) give   d) grow stronger

___c___ 43. **random**   a) believable   b) not wanted   c) planned   d) pleasant

___d___ 44. **remedy**   a) thought   b) distance   c) purpose   d) disease

___a___ 45. **shallow**   a) deep   b) crowded   c) weak   d) least

___c___ 46. **significant**   a) not real   b) done on purpose   c) not important
d) not steady

___d___ 47. **strive**   a) give advice   b) put in   c) ask for   d) give up

___a___ 48. **temporary**   a) long-lasting   b) not qualified   c) weak   d) not typical

___d___ 49. **thrive**   a) know   b) argue   c) change   d) grow weak

___d___ 50. **triumph**   a) suggestion   b) patience   c) distance   d) loss

Score   (Number correct) _____ × 2 = _____ %

Enter your score above and in the vocabulary performance chart on the inside back cover of the book.

Unit Four

apparent	fulfill
automatic	influence
burden	security
economical	sympathize
extravagant	transfer

Ten Words in Context

In the space provided, write the letter of the meaning closest to that of each **boldfaced** word. Use the context of the sentences to help you figure out each word's meaning.

1 apparent
(ə-păr′ənt)
– *adjective*

- Marcie's smile made it **apparent** that she had done well on the test.
- It's **apparent** that Leon and Bess have settled their quarrel, since they are dating steadily again.

_b_ *Apparent* means   a. helpful.   b. clear.   c. secret.

2 automatic
(ô′tə-măt′ĭk)
– *adjective*

- Our new coffeemaker is **automatic**. We set it at night, and it turns on by itself in the morning.
- Before the **automatic** washing machine, laundering clothes was not so easy.

_a_ *Automatic* means   a. self-operating.   b. unusual.   c. low in cost.

3 burden
(bûr′dn)
– *noun*

- Although others think raising a handicapped child must be a **burden**, my neighbor says she has found joy, not hardship, in caring for her son.
- At first Louie was proud that he had stolen the money, but in time, his crime became a great **burden** to him.

_c_ *Burden* means   a. freedom.   b. protection.   c. heavy load.

4 economical
(ĕk′ə-nŏm′ĭ-kəl)
– *adjective*

- It's usually more **economical** to buy food and soap in large packages. Smaller packages will cost more per ounce.
- To decide which car is most **economical**, compare prices, gas mileage, and repair costs.

_b_ *Economical* means   a. difficult.   b. money-saving.   c. easy to see.

5 extravagant
(ĭk-străv′ə-gənt)
– *adjective*

- I think it's **extravagant** to buy a prom dress that will be worn only once, so I borrowed one from a friend.
- Rhoda's budget is so tight that she felt it would be **extravagant** to buy herself a ten-dollar pair of earrings.

_c_ *Extravagant* means   a. not effective.   b. obvious.   c. spending too much.

6 fulfill
(fŏŏl-fĭl′)
– *verb*

- One day, Chen hopes to **fulfill** his dream of visiting China again and renewing ties with his family there.
- Jill doesn't like her job, but she promised to stay with it at least one year, and she plans to **fulfill** that promise.

_b_ *Fulfill* means   a. repeat.   b. carry out.   c. have an effect on.

7 **influence**
(ĭn′flōō-əns)
– *verb*

- My father thinks my friends **influence** me too much. He says they are the reason that I study so little and party so often.
- Do advertisements **influence** what you buy?

_c_ *Influence* means   a. delay.   b. protect.   c. affect.

8 **security**
(sĭ-kyŏŏr′ĭ-tē)
– *noun*

- For nighttime **security**, the owner of the jewelry shop turns on a burglar alarm.
- People with homes near the river like the **security** of flood insurance.

_c_ *Security* means   a. hardship.   b. expense.   c. safety.

9 **sympathize**
(sĭm′pə-thīz′)
– *verb*

- The whole town **sympathized** with the family whose house burned down.
- To show he **sympathized** with Mrs. Jackson when her husband died, Scott sent her flowers and a card.

_a_ *Sympathized with* means   a. felt sorry for.   b. sent for.   c. talked to.

10 **transfer**
(trăns-fûr′)
– *verb*

- Before I can paint the bookcase, I have to **transfer** all the books into boxes.
- In April, the Army will **transfer** Jamal from a base in South Carolina to one in Virginia.

_b_ *Transfer* means   a. reach.   b. move.   c. see.

Matching Words with Definitions

Following are definitions of the ten words. **Print** each word next to its definition. If you look closely at each word in context, you will be able to figure out its meaning.

1. _____economical_____   Costing or spending little; thrifty

2. _____transfer_____   To move or send from one place to another

3. _____automatic_____   Moving or operating by itself

4. _____influence_____   To have an effect on

5. _____sympathize_____   To feel or express sorrow or pity for

6. _____fulfill_____   To carry out; achieve; do

7. _____burden_____   A hardship; something difficult to bear

8. _____apparent_____   Obvious; easy to see

9. _____security_____   Protection; freedom from danger, fear, or worry

10. _____extravagant_____   Spending much more than is necessary or wise; wasteful

CAUTION: Do not go any further until you are sure the above answers are correct. Then you can use the definitions to help you in the following practices. Your goal is eventually to know the words well enough so that you don't need to check the definitions at all.

➤ *Check 1*

Using the answer line, complete each item below with the correct word from the box.

a. **apparent**	b. **automatic**	c. **burden**	d. **economical**	e. **extravagant**
f. **fulfill**	g. **influence**	h. **security**	i. **sympathize**	j. **transfer**

_____*transfer*_____ 1. My boss intends to assign me to another office. In other words, he wants to ___ me there.

_____*burden*_____ 2. A ___ may be a physical or a mental hardship, or both.

_____*influence*_____ 3. Political candidates try to ___ elections with numerous ads.

_____*extravagant*_____ 4. An ___ person enjoys spending a lot of money.

_____*sympathize*_____ 5. When we've had the same difficult experience as someone else, it's easier for us to ___ with him or her.

_____*apparent*_____ 6. Because Kira was smiling, it was ___ that she was happy about something.

_____*fulfill*_____ 7. When you make an agreement with people, they expect you to ___ your part of the deal.

_____*security*_____ 8. After people are robbed, they often feel a greater need for ___.

_____*economical*_____ 9. An ___ person doesn't like to waste money.

_____*automatic*_____ 10. Do you think there will ever be a fully ___ car, one that needs no driver?

NOTE: Now check your answers to these questions by turning to page 250. Going over the answers carefully will help you prepare for the remaining practices, for which answers are not given.

➤ *Check 2*

Using the answer lines, complete each item below with **two** words from the box.

_____*transfer*_____
_____*sympathize*_____ 1–2. Because we are moving, our children will have to ___ to different schools. I can ___ with them because I went through the same experience as a child.

_____*Automatic*_____
_____*security*_____ 3–4. ___ yard lights, which go on by themselves at dark, can add to the ___ of a home.

_____*economical*_____
_____*fulfill*_____ 5–6. Clark had to think of an ___ way to ___ his promise to give each of his twelve nieces and nephews a gift, so he baked them each a pie.

_____*apparent*_____
_____*burden*_____ 7–8. From the young hiker's slowed walk, it was ___ that his large backpack had become a ___.

_____*influence*_____
_____*extravagant*_____ 9–10. Having a credit card has ___d Barry in a sad way. He has become so ___ that he now has a closet full of more clothes than he can wear— and a huge credit-card bill.

➤ *Related Words*

Once you learn a new word, you can more easily understand many related words. Below are ten words related to the core words of this chapter. Use their definitions to help you write in the word that best completes each item.

a. **automation**, *noun*	The use of machines instead of people or animals
b. **economize**, *verb*	To cut down on spending
c. **influential**, *adjective*	Having the power to affect someone or something
d. **insecure**, *adjective*	Not safe; not protected enough
e. **sympathy**, *noun*	Pity; sorrow for another

_____*insecure*_____   1. Walking through a dangerous neighborhood alone at night makes most people feel ___.

_____*economize*_____   2. The newlyweds ___ by using coupons and buying secondhand clothes.

_____*sympathy*_____   3. Having great ___ for the flood victims, people throughout the country sent money to help them.

_____*Automation*_____   4. ___ has greatly affected farming; for instance, the workhorse has been replaced by the tractor.

_____*influential*_____   5. The *Daily Mirror* is such an ___ newspaper that the political candidates it supports almost always win.

f. **economy**, *noun*	The business affairs of a region, town, or country
g. **fulfillment**, *noun*	Achievement; completion
h. **secure**, *adjective*	Safe; protected
i. **sympathetically**, *adverb*	In a kindly way
j. **unfulfilled**, *adjective*	Not done; not achieved; not carried out

_____*fulfillment*_____   6. For the young gymnast, competing at the Olympics was the ___ of a lifelong dream.

_____*economy*_____   7. When a factory closes down, it affects the whole town's ___, as the laid-off workers have little money to spend in local stores.

_____*secure*_____   8. Dad always buys more groceries than we need; it makes him feel ___ to know the cupboards are full of food.

_____*sympathetically*_____   9. The minister spoke to the crying child very ___.

_____*unfulfilled*_____   10. The carpenters promised to fix the garage door four weeks ago, but so far, their promise is ___.

➤ *Word Work*

A. Write each word next to the examples that best match it.

a. **automatic**	b. **economize**	c. **extravagant**
d. **security**	e. **sympathy**	

_____*extravagant*_____ 1. Eating in fancy restaurants every night
Buying two dresses for the same party because you can't decide between them
Purchasing a sterling-silver dog collar

_____*automatic*_____ 2. A stoplight
A door that slides open when a person approaches it
An oven that cleans itself

_____*security*_____ 3. A burglar alarm
Fire insurance
Armed guards

_____*sympathy*_____ 4. Sending a card when a friend's mother dies
Hugging a crying child
Taking a friend who's lost her job out to dinner

_____*economize*_____ 5. Figure out the best grocery buys
Turn off lights when you leave a room
Use old envelopes for shopping lists

B. In the space provided, write the letter of the choice that best completes each item.

_c_ 6. The outside porch light comes on at the same time every evening.

    a. extravagant   b. unfulfilled   c. automatic

_b_ 7. To make up for being sick last semester, the student is taking a full load plus two extra classes.

    a. automation   b. burden   c. transfer

_a_ 8. When I saw an ad for chocolate-chip cookies, I immediately went to the kitchen and baked some.

    a. influence   b. automation   c. burden

_c_ 9. An electric toothbrush does a better job of brushing your teeth than you do.

    a. transfer   b. burden   c. automatic

_b_ 10. When Jen moved into the attic bedroom, she spent hours carrying her belongings up there.

    a. automatic   b. transfer   c. influence

➤ *Word Parts*

A. The suffix *-ment* often means "the result, state, act, or process of ___."

Examples: *fulfillment* — the result of fulfilling
enjoyment — the state of enjoying

On each answer line, write the word from the box that means the same as the *italicized* words.

a. **astonishment°**	b. **fulfillment**	c. **management**
d. **replacement**	e. **statement**	

_____astonishment_____ 1. The magician's surprising act filled us with a *state of being astonished°*.

_____replacement_____ 2. The *act of replacing* of our old kitchen floor was not easy. First we had to tear the old floor out before the new one could be put in.

_____management_____ 3. It is obvious that the *process of managing* of this company is excellent. The company is very successful, and the workers are very happy

_____fulfillment_____ 4. For me, a small home in the country would be the *result of fulfilling* of a dream.

_____statement_____ 5. Kareem likes to study for tests with another person. He says that the *act of stating* of an idea out loud to someone else helps him remember it better.

B. The suffixes *-ly* and *-ally* mean "in a certain way."

Examples: *economical* — thrifty   *secure* — safe
economically — in a thrifty way   *securely* — in a safe way

On each answer line, write the word from the box that best completes the item.

f. **consistently°**	g. **economically°**	h. **exactly**
i. **extravagantly°**	j. **securely**	

_____consistently_____ 6. Ralph may not be the perfect worker, but at least he is steady about one thing—he is ___ late for work each day.

_____securely_____ 7. Before leaving on vacation, make sure the doors and windows are closed ___.

_____extravagantly_____ 8. Wanting to impress his date, Dan spent money ___ on lobster, champagne, and a hired limousine.

_____exactly_____ 9. If a math answer is not ___ right, you may not get full credit for it.

_____economically_____ 10. The three families got a new lawn mower ___ by buying it together, then sharing it.

➤ *Final Check*

Read the passages carefully. Then fill in each blank with the word that best fits the context.

A. A Mismatched Couple

a. **burden**	b. **economical**	c. **extravagant**
d. **security**	e. **sympathize**	

Stacy and Ken have completely different attitudes° toward money. She is (1)_____*economical*_____ to an extreme, always trying to get the best price on even the smallest purchase. Ken, on the other hand, is very (2)_____*extravagant*_____. He loves to spend money on anything that catches his eye. If there's a dime in his pocket, he feels that it's a (3)_____*burden*_____, as hard to carry around as a heavy load. He'll find something to spend it on just to be rid of it. Knowing she has money in case of accident or illness gives Stacy a feeling of (4)_____*security*_____, but Ken doesn't worry about the future. Each is puzzled by the other's "strange" behavior. Stacy sees Ken as wasteful and irresponsible, and Ken calls Stacy cheap. He can't (5)_____*sympathize*_____ with her when she's worried about an empty bank account. Since they have very little tolerance° for each other's views on money, no one was surprised when these two got divorced.

B. A Campaign to Become Class President

f. **apparent**	g. **automatic**	h. **fulfill**
i. **influence**	j. **transfer**	

In her senior year, Holly wanted very much to be elected class president. But she knew that the other girl who was competing for the office was much better known and had more experience in student government. As a result, Holly began to do all she could to (6)_____*influence*_____ her classmates so that they would vote for her. She found herself promising them anything they asked for. "If I'm elected," she told one student, "I will see that the school puts in (7)_____*automatic*_____ doors to make it easy to enter when our arms are full of books." To another, she said that a hot tub would be installed in the school gym. She promised a third student that he could (8)_____*transfer*_____ to the school across town that his girlfriend attended. As the election drew near, it became (9)_____*apparent*_____ that Holly had a good chance of winning. This scared her because she realized that she could not (10)_____*fulfill*_____ all her promises. Finally, she quit the race, saying she couldn't maintain° her grades and serve as class president too. She felt foolish for having let her desire to win run away with her good sense.

➤ *Questions for Discussion*

1. What gives you a sense of **security** at home? What makes you feel insecure?

2. Once people had to do their laundry by hand. Now there are **automatic** washers to do it for them. What automatic machine do you wish someone would invent to help you with some other task?

3. Think of one person who has had a big **influence** on your life. Describe how he or she has affected you.

4. Have you ever made a promise that was difficult to **fulfill**, yet you kept it? What was it?

5. Describe one way that your family tries to be **economical**.

➤ *Ideas for Writing*

1. Write about a time when it was **apparent** that something was bothering a friend. What made it so apparent to you that something was bothering him or her? How did you help your friend deal with that **burden**? Did you just express your **sympathy**, or did you assist in some more active way?

2. If you had one day in which you could be as **extravagant** as you liked, what would you do? What dreams would you **fulfill** during that day?

Check Your Performance			CHAPTER 16
Activity	*Number Right*	*Points*	*Total*
Check 2	_____	× 10 =	_____
Related Words	_____	× 10 =	_____
Word Work	_____	× 10 =	_____
Word Parts	_____	× 10 =	_____
Final Check	_____	× 10 =	_____

Enter your scores above and in the vocabulary performance chart on the inside back cover of the book.

CHAPTER

17

appropriate	emotion
bewilder	fiction
communicate	investigate
deceive	legible
earnest	theory

Ten Words in Context

In the space provided, write the letter of the meaning closest to that of each **boldfaced** word. Use the context of the sentences to help you figure out each word's meaning.

1 appropriate
(ə-prō′prē-ĭt)
– *adjective*

- While it's **appropriate** to scream at a football game, such behavior is not considered proper at the ballet.
- Hiking boots aren't **appropriate** for jogging—they are too stiff and heavy.

_c_ *Appropriate* means   a. legal.   b. unusual.   c. correct.

2 bewilder
(bĭ-wĭl′dər)
– *verb*

- The large new school at first **bewildered** Chung, but after a day or two, getting around was no longer confusing to him.
- My grandmother's poor health **bewildered** her doctor until he found out she wasn't taking her medicines.

_b_ *Bewilder* means   a. to calm.   b. to puzzle.   c. to attract.

3 communicate
(kə-myōō′nĭ-kāt′)
– *verb*

- Alice and I rarely see each other, but we **communicate** often by sending letters and making phone calls.
- Today, many people **communicate** with each other by using the electronic mail service on their computers.

_b_ *Communicate* means   a. to call.   b. to exchange information.   c. to visit.

4 deceive
(dĭ-sēv′)
– *verb*

- Linda **deceived** Jason by dating him without telling him that she was married.
- A business owner who tries to **deceive** customers should be reported to the police.

_c_ *Deceive* means   a. to help.   b. to find.   c. to fool.

5 earnest
(ûr′nĭst)
– *adjective*

- I like our new baby sitter because she is very **earnest**; she clearly takes her job very seriously.
- Jimmy seemed **earnest** when he promised to clean the windows by Friday, so I was surprised to see he hadn't done them.

_c_ *Earnest* means   a. confused.   b. quiet.   c. serious.

6 emotion
(ĭ-mō′shən)
– *noun*

- Stan rarely shows his **emotions**. We have to guess what he is really feeling.
- Many people have trouble talking about their **emotions**, especially anger and fear.

_a_ *Emotion* means   a. feeling.   b. explanation.   c. movement.

7 fiction
(fĭk′shən)
– *noun*

- One of Mark Twain's most amusing pieces of **fiction** is his story about a Connecticut man who travels back to the time of King Arthur.
- Some newspapers print obvious **fiction**, such as, "Nine-year-old girl has triplets who weigh 100 pounds more than she does!"

_b_ *Fiction* means   a. news.   b. made-up writing.   c. facts.

8 investigate
(ĭn-vĕs′tĭ-gāt′)
– *verb*

- The FBI has been called in to **investigate** the disappearance of the baby from the hospital.
- When I heard a noise downstairs at 3 a.m., I lay still in bed, too frightened to get up and **investigate** the situation.

_a_ *Investigate* means   a. look into.   b. delay.   c. exchange.

9 legible
(lĕj′ə-bəl)
– *adjective*

- My father used to make me rewrite my sloppy homework. "I can barely read this," he would say. "Make it **legible**."
- The fancy script on that new restaurant sign isn't very **legible**. Does it say "Peretti's," "Perelli's," or "Pepetti's"?

_b_ *Legible* means   a. easy to believe.   b. easy to read.   c. easy to prove.

10 theory
(thē′ə-rē)
– *noun*

- According to the **theory** of evolution, plants and animals have developed in ways that help them do well in their environment.
- The police's **theory** was that the killer was a short man with dark hair, but the murderer turned out to be a blond woman wearing a dark wig.

_b_ *Theory* means   a. action.   b. explanation.   c. question.

Matching Words with Definitions

Following are definitions of the ten words. **Print** each word next to its definition. If you look closely at each word in context, you will be able to figure out its meaning.

1. _____communicate_____   To exchange or give information
2. _____bewilder_____   To confuse; puzzle
3. _____earnest_____   Serious and sincere
4. _____emotion_____   A strong feeling
5. _____theory_____   A statement that explains events or facts; an explanation, often unproven
6. _____legible_____   Clear enough to be read
7. _____fiction_____   Literature consisting of imaginary stories; anything made up
8. _____appropriate_____   Proper; suited to a certain use or purpose
9. _____deceive_____   To make (someone) believe something that is not true
10. _____investigate_____   To explore or examine carefully in order to learn the facts

CAUTION: Do not go any further until you are sure the above answers are correct. Then you can use the definitions to help you in the following practices. Your goal is eventually to know the words well enough so that you don't need to check the definitions at all.

➤ *Check 1*

Using the answer line, complete each item below with the correct word from the box.

a. **appropriate**	b. **bewilder**	c. **communicate**	d. **deceive**	e. **earnest**
f. **emotion**	g. **fiction**	h. **investigate**	i. **legible**	j. **theory**

_____appropriate_____ 1. At the fancy dinner, Sheila watched her hostess to see which fork was ___ for each course.

_____deceive_____ 2. Charlotte's sweet smiles don't ___ me. I know that she really dislikes me.

_____communicate_____ 3. Dolphins ___ with one another through a language of squeaks and grunts.

_____bewilder_____ 4. At first, the many noises, flashing lights, and whirling rides at the fair ___ed the children.

_____theory_____ 5. Murphy has a ___ about life. He believes that everything that can possibly go wrong, will.

_____investigate_____ 6. When we go on our walks, my dog ___s every bush and tree we come across.

_____legible_____ 7. Ten years ago, I carved my initials in a tree. Recently I was surprised to see that they were still ___.

_____earnest_____ 8. When Gordon begged his boss for another chance, he seemed so ___ that his employer decided to give him his job back.

_____fiction_____ 9. When I want to relax, I read love stories, mysteries, and other kinds of ___.

_____emotion_____ 10. Which do you think is the more powerful ___, love or hate?

NOTE: Now check your answers to these questions by turning to page 250. Going over the answers carefully will help you prepare for the remaining practices, for which answers are not given.

➤ *Check 2*

Using the answer lines, complete each item below with **two** words from the box.

_____fiction_____
_____investigate_____ 1–2. Agatha Christie wrote wonderful works of ___ about Miss Marple, a woman who loved to ___ crimes the police could not solve.

_____theory_____
_____legible_____ 3–4. Some people believe the ___ that you can teach yourself to write well with either hand, but when I use my left hand, what I write is not ___.

_____communicate_____
_____bewilder_____ 5–6. The lost little girl spoke no English, so the police officer's attempts to ___ with her only ___ed her more.

_____earnest_____
_____deceive_____ 7–8. The man claiming to have lost his wallet seemed so ___ that I believed him and gave him money, but when I saw him doing the same thing a week later, I knew he had ___d me.

_____emotion_____
_____appropriate_____ 9–10. Many people feel a powerful mixture of ___s at special events; for example, it is considered ___ to cry at a weddings, even though it is a happy time.

➤ *Related Words*

Once you learn a new word, you can more easily understand many related words. Below are ten words related to the core words of this chapter. Use their definitions to help you write in the word that best completes each item.

a. **bewilderment**, *noun*	Confusion
b. **communication**, *noun*	Making information known
c. **deception**, *noun*	An act of making someone believe something that is not true; a lie or trick
d. **investigator**, *noun*	A person who studies facts or a situation in order to learn the truth
e. **nonfiction**, *noun*	Writing that is about real life, not made-up ideas

communication 1. Radio, television, newspapers, letters, and, of course, conversation, are all forms of ___.

deception 2. The museum officials who paid millions of dollars for the fake Picasso painting were angry and embarrassed when they discovered the ___.

investigator 3. When Mr. Burns's wife became suspicious, she hired an ___, who learned that Mr. Burns had three wives in three different cities. When she confronted° him with this fact, she had some harsh° things to say.

nonfiction 4. Truman Capote's book *In Cold Blood: The True Story of a Multiple Murder* is a piece of ___ that tells the story of the 1959 killing of a farm family in Kansas.

bewilderment 5. Imagine my ___ when I came home to what I thought was an empty house and heard voices call out, "Surprise! Happy Birthday!"

f. **emotional**, *adjective*	Having to do with feelings
g. **fictional**, *adjective*	Made-up; not true
h. **illegible**, *adjective*	Not able to be read
i. **investigation**, *noun*	The act of examining or exploring something
j. **theorize**, *verb*	To think up a possible explanation for something

illegible 6. Professor Chaplin talks too quickly. When I try to take notes on her lectures, I have to hurry so much that my writing is ___.

emotional 7. Certain musical notes and chords make many people feel like crying. Why is it that music can have such a strong ___ effect?

investigation 8. The reporters spent a year on an ___ to prepare for their series of articles about why the city's crime rate is so high.

theorize 9. Over the years, many people have claimed to see a huge animal in a lake in Scotland; some people ___ that it is some sort of dinosaur.

fictional 10. In the novel *Lost Horizon*, the author wrote of the ___ land of Shangri-La, where people stay young for hundreds of years.

➤ *Word Work*

A. Write each word next to the examples that best match it.

| a. **communicate** | b. **deceive** | c. **theory** |
| d. **appropriate** | e. **fiction** | |

_____*appropriate*_____ 1. Wearing a swimsuit to the beach
Wearing jeans and a sweatshirt to a football game
Wearing a fancy dress to a New Year's Eve party

_____*deceive*_____ 2. Pretending to be collecting money for a charity and then keeping the money yourself
Faking an accident in order to collect insurance money
Saying your dog ate your homework when you really didn't do it

_____*communicate*_____ 3. Talking on the phone about a problem
Writing notes about a date to friends
Discussing an assignment with a teacher

_____*fiction*_____ 4. "Goldilocks and the Three Bears"
A movie about a talking donkey
An imagined meeting between Abraham Lincoln and Oprah Winfrey

_____*theory*_____ 5. Maybe dinosaurs were wiped out by a meteor that hit the Earth.
It's possible that Lee Harvey Oswald did not act alone when he shot President Kennedy.
Police think the person who stole the jewels may have once worked in the store.

B. In the space provided, write the letter of the choice that best completes each item.

_c_ 6. An **earnest** person is likely to tell you

    a. a lie.   b. what he or she thinks you want to hear.   c. the truth.

_a_ 7. If algebra **bewilders** you, that probably means

    a. you are having trouble with that class.
    b. you find algebra easy to do.
    c. the class was too full and you had to take another class instead.

_c_ 8. **Emotions** are likely to be strong during

    a. a nap.   b. an elevator ride.   c. an argument.

_b_ 9. A person whose job is largely to **investigate** is a

    a. pet shop owner.   b. store detective.   c. gardener.

_c_ 10. A second-grader whose writing is very **legible** can expect

    a. criticism from his or her teacher.
    b. to be asked to write smaller.
    c. praise from his or her teacher.

➤ *Synonyms and Antonyms*

A. Synonyms. Write the letter of the word or phrase that most nearly means the **same** as each boldfaced word.

_d_ 1. **bewilder**

    a. make certain   b. release

    c. insist   d. confuse

_b_ 2. **communicate**

    a. hide   b. make known

    c. remove   d. forget

_a_ 3. **emotion**

    a. feeling   b. energy

    c. excuse   d. movement

_c_ 4. **investigate**

    a. puzzle   b. write

    c. inspect   d. fool

_c_ 5. **theory**

    a. agreement   b. problem

    c. explanation   d. question

B. Antonyms. Write the letter of the word or phrase that most nearly means the **opposite** of each boldfaced word.

_b_ 6. **appropriate**

    a. not healthy   b. not proper

    c. not believable   d. not ready

_c_ 7. **deceive**

    a. stay away from   b. argue

    c. tell the truth to   d. find

_a_ 8. **earnest**

    a. not sincere   b. unusual

    c. not accurate   d. not perfect

_d_ 9. **fiction**

    a. justice   b. ability

    c. reason   d. fact

_d_ 10. **legible**

    a. not for sale   b. not lasting

    c. not on purpose   d. not readable

➤ *Final Check*

Read the passages carefully. Then fill in each blank with the word that best fits the context.

A. The Famous Detective

| a. **deceive** | b. **emotion** | c. **fiction** |
| d. **investigate** | e. **theory** | |

One of the most famous characters from the world of (1)_____*fiction*_____ is Sherlock Holmes, created by the writer Arthur Conan Doyle. Holmes first appeared in a story Doyle wrote in 1887. It was called "A Study in Scarlet." Holmes was a detective. No criminal, no matter how clever, could (2)_____*deceive*_____ him for long. Rather than being affected by (3)_____*emotion*_____s such as fear or hate, he used his great powers of thinking to solve crimes. As he (4)_____*investigate*_____d crimes, he noticed important small details that were not apparent° to others. Then it would not be long before he developed a perfect (5)_____*theory*_____ to explain the crime.

B. Why So Quiet?

| f. **appropriate** | g. **bewilder** | h. **communicate** |
| i. **earnest** | j. **legible** | |

I still remember my first day in first grade. My first-grade teacher probably does, too. I had grown up in a very large, very noisy family. Everybody yelled, all the time. It wasn't because we were angry. There were just so many of us that we thought it was the only way to (6)_____*communicate*_____. I didn't realize that our characteristic° loudness wasn't typical of all families. So I went into school believing that when you wanted to be heard, the (7)_____*appropriate*_____ thing to do was yell your head off. My teacher was a very gentle person. She talked slowly and never, ever raised her voice. I remember her writing her name on the board in large, (8)_____*legible*_____ letters and saying, "My name is Mrs. Henderson. Can you say 'Mrs. Henderson,' boys and girls?" My shy classmates whispered, "Mrs. Henderson." I shouted, "MRS. HENDERSON!!" at the top of my lungs (I don't exaggerate°—I was really loud). Throughout the day, my classmates continued to whisper, and I continued to shout. By the end of the first day, school had totally (9)_____*bewilder*_____ed me. I was so confused that I thought I had been assigned to the wrong class. I went home and told my parents I wanted to be in class with people who "talked right." I wasn't kidding—I was completely (10)_____*earnest*_____. It took a couple of weeks for me to figure out how to fit in with my quieter classmates.

➤ *Questions for Discussion*

1. Describe two places that have very different requirements for **appropriate** behavior. For example, you might talk about what is suitable° behavior at a football game and in a fancy restaurant.

2. Think of a friend who has moved away, but with whom you have stayed in touch. In what ways do the two of you **communicate**?

3. Tell about a time when a person seemed to you to be **earnest**, but then did something that showed he or she was not sincere at all. How did that person **deceive** you, and how did you discover the truth?

4. Describe a work of **fiction** that you have read and enjoyed. What about it held your interest?

5. Lots of television shows are based on police or detectives or even scientists who **investigate** crimes or unusual events. What is one such show that you've watched? How do the people in the show go about their work?

➤ *Ideas for Writing*

1. Things that puzzle us happen from time to time, but we usually figure out the puzzle before long. But have you ever been involved in a mystery that was never solved? It might be the disappearance of something that belonged to you or a change in a friend that you never understood. What happened to **bewilder** you? Do you have any **theory** about what might have really happened?

2. Select a particular **emotion**, such as sadness, embarrassment, joy, fear, or another feeling. Write about a time when you experienced that emotion strongly. Tell what happened, how you felt, and why you felt that way.

Check Your Performance			**CHAPTER 17**
Activity	*Number Right*	*Points*	*Total*
Check 2	_____	× 10 =	_____
Related Words	_____	× 10 =	_____
Word Work	_____	× 10 =	_____
Synonyms and Antonyms	_____	× 10 =	_____
Final Check	_____	× 10 =	_____

Enter your scores above and in the vocabulary performance chart on the inside back cover of the book.

assure	humiliate
crucial	impulse
distract	perceive
extraordinary	revive
hostile	timid

Ten Words in Context

In the space provided, write the letter of the meaning closest to that of each **boldfaced** word. Use the context of the sentences to help you figure out each word's meaning.

1 **assure**
(ə-shŏŏr′)
– *verb*

- If you leave jewelry in your hotel room, the hotel cannot **assure** you that it will be safe.
- I asked the salesclerk, "Can you **assure** me that this watch is really waterproof?"

c *Assure* means   a. to remind.   b. to agree with.   c. to promise.

2 **crucial**
(krŏŏ′shəl)
– *adjective*

- The trial had to stop when a **crucial** witness suddenly disappeared.
- Protein is a **crucial** part of a healthy diet.

b *Crucial* means   a. rare.   b. necessary.   c. useless.

3 **distract**
(dĭ-străkt′)
– *verb*

- I have trouble studying when noises from outside **distract** me.
- The children made funny faces at the actress, trying to **distract** her as she performed her part.

b *Distract* means   a. to frighten greatly.   b. to draw away the attention of.   c. to give support to.

4 **extraordinary**
(ĭk-strôr′dn-ĕr-ē)
– *adjective*

- The restaurant made **extraordinary** attempts to attract new customers, even giving away free meals on certain days.
- The cancer patient inspired others with the **extraordinary** courage she showed in dealing with her illness.

c *Extraordinary* means   a. unfriendly.   b. normal.   c. very unusual.

5 **hostile**
(hŏs′təl)
– *adjective*

- The **hostile** crowd threw tomatoes and eggs at the speaker.
- The cat acted **hostile** towards the new kitten, snarling and spitting at it.

b *Hostile* means   a. fearful.   b. unfriendly.   c. embarrassed.

6 **humiliate**
(hyŏŏ-mĭl′ē-āt′)
– *verb*

- Good teachers do not **humiliate** students for making mistakes by calling them names or holding up their work for everyone to see.
- In dreams, people often **humiliate** themselves by doing things like going outdoors without their clothing on.

a *Humiliate* means   a. to shame.   b. to show off.   c. to misunderstand.

7 impulse
(ĭm′pŭls′)
– *noun*

- People who go food shopping when they are hungry often get an **impulse** to buy something they don't really need.
- Carmen had planned on staying home alone, but at the last minute she had an **impulse** to phone her new neighbors and invite them to come over that evening for coffee and cake.

_a_ *Impulse* means   a. unplanned desire.   b. view.   c. fear.

8 perceive
(pər-sēv′)
– *verb*

- I **perceive** from the wonderful smell that someone is barbecuing ribs.
- Hawks have such good eyesight that they can **perceive** a tiny mouse from hundreds of feet in the air.

_c_ *Perceive* means   a. to remember.   b. to include.   c. to notice.

9 revive
(rĭ-vīv′)
– *verb*

- If you've lost all desire to learn biology, Professor Berg, who is a wonderful teacher, will **revive** your interest in that subject.
- No matter how tired our dog is, the question "Want to go for a walk?" will **revive** him.

_b_ *Revive* means   a. to show.   b. to bring back to life.   c. to embarrass.

10 timid
(tĭm′ĭd)
– *adjective*

- When her parents tried to introduce her to guests, the **timid** child hid under the table.
- Ever since he almost drowned in a boating accident, Jared has been **timid** about going in the water.

_a_ *Timid* means   a. frightened.   b. careless.   c. full of energy.

Matching Words with Definitions

Following are definitions of the ten words. **Print** each word next to its definition. If you look closely at each word in context, you will be able to figure out its meaning.

1. _____assure_____ To make (someone) sure about something; tell with certainty
2. _____timid_____ Fearful or shy; lacking in self-confidence
3. _____humiliate_____ To make ashamed; embarrass
4. _____crucial_____ Extremely important
5. _____hostile_____ Unfriendly; having or showing ill will
6. _____revive_____ To give new energy, spirit, or strength
7. _____impulse_____ A sudden urge to do something
8. _____extraordinary_____ Beyond the ordinary; special
9. _____distract_____ To cause to turn away from what one was paying attention to
10. _____perceive_____ To be or to become aware of through one's senses; see, hear, feel, taste, or smell

CAUTION: Do not go any further until you are sure the above answers are correct. Then you can use the definitions to help you in the following practices. Your goal is eventually to know the words well enough so that you don't need to check the definitions at all.

➤ *Check 1*

Using the answer line, complete each item below with the correct word from the box.

a. **assure**	b. **crucial**	c. **distract**	d. **extraordinary**	e. **hostile**
f. **humiliate**	g. **impulse**	h. **perceive**	i. **revive**	j. **timid**

humiliate   1. Bullies ___ other people in order to make themselves feel powerful.

distract   2. The football game on TV ___ed Tyrell from his homework.

assure   3. My boss ___s me that I will get a raise soon.

revive   4. The flowers in the garden were beginning to droop in the dry weather, but a heavy rain shower soon ___d them.

impulse   5. Grocery store managers often place candy bars, combs, and other small, inexpensive items near the checkout, hoping that shoppers will have an ___ to buy them.

crucial   6. To succeed at a job interview, it is ___ that you arrive on time.

perceive   7. Because parents know their children so well, they can often ___ that the children are not feeling well just by looking at them.

hostile   8. Two of my coworkers are very ___ toward each other; their unfriendly relationship makes work difficult for others as well.

timid   9. Thea felt too ___ to raise her hand when the magician asked for volunteers.

extraordinary   10. The newspaper carried a story about an ___ woman who uses a wheelchair and is still a terrific tennis player.

NOTE: Now check your answers to these questions by turning to page 250. Going over the answers carefully will help you prepare for the remaining practices, for which answers are not given.

➤ *Check 2*

Using the answer lines, complete each item below with **two** words from the box.

humiliate
impulse   1–2. When Len's boss ___d him in front of his coworkers, he felt a sudden ___ to grab the man's necktie and snip it off with scissors.

perceive
distract   3–4. Once I began to ___ the aroma of fried chicken, I stopped doing my homework because I was so ___ed by the wonderful smell.

crucial
assure   5–6. The builders know it is ___ that the bathroom be finished before our visitors arrive next week, and they have ___d us the work will be done.

extraordinary
revive   7–8. When Sandra got the chance to work with an ___ coach—one who had coached many champions—it ___d her dream of someday competing in the Olympics.

hostile
timid   9–10. The more ___ the angry, impatient bus driver became, the more he frightened the ___ little girl who had lost her bus ticket.

➤ *Related Words*

Once you learn a new word, you can more easily understand many related words. Below are ten words related to the core words of this chapter. Use their definitions to help you write in the word that best completes each item.

a. **assurance**, *noun*	A promise
b. **distraction**, *noun*	Something that draws one's attention in another direction
c. **humiliation**, *noun*	Shame; embarrassment
d. **reassure**, *verb*	To make less fearful or worried
e. **revival**, *noun*	A new presentation of an old play, opera, etc.

_____*reassure*_____ 1. Although the company was sold, the new owner ___d the workers that they would not lose their jobs.

_____*distraction*_____ 2. The wall between the two theaters is thin, so moviegoers have to put up with the ___ of hearing the other movie going on next door.

_____*assurance*_____ 3. Can you give me your ___ that my car will be fixed today?

_____*revival*_____ 4. I'd like to see a ___ of the musical *Peter Pan* with Whitney Houston playing the part of Tinkerbell.

_____*humiliation*_____ 5. During his cooking demonstration, Chris experienced the ___ of dropping a dozen eggs on the floor in front of his entire class.

f. **hostility**, *noun*	Unfriendliness; anger
g. **impulsive**, *adjective*	Likely to take action quickly, without much thought
h. **perception**, *noun*	Becoming aware through use of the senses; awareness
i. **perceptive**, *verb*	Quick to notice things and understand situations
j. **timidity**, *noun*	Shyness; fear; lack of confidence

_____*impulsive*_____ 6. Jessie is often ___. She does things without thinking—such as suddenly painting her kitchen purple—and then is sorry.

_____*perception*_____ 7. Animals' ___ of colors differs from people's ability to see colors. For example, bees cannot see red, but they can see ultraviolet light.

_____*hostility*_____ 8. Although Rita said, "I forgive you," her voice was so full of ___ that it was clear she wasn't earnest°. She wasn't ready to forgive.

_____*perceptive*_____ 9. A good detective is very ___, not missing a detail as he investigates° a crime.

_____*timidity*_____ 10. As a teenager, I often had to deal with ___. I would frequently stay in my room rather than speak to someone I didn't know well.

➤ *Word Work*

A. In the space provided, write the letter of the word that most closely relates to the situation in each item.

___c___ 1. These beautiful paintings are the work of a nine-year-old artist with amazing talent.

      a. timid   b. revive   c. extraordinary

___c___ 2. "I've got an idea!" said Nelson, jumping up from his desk. "Let's take a break and all go get some ice cream."

      a. timid   b. perceive   c. impulse

___c___ 3. As Tom stood waiting for someone to pick him to join a softball team, he heard one team captain mumble, "I hope we don't get stuck with that wimp."

      a. assure   b. crucial   c. humiliate

___a___ 4. The first two years of life greatly affect the mental and emotional development of a child.

      a. crucial   b. perceive   c. hostile

___b___ 5. Aisha came home from work feeling tired, but a short nap made her refreshed and energetic.

      a. perceive   b. revive   c. extraordinary

B. In the space provided, write the letter of the choice that best completes each item.

___b___ 6. A common **hostile** comment is

      a. "Nice to meet you."   b. "Mind your own business."   c. "See you later."

___a___ 7. A **timid** man is likely to find it difficult to

      a. ask a girl for a date.   b. study.   c. eat a healthy diet.

___b___ 8. Something that may **distract** a person studying late at night is

      a. a textbook.   b. a dripping faucet.   c. coffee.

___c___ 9. While eating pizza for dinner, Chang **perceived**

      a. the events of his day.
      b. a thought about his girlfriend.
      c. a dash of hot pepper in the sauce.

___a___ 10. The company president **assured** the workers that

      a. there would be no layoffs.
      b. the company might be for sale.
      c. everyone might have to take a pay cut.

➣ *Word Parts*

A. The suffix *-ity* means "the quality or state of being ___."

Examples: *timid* — shy
         timidity — the quality or state of being shy

On each answer line, write the word from the box that best completes the item.

a. **brutality**°	b. **generosity**	c. **hostility**
d. **security**°	e. **timidity**	

_____*security*_____   1. Mrs. Lee likes the ___ of living in an apartment that's on the tenth floor, where no thieves can enter through the windows.

_____*generosity*_____   2. Everyone was amazed by the ___ of the man who won a huge lottery prize and then gave it all away to charity.

_____*brutality*_____   3. There are laws to protect animals from ___; it is against the law to beat or otherwise harm them.

_____*hostility*_____   4. Ever since Margo asked Rose's boyfriend out on a date, there has been ___ between the two women.

_____*timidity*_____   5. If you suffer from ___, you can learn to be less shy through practice. Every day, try to do one brave thing, such as speaking up at work or starting a conversation.

B. The suffixes *-able* and *-ible* can mean "able to be ___."

Examples: *perceive* — to notice through one's senses
         perceptible — able to be noticed through use of the senses

On each answer line, write the word from the box that best completes the item.

f. **manageable**	g. **perceptible**	h. **readable**
i. **transferable**	j. **usable**	

_____*readable*_____   6. Nadia's handwriting is so bad that it is usually not even ___.

_____*transferable*_____   7. If you decide to leave this college and go to another, you may lose some credits—some of your credits may not be ___.

_____*manageable*_____   8. I have tons of homework to do this weekend, but it is ___. If I use my time well, I can handle it.

_____*perceptible*_____   9. The odor of fried fish is ___ in the house even hours after we've had dinner.

_____*usable*_____   10. These bananas are too ripe, but they are still ___ for banana bread. You could also freeze them and utilize° them later in fruit drinks.

➤ *Final Check*

Read the passages carefully. Then fill in each blank with the word that best fits the context.

A. Fear of Speaking

a. **distract**	b. **hostile**	c. **humiliate**
d. **impulse**	e. **timid**	

Some people are afraid of spiders. Others fear heights. But for many people, the scariest thing of all is having to speak in front of a group of strangers. Even people who are not usually (1)_____*timid*_____ often have an intense° fear of speaking in public. They often imagine that the audience will be (2)_____*hostile*_____, even when it is actually friendly. Because they are so sure that they will (3)_____*humiliate*_____ themselves, they usually manage to do just that. They are so awkward° when they walk to the front of the room that they almost trip over their own feet. When they begin to speak, their hands flutter, causing the papers they are holding to shake loudly. This annoying noise (4)_____*distract*_____s the audience from what the speakers are trying to say. Embarrassed by their poor performance, the unfortunate speakers have to fight the (5)_____*impulse*_____ to crawl under a chair and hide. One of the best things people like this can do for themselves is take a course in public speaking. Even if they never learn to love public speaking, they can learn to face an audience without feeling frightened.

B. Do You Believe in Magic?

f. **assure**	g. **crucial**	h. **extraordinary**
i. **perceive**	j. **revive**	

Have you ever wondered how magic tricks work? Magicians work hard to make their tricks look like authentic° magic. But no magician has done what Horace Goldin did to make a trick look real. Goldin performed the well-known act in which a volunteer from the crowd is placed in a box, cut in half, and then reconnected right in front of the audience. But Goldin's trick was (6)_____*extraordinary*_____ because of a special added twist. After the victim was sawed in half and reconnected, the audience was (7)_____*assure*_____d that the volunteer was fine and could return to his seat. When the man stood up, however, the top half of his body appeared to separate and fall to the floor. Meanwhile the bottom half also fell, but then it (8)_____*revive*_____d, got up, and ran off the stage! The trick totally bewildered° the audience.

How did Goldin do it? The secret was the volunteer, a close friend of Goldin's. The volunteer had a twin brother who had no legs. What the audience (9)_____*perceive*_____d as the volunteer's upper half was really the legless twin. The separate walking legs were just a short person wearing normal-sized pants. In 1921, however, the legless twin brother demanded a higher salary. When Goldin refused to pay, the twin quit the act. With a (10)_____*crucial*_____ part of the act gone, Goldin had to stop performing the trick.

➤ *Questions for Discussion*

1. Of all the friendships you've had, which one seems the most **crucial** to you? Why has that one friendship been so important to you?

2. Describe a person you are acquainted with who often seems **hostile**. Is this person unfriendly to everyone or only to certain people? How does the person express his or her hostility?

3. When have you seen one person try to **humiliate** another? What did he or she do in order to embarrass the other person? Describe what the first person did and how the other person reacted.

4. Tell a story about a time when you spoke or acted because of an **impulse**. Did you feel OK later about what you had said or done, or did you wish you had thought it through more carefully first?

5. When you were a child, what made you feel **timid**? How did you act when you were feeling so shy and frightened? (If you can't remember, think of a young child you know, and describe what makes this child feel timid and how he or she acts when shy and frightened.)

➤ *Ideas for Writing*

1. Write about how and where you like to study. Where do you prefer to sit? What do you like to have around you? Do you like to have music playing and people around, or do those things **distract** you? When you get sleepy or bored as you study, what do you do to **revive** yourself?

2. Write about the trip that you take to reach school. What route do you follow? Do you walk or travel in a car or bus? Describe some of the sights, smells, and sounds that you usually **perceive** in the course of your trip. What **extraordinary** things have you ever seen or experienced along the way?

Check Your Performance			CHAPTER 18
Activity	*Number Right*	*Points*	*Total*
Check 2	_____	× 10 =	_____
Related Words	_____	× 10 =	_____
Word Work	_____	× 10 =	_____
Word Parts	_____	× 10 =	_____
Final Check	_____	× 10 =	_____

Enter your scores above and in the vocabulary performance chart on the inside back cover of the book.

abandon	function
alert	idle
circumstances	overcome
devote	primary
dominate	theme

Ten Words in Context

In the space provided, write the letter of the meaning closest to that of each **boldfaced** word. Use the context of the sentences to help you figure out each word's meaning.

1 **abandon**
(ə-băn′dən)
– *verb*

- When it got dark out, the divers had to **abandon** their search for the body of the woman who had drowned.
- Because they ran out of money, the scientists had to **abandon** their research project.

c *Abandon* means   a. to begin.   b. to sell.   c. to quit.

2 **alert**
(ə-lûrt′)
– *adjective*

- If you are riding a bicycle on a busy city street, you need to be **alert** at all times.
- Many people need a cup of coffee in the morning to make them feel really **alert**.

c *Alert* means   a. bad-tempered.   b. well dressed.   c. fully awake.

3 **circumstances**
(sûr′kəm-stăns′əz)
– *noun*

- My sister and brother-in-law had a big argument about something yesterday, but I do not know the exact **circumstances**.
- Here are the main **circumstances** of the robbery: A man wearing a Santa Claus mask took some money from a toy store.

a *Circumstances* means   a. facts.   b. answers.   c. people.

4 **devote**
(dĭ-vōt′)
– *verb*

- The kids **devoted** the entire evening to playing video games.
- Professor Morales **devoted** her life to the study of ancient Egypt.

b *Devote* means   a. to look over.   b. to give over.   c. to win over.

5 **dominate**
(dŏm′ə-nāt′)
– *verb*

- McDonald's and Burger King seem to **dominate** the country's burger market.
- My brother likes to dream about a time when his favorite team will be so good that it will **dominate** football.

b *Dominate* means   a. to take pity on.   b. to be a leader in.   c. to lose interest in.

6 **function**
(fŭngk′shən)
– *noun*

- A waiter's **function** is to take the diners' orders and then to bring them their food.
- What is the **function** of that red button on the front of the VCR?

a *Function* means   a. purpose.   b. subject.   c. length of time.

7 idle
(īd′l)
– adjective

- After being at home for a week with the flu, I was sick of being **idle** and happy to get back to work.
- When the boss is out of town, many of the workers in this store are **idle** much of the time.

_a_ *Idle* means   a. not busy.   b. outside.   c. in a group.

8 overcome
(ō′vər-kŭm′)
– verb

- My brother had to **overcome** a learning disability to become a successful student.
- With the help of swimming lessons, I **overcame** my fear of water.

_d_ *Overcome* means   a. to know.   b. to write about.   c. to beat.

9 primary
(prī′mĕr′ē)
– adjective

- My brother's **primary** interest in life seems to be playing basketball—he practices day and night.
- The **primary** reason for the family reunion is to celebrate Grandma's ninetieth birthday.

_d_ *Primary* means   a. easiest.   b. forgotten.   c. main.

10 theme
(thēm)
– noun

- The writing assignment is a five-hundred-word paper on the **theme** "a surprising event."
- *Romeo and Juliet* and *West Side Story* share the same **theme**: young lovers separated by the hatred of others.

_c_ *Theme* means   a. answer.   b. rule.   c. idea.

Matching Words with Definitions

Following are definitions of the ten words. **Print** each word next to its definition. If you look closely at each word in context, you will be able to figure out its meaning.

1. _____ *primary* _____   Most important; major
2. _____ *overcome* _____   To win in a struggle over; defeat
3. _____ *abandon* _____   To stop trying to continue; discontinue; quit
4. _____ *devote* _____   To give one's time or attention completely to something or someone
5. _____ *function* _____   The expected activity of a person or thing; purpose; role
6. _____ *alert* _____   Wide-awake and watchful; highly aware
7. _____ *idle* _____   Not doing anything; inactive
8. _____ *dominate* _____   To have a leading place or position in; be at the head of
9. _____ *circumstances* _____   Condition or facts of a particular situation or happening
10. _____ *theme* _____   The main subject; the topic around which something is organized

CAUTION: Do not go any further until you are sure the above answers are correct. Then you can use the definitions to help you in the following practices. Your goal is eventually to know the words well enough so that you don't need to check the definitions at all.

➤ *Check 1*

Using the answer line, complete each item below with the correct word from the box.

a. **abandon**	b. **alert**	c. **circumstances**	d. **devote**	e. **dominate**
f. **function**	g. **idle**	h. **overcome**	i. **primary**	j. **theme**

_____*alert*_____ 1. An ___ person is wide-awake and very much aware of his or her surroundings.

_____*primary*_____ 2. It is clear that the ___ reason my aunt's boyfriend likes her is her money.

_____*idle*_____ 3. When my boss is just staring out the window, she looks ___, but she is really trying to figure out a problem.

_____*theme*_____ 4. Dances often have a special ___, such as "Winter Wonderland."

_____*overcome*_____ 5. Before Cara can visit her grandparents in Italy, she needs to ___ her fear of flying in an airplane.

_____*abandon*_____ 6. When a friend called to ask if I wanted to go to the movies, I quickly ___ed my ironing and got ready to go out.

_____*devote*_____ 7. The young skater ___s five hours each day to practicing.

_____*circumstances*_____ 8. At first I thought Jorge was unfriendly, but when I learned the ___ of his life—he is a single parent who is also caring for his elderly father—I understood that he doesn't have much time to chat.

_____*function*_____ 9. A pen and a pencil have the same ___.

_____*dominate*_____ 10. Coca Cola and Pepsi ___ the cola market.

NOTE: Now check your answers to these questions by turning to page 250. Going over the answers carefully will help you prepare for the remaining practices, for which answers are not given.

➤ *Check 2*

Using the answer lines, complete each item below with **two** words from the box.

_____*circumstances*_____
_____*abandon*_____ 1–2. During the Depression of the 1930s, ___ were so bad that many young people had to ___ their education and go to work full-time.

_____*function*_____
_____*idle*_____ 3–4. The boss was angry when he found us taking a long break. "Your ___ is to get work done," he snapped—"not to sit around ___!"

_____*theme*_____
_____*alert*_____ 5–6. "You'll have to read carefully to find the ___ of this story," our instructor said. Then he assured° us, "But if you are ___ and pay attention to every clue, I think you can figure out the author's true topic."

_____*primary*_____
_____*devote*_____ 7–8. Some women's ___ interest is their careers, and some ___ themselves to their families; others manage to do both.

_____*overcome*_____
_____*dominate*_____ 9–10. There are many true stories of very successful people who have ___ serious physical problems and gone on to ___ a sport.

➢ *Related Words*

Once you learn a new word, you can more easily understand many related words. Below are ten words related to the core words of this chapter. Use their definitions to help you write in the word that best completes each item.

a. **devotion**, *noun*	Deep affection and loyalty
b. **dominant**, *adjective*	Having more influence or power than others
c. **idleness**, *noun*	The state of being inactive
d. **primarily**, *adverb*	Mainly; chiefly
e. **theme song**, *noun*	A melody which is regularly used on a TV show or movie or by an individual and which comes to stand for that show or movie or person

_____primarily_____ 1. In my home, we ___ speak Spanish, unless we have English-speaking visitors. Then, of course, we communicate° in English.

_____devotion_____ 2. When I was a teenager, it was the style to sign a love letter to your girlfriend or boyfriend with this rhyme: "Yours with an ocean of ___."

_____idleness_____ 3. When I'm on vacation, I like to spend some time in total ___. I sleep late and rest all day.

_____dominant_____ 4. Tim is the ___ partner in his marriage. He makes all the decisions, and his wife just says, "Yes, dear."

_____theme song_____ 5. If Tim's wife had a ___, it would have to be "Stand By Your Man."

f. **alertness**, *noun*	State or condition of being wide awake; full or intense awareness
g. **functional**, *adjective*	Working well
h. **idler**, *noun*	A lazy person
i. **prime**, *adjective*	First in importance or value
j. **theme park**, *noun*	An amusement park in which all the buildings, exhibits, and rides are built around a central subject

_____idler_____ 6. Barry is a terrible ___: he is at the water fountain, on the phone with friends, and on coffee breaks more often than he actually works.

_____alertness_____ 7. When my son woke up after his operation, the nurse tested his ___ by asking questions such as "Where are you, Billy?" and "Do you know what day it is?"

_____functional_____ 8. My old car looks terrible, but it's still ___, taking me wherever I want to go.

_____theme park_____ 9. I took my little niece to a ___ that is based on *Sesame Street*. The ideas of the rides and games are all from that show.

_____prime_____ 10. TV broadcasters can charge the most for ads that appear during ___ time, when most people are watching.

➤ *Word Work*

A. In the space provided, write the letter of the choice that best completes each item.

___b___ 1. Today at the store, the other salespeople and I were **idle** most of the day because
        a. there were so many customers to take care of.
        b. there were very few customers.
        c. we didn't have time for a lunch break.

___a___ 2. If someone says that Mindy always tries to **dominate** the conversation, you can guess that Mindy
        a. doesn't let anyone else speak much.   b. is very funny.
        c. is too shy to speak up.

___c___ 3. Your **primary** goal in life is
        a. something that doesn't matter much to you.
        b. the goal you would say is second or third in importance.
        c. your most important goal.

___c___ 4. A student might **abandon** her homework one night if she
        a. really needed a good grade.
        b. had a friend who wanted to study together.
        c. had a big date that night.

___b___ 5. "Look **alert**!" my father sometimes said to us. He meant
        a. Quiet down and go to sleep this minute!   b. Pay attention!
        c. Comb your hair!

B. Write each word next to the examples that best match it.

a. **circumstances**	b. **devote**	c. **function**
d. **overcome**	e. **theme**	

_____overcome_____ 6. Wheelchair users compete in tennis and basketball.
        Someone gets over a stutter to become a fine public speaker.
        An alcoholic stays sober for many years.

_____devote_____ 7. People spend many hours with and for their children.
        People put in a lot of time and energy at their jobs.
        People contribute much effort to the cause of civil rights.

_____theme_____ 8. A student paper on the topic of cheating
        A book about how to survive a divorce
        A kid's birthday party with a circus cake and circus decorations

_____circumstances_____ 9. The details of Anna's financial situation
        Living conditions in Betsy's house
        The realities of life in Cory's neighborhood

_____function_____ 10. Of a bathroom scale: to measure people's weight
        Of the red light on the dashboard: to let you know the oil is low
        Of a traffic police officer: to control traffic

➤ *Synonyms and Antonyms*

A. Synonyms. Write the letter of the word or phrase that most nearly means the **same** as each boldfaced word.

__*a*__ 1. **circumstances**

      a. conditions   b. jobs

      c. activities   d. abilities

__*a*__ 2. **dominate**

      a. lead   b. follow

      c. be active   d. leave

__*d*__ 3. **devote**

      a. get rid of   b. win over

      c. hide from   d. give over to

__*c*__ 4. **function**

      a. subject   b. fact

      c. purpose   d. rule

__*d*__ 5. **theme**

      a. fact   b. safety

      c. use   d. subject

B. Antonyms. Write the letter of the word or phrase that most nearly means the **opposite** of each boldfaced word.

__*b*__ 6. **abandon**

      a. leave   b. continue

      c. lose   d. work badly

__*a*__ 7. **alert**

      a. sleepy   b. curious

      c. complete   d. late

__*c*__ 8. **idle**

      a. new   b. stiff

      c. active   d. grateful

__*d*__ 9. **overcome**

      a. win   b. follow

      c. continue   d. give in to

__*b*__ 10. **primary**

      a. least expensive   b. least important

      c. not enough   d. not prepared

➤ *Final Check*

Read the passages carefully. Then fill in each blank with the word that best fits the context.

A. The Miracle Runner

a. **devote**	b. **dominate**	c. **idle**
d. **primary**	e. **overcome**	

Glenn Cunningham was one of the most famous and extraordinary° athletes of the 1930s. To succeed, he had to (1)_____*overcome*_____ difficulties that might have stopped anyone. When Glenn was 8, he and his older brother Floyd were trapped in a burning building. Floyd was killed, and Glenn was badly burned. The fire had eaten deep into his legs, and the toes of one foot were gone. In fact, doctors advised° his parents to have Glenn's legs taken off. Glenn lay in bed for months, his legs thin as sticks. He hated being (2)_____*idle*_____, so he struggled to learn to stand and then to take a few steps. Then he began to run. At first, his (3)_____*primary*_____ goal in running was just to get rid of his limp. Then he discovered that he was a very good runner.

At age 13, Glenn entered a mile race at a local fair and won easily. From then on, he (4)_____*devote*_____d himself to running—and to winning. In high school, then in college, and later when he was a member of the United States Olympic team, he (5)_____*dominate*_____d his sport. He set a world-record time for running the mile: 4 minutes, 4.4 seconds. And this was someone who had been told he would never walk again!

B. One of Those Days

f. **abandon**	g. **alert**	h. **circumstances**
i. **function**	j. **theme**	

Did you ever have a day whose (6)_____*theme*_____ seems to be "things that go wrong"? I had one such day last Friday. This is the only day I have a class at 8 a.m. But my alarm clock did not perform its (7)_____*function*_____—it did not make a sound. I had no time to eat, but because I was sleepy, I made a cup of coffee to help me feel more (8)_____*alert*_____. When I poured milk into the coffee, though, I found that the milk was sour. Yuck! So I (9)_____*abandon*_____ed my effort to have a cup of coffee, grabbed my car keys, and ran out. Then I remembered my car was in the shop for repairs. So I raced to the bus stop, but got there just as the bus drove off. Desperate° to get to school, I decided to continue on foot, so I began running again. Then along came a car that hit a deep puddle and splashed me from head to foot with mud.

At school, I told the instructor the (10)_____*circumstances*_____ that had made me late, muddy, and out of breath. Looking annoyed that I had disrupted° the class, he told me to hand in my assignment. At that point, I discovered I had brought the wrong textbook and notebook. I decided then and there that the next time I oversleep, I'll just stay in bed!

➤ *Questions for Discussion*

1. Have you ever wished you could **abandon** your responsibilites—school, family, work—and just take off somewhere? Explain what **circumstances** made you feel that way.

2. When you have free time, do you **devote** yourself to some activity, or do you prefer to be **idle**? Why?

3. Prisons are the topic of many arguments these days. What do you think the **function** of a prison should be? To help criminals become better citizens? To punish them? Or just to keep them where they can't do any more harm?

4. "We Shall **Overcome**" became the **theme song** of the civil-rights movement. Why do you think the song was so powerful? What does it mean to you?

5. Have you ever been to a **theme park**? If so, what was the **theme**, and how was it carried out?

➤ *Ideas for Writing*

1. When you are bored or sleepy, what do you do to make yourself more **alert**? Do you drink coffee? Go for a fast walk? Take a shower? Describe something that wakes you up when you need a lift.

2. Write about your **primary** goal in getting an education. Is it a better job? Personal growth? To please your family? Self-respect?

Check Your Performance   CHAPTER 19

Activity	Number Right	Points	Total
Check 2	_____	× 10 =	_____
Related Words	_____	× 10 =	_____
Word Work	_____	× 10 =	_____
Synonyms and Antonyms	_____	× 10 =	_____
Final Check	_____	× 10 =	_____

Enter your scores above and in the vocabulary performance chart on the inside back cover of the book.

disregard	monotonous
excerpt	obtain
exclude	prey
hinder	seize
misleading	severe

Ten Words in Context

In the space provided, write the letter of the meaning closest to that of each **boldfaced** word. Use the context of the sentences to help you figure out each word's meaning.

1 disregard
(dĭs′rĭ-gärd′)
– verb

- I suggested that Patty put some of her money in a savings account, but she **disregarded** my idea and spent it all.
- The drive with Luis was frightening—he **disregarded** the speed limit, even though the road was icy.

_b_ *Disregard* means   a. to follow.   b. to ignore.   c. to get in the way of.

2 excerpt
(ĕk′sûrpt′)
– noun

- The *New York Times* printed all of the President's speech, but most newspapers printed only **excerpts** from it.
- Previews advertise films by showing several **excerpts**, parts that will make people want to come see the whole movie.

_a_ *Excerpt* means   a. part.   b. price.   c. speech.

3 exclude
(ĭk-sklo͞od′)
– verb

- In making pickles that will be stored for a long time, air must be **excluded** from the jars.
- The little boy ran crying to his teacher after other children **excluded** him from their game.

_c_ *Exclude* means   a. to watch.   b. to invite.   c. to keep out.

4 hinder
(hĭn′dər)
– verb

- Not having computer skills **hindered** Jane in her search for an office job.
- Bad weather **hindered** the climbers on their hike up the mountain.

_a_ *Hinder* means   a. to get in the way of.   b. to cheer up.   c. to find.

5 misleading
(mĭs-lē′dĭng)
– adjective

- The fact that the two close friends have the same last name is **misleading**. Many people think they are really sisters.
- My cousin may appear rich, but his fancy car and nice clothes are **misleading**. In reality, he owes thousands of dollars on his credit card.

_c_ *Misleading* means   a. hard to find.   b. recent.   c. giving the wrong idea.

6 monotonous
(mə-nŏt′n-əs)
– adjective

- The child in the supermarket kept up a **monotonous** request—"I want some candy. I want some candy. I want some candy."
- My days had become **monotonous**: I got up, went to work, came home, slept, then did it all over again.

_a_ *Monotonous* means   a. dull.   b. pleasant.   c. messy.

7 obtain
(əb-tān′)
– *verb*

- After completing the Driver's Education class, Maria **obtained** a driver's license.
- The soldier **obtained** a three-day pass in order to attend his sister's wedding.

_b_ *Obtain* means   a. to grab.   b. to get.   c. to give away.

8 prey
(prā)
– *noun*

- Because a cat's **prey** includes mice, farmers like to keep cats in their barns.
- Movie stars are the **prey** of thoughtless photographers who will do anything to get a photo.

_a_ *Prey* means   a. those that are hunted.   b. part of a whole.   c. sickness.

9 seize
(sēz)
– *verb*

- The woman screamed when a thief **seized** her pocketbook.
- Before anyone could stop him, the baby **seized** the cat's tail and pulled.

_b_ *Seize* means   a. to laugh at.   b. to grab.   c. to know.

10 severe
(sə-vîr′)
– *adjective*

- A **severe** storm hit our area, causing great damage and several deaths.
- Patients with the most **severe** illnesses are kept in a separate part of the hospital, where they receive special care.

_b_ *Severe* means   a. fair.   b. dangerous.   c. boring.

Matching Words with Definitions

Following are definitions of the ten words. **Print** each word next to its definition. If you look closely at each word in context, you will be able to figure out its meaning.

1. _____prey_____   A creature or creatures that are hunted by another animal; the victim or victims of an attack

2. _____excerpt_____   Part of a whole work (such as a book, speech, or film)

3. _____disregard_____   To pay no attention to

4. _____exclude_____   To refuse to allow in; not include

5. _____obtain_____   To get something through planning or effort

6. _____misleading_____   Leading to a mistake in thought or action

7. _____monotonous_____   Boring because of lack of change or differences

8. _____severe_____   Causing great physical or mental suffering; very serious

9. _____seize_____   To take hold of suddenly or with force

10. _____hinder_____   To stop or slow down (someone or something); block; interfere with

CAUTION: Do not go any further until you are sure the above answers are correct. Then you can use the definitions to help you in the following practices. Your goal is eventually to know the words well enough so that you don't need to check the definitions at all.

➤ *Check 1*

Using the answer line, complete each item below with the correct word from the box.

a. **disregard**	b. **excerpt**	c. **exclude**	d. **hinder**	e. **misleading**
f. **monotonous**	g. **obtain**	h. **prey**	i. **seize**	j. **severe**

_____*misleading*_____ 1. Cynthia's bright smile is ___; actually, she is feeling quite angry.

_____*prey*_____ 2. The robbers' usual ___ were newlyweds whose houses might contain expensive wedding gifts.

_____*exclude*_____ 3. My aunt is a vegetarian and ___s all meat from her house.

_____*hinder*_____ 4. A huge snowstorm ___ed Thanksgiving travelers.

_____*severe*_____ 5. Although the car wasn't damaged much in the crash, the driver had ___ injuries.

_____*monotonous*_____ 6. No matter how much you like your favorite food, having it at every meal would soon become ___.

_____*obtain*_____ 7. Members of the Environmental Club went door-to-door to ___ signatures for their request to set up a recycling center in town.

_____*excerpt*_____ 8. The video called *The Best of Johnny Carson* contains funny ___s from ten years of the *Tonight* show.

_____*seize*_____ 9. When she realized her train would leave in just an hour, Rita ___d her suitcase from the shelf and began stuffing clothes into it.

_____*disregard*_____ 10. Phil lost his money when he ___ed the "Out of Order" sign and put two quarters in the jukebox.

NOTE: Now check your answers to these questions by turning to page 250. Going over the answers carefully will help you prepare for the remaining practices, for which answers are not given.

➤ *Check 2*

Using the answer lines, complete each item below with **two** words from the box.

_____*seize*_____
_____*prey*_____ 1–2. It is striking to see a hawk drop out of the sky and ___ a field mouse, then fly away with its ___ in its claws.

_____*severe*_____
_____*exclude*_____ 3–4. When my uncle had a ___ illness, the doctor ___ed everyone from his hospital room except my aunt.

_____*excerpt*_____
_____*misleading*_____ 5–6. The TV ads for the movie used an ___ from the film that was ___. It was funny, but the movie was not a comedy at all.

_____*obtain*_____
_____*hinder*_____ 7–8. Yolanda wanted to be first in line to ___ tickets for a very special concert, but the snowstorm ___ed her.

_____*disregard*_____
_____*monotonous*_____ 9–10. Because Wendy is so shy, she ___s invitations to go out, and as a result she stays home night after night and leads a very ___ life.

➤ *Related Words*

Once you learn a new word, you can more easily understand many related words. Below are ten words related to the core words of this chapter. Use their definitions to help you write in the word that best completes each item.

a. **exclusive**, *adjective*	Letting only certain people in
b. **hindrance**, *noun*	Something that gets in the way or holds back
c. **include**, *verb*	To take in (someone or something) as part of something larger
d. **monotony**, *noun*	Boredom
e. **severity**, *noun*	Seriousness

_____ *hindrance* _____ 1. The icy sidewalk was such a ___ that I missed my bus.

_____ *severity* _____ 2. When we heard our friend had been in an accident, we called the hospital to try to learn the ___ of her injuries.

_____ *monotony* _____ 3. I don't enjoy going to the zoo because I am bothered by the ___ of the animals' lives—they spend day after day idle° in the same small cages.

_____ *exclusive* _____ 4. The Honor Club at our school is so ___ that only 5 percent of the student body is qualified to join.

_____ *include* _____ 5. The Honor Club ___s top students from the tenth, eleventh, and twelfth grades.

f. **exclusion**, *noun*	The act of leaving something out
g. **mislead**, *verb*	To lead (someone) to think what is not so
h. **monotone**, *noun*	A single, unchanging sound
i. **predator**, *noun*	An animal that lives by hunting other animals for food
j. **regardless of**, *preposition*	Without considering anyone or anything else; in spite of

_____ *monotone* _____ 6. Professor Woodworth speaks in such a dull ___ that students have a hard time staying alert° in his class.

_____ *predator* _____ 7. It's easy to see that the tiger is a ___. Its sharp teeth are designed for ripping other animals to pieces.

_____ *mislead* _____ 8. Some advertisements purposely ___ people, making them believe the products are better than they really are. Companies should not be allowed to deceive° people that way.

_____ *exclusion* _____ 9. Becoming a vegetarian means more than the ___ of meat from the diet. It also means creating a balanced diet that doesn't involve meat.

_____ *regardless of* _____ 10. I don't enjoy working with Vic because he does what he likes ___ anyone else's opinions.

➢ *Word Work*

A. In the space provided, write the letter of the choice that best completes each item.

_b_ 1. If someone **seizes** a book from you, then probably
   a. you gave that person the book.
   b. the person took the book without permission.
   c. the person bought the book from you.

_a_ 2. One way to **hinder** a friend who is housecleaning is to
   a. hide the vacuum cleaner.
   b. hire a cleaning company.
   c. do the dusting for him or her.

_c_ 3. A job that is **monotonous** will involve
   a. danger.   b. no boss.   c. the same duties day after day.

_b_ 4. An animal goes looking for **prey** when the animal is feeling
   a. sleepy.   b. hungry.   c. playful.

_c_ 5. A person who **disregards** a "No Smoking" sign
   a. will wait and smoke somewhere else.
   b. will put the sign in his or her pocket and leave.
   c. will smoke in spite of the sign.

B. Write each word next to the examples that best match it.

a. **excerpt**	b. **exclude**	c. **misleading**
d. **obtain**	e. **severe**	

misleading   6. An ad for a broken-down old car that says, "Classic antique; needs a little work."
   A man who takes off his wedding ring when he goes to a nightclub
   A letter that says in big type, "You have won the grand prize!" and in tiny type, "if you have the winning number."

excerpt   7. A chapter from a novel
   A scene from a movie
   A paragraph from a short story

obtain   8. Earning a high-school diploma
   Getting a job
   Getting a license to drive a semitrailer

severe   9. A hailstorm that breaks car windows and destroys crops
   AIDS
   Being robbed at gunpoint

exclude   10. A diet is free of salt.
   A club does not allow everyone to join.
   A bar does not let underage people in.

➤ *Analogies*

Each item below starts with a pair of words in CAPITAL LETTERS. For each item, figure out the relationship between these two words. Then decide which of the choices (*a*, *b*, *c*, or *d*) expresses a similar relationship. Write the letter of your choice on the answer line. (All the repeated words in these items are from this unit.)

___d___ 1. MONOTONOUS : EXCITING ::

    a. healthy : strong   b. film : camera
    c. five : fifteen   d. hinder : help

___b___ 2. PREY: VICTIM ::

    a. artist : painting   b. baby : infant
    c. security° : lock   d. doctor : patient

___a___ 3. SEVERE : MILD ::

    a. painful : pleasant   b. angry : frowning
    c. harmful : dangerous   d. loud : noisy

___c___ 4. COMMUNICATE° : TELEPHONE ::

    a. fiction° : book   b. distract° : attention
    c. sweep : broom   d. screwdriver : nail

___d___ 5. EXTRAORDINARY° : COMMON ::

    a. assure° : promise   b. chew : gum
    c. mask : face   d. hostile° : friendly

___a___ 6. DISREGARD : IGNORE ::

    a. recall : remember   b. important : silly
    c. protect : reveal   d. sing : choir

___d___ 7. ECONOMICAL° : EXTRAVAGANT° ::

    a. country : map   b. earnest° : sincere
    c. pitch : ball   d. calm : worried

___b___ 8. PRETTY : UGLY ::

    a. friendly : nice   b. timid° : brave
    c. important : crucial°   d. difficult : burden°

___b___ 9. SEIZE : TAKE ::

    a. exclude : include   b. embarrass : humiliate°
    c. pull : push   d. shout : whisper

___d___10. PERCEIVE° : SENSES ::

    a. lazy : idle°   b. song : music
    c. write : letter   d. run : legs

➤ *Final Check*

Read the passages carefully. Then fill in each blank with the word that best fits the context.

A. Pregnancy and Alcohol

| a. **excerpt** | b. **exclude** | c. **hinder** |
| d. **misleading** | e. **severe** | |

If all goes well, an unborn baby thrives°, growing from a few cells into a healthy child. However, not all pregnancies go well. Sometimes, problems arise that (1)_____*hinder*_____ the baby's development. Most of those problems just happen and are not within anyone's control. But one common cause of a baby's problems can be prevented: the mother's use of alcohol.

Here is an (2)_____*excerpt*_____ from a textbook discussion of alcohol and pregnancy: "A woman who drinks heavily during pregnancy can injure the brain of her unborn child." A child born to a heavy drinker is likely to have (3)_____*severe*_____ health problems, including a small head, unusual facial features, low intelligence, and a damaged heart.

But it would be (4)_____*misleading*_____ to say that only heavy drinking is a problem during pregnancy. Even if a mother-to-be has just two drinks a week, she can harm her child's ability to pay attention and learn easily.

Exactly how much alcohol is too much for a pregnant woman? No one knows for sure. Until we know more, a pregnant woman is wise to (5)_____*exclude*_____ alcohol from her life.

B. A Criminal with a Tail

| f. **disregard** | g. **monotonous** | h. **obtain** |
| i. **prey** | j. **seize** | |

One of the best-known, most extraordinary° criminals ever sentenced to Pennsylvania's Graterford Prison was not a thief, a murderer, or a cheat. In fact, he was not even human. Prisoner #C2559, also known as Pep, was a dog who was (6)_____*seize*_____d by police in 1924 and forced to spend the rest of his days behind bars. Pep got into trouble by attacking his neighbor's cat one hot summer afternoon. Unfortunately for Pep, his furry (7)_____*prey*_____ happened to belong to Gifford Pinchot, the governor of Pennsylvania. The angry governor (8)_____*disregard*_____ed the fact that Pep was a dog and ordered an immediate trial. Without the ability to speak or (9)_____*obtain*_____ a lawyer for himself, Pep was sent to jail for life.

In prison, however, Pep was treated more kindly. His fellow prisoners were very fond of him. Even though he was assigned to a cell and expected to work every day, Pep was allowed to transfer° from one cell to another whenever he wanted. His furry face and wagging tail were a welcome change in the otherwise (10)_____*monotonous*_____ world of the prison, where each day seemed like the one before it. When he died six years later, Pep was the most popular inmate in the entire prison.

➤ *Questions for Discussion*

1. When have you **disregarded** the advice someone gave you, and then wished you had paid attention to it? Tell about what happened.

2. How do you feel about the previews that are shown in theaters before the feature? Do you think that the **excerpts** shown give a good idea of what those movies will be like?

3. Tell about a time when you were trying to leave the house to get to work or school, but something **hindered** you. What was it that got in the way of your leaving?

4. Do you ever see advertisements for products or hear claims that you think are **misleading**? Describe one such ad or claim. In what way do you believe it leads people to a mistaken conclusion?

5. What was the most **severe** weather you have ever experienced? How bad was it, and how did you deal with it?

➤ *Ideas for Writing*

1. What is the most **monotonous** job—either a paid job or a household chore—that you have ever had to do? Did you make it more exciting by playing music? By watching TV? Describe the job and what was so boring about it, and then tell how you made it more fun for yourself.

2. How do you feel about hunting? Would you enjoy following your **prey**—perhaps a deer or a goose—and hoping to get a clear shot at it? Do you think that hunting is an acceptable way to **obtain** food? Or are you bothered by the idea of hunting wild animals? Write about your attitude° toward hunting.

Check Your Performance			CHAPTER 20
Activity	*Number Right*	*Points*	*Total*
Check 2	_____	× 10 =	_____
Related Words	_____	× 10 =	_____
Word Work	_____	× 10 =	_____
Analogies	_____	× 10 =	_____
Final Check	_____	× 10 =	_____

Enter your scores above and in the vocabulary performance chart on the inside back cover of the book.

UNIT FOUR: *Review*

The box at the right lists twenty-five words from Unit Four. Using the clues at the bottom of the page, fill in these words to complete the puzzle that follows.

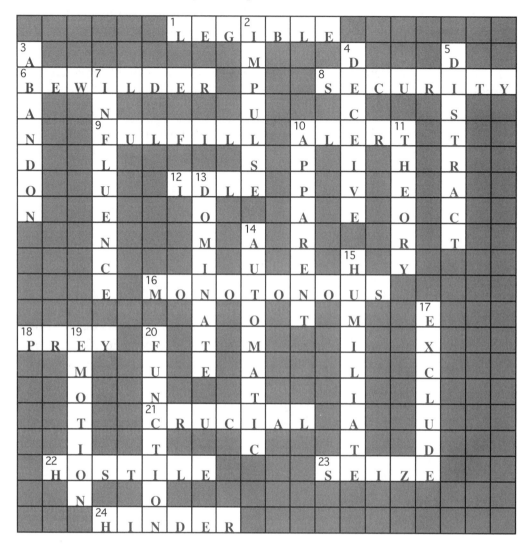

abandon
alert
apparent
automatic
bewilder
crucial
deceive
distract
dominate
emotion
exclude
fulfill
function
hinder
hostile
humiliate
idle
impulse
influence
legible
monotonous
prey
security
seize
theory

ACROSS

1. Clear enough to be read
6. To confuse; puzzle
8. Protection; freedom from danger, fear, or worry
9. To carry out; achieve; do
10. Wide-awake and watchful
12. Not doing anything; inactive
16. Boring because of lack of change or differences
18. A creature or creatures that are hunted by another animal
21. Extremely important
22. Unfriendly; having or showing ill will
23. To take hold of suddenly or with force
24. To stop or slow down; block

DOWN

2. A sudden urge to do something
3. To discontinue; quit
4. To make (someone) believe something that is not true
5. To cause to turn away from what one was paying attention to
7. To have an effect on
10. Obvious; easy to see
11. A statement that explains events or facts
13. To have a leading place or position in; be at the head of
14. Moving or operating by itself
15. To make ashamed; embarrass
17. To refuse to allow in; not include
19. A strong feeling
20. The expected activity of a person or thing; purpose

UNIT FOUR: Test 1

PART A
Choose the word that best completes each item and write it in the space provided.

_____appropriate_____ 1. When the children began screaming and throwing things on the bus, the driver yelled, "This is not ___ behavior!"

    a. primary   b. legible   c. alert   d. appropriate

_____bewildered_____ 2. English police are still ___ by the 1934 murder of a woman whose body parts were found in two wooden trunks. Not only is the crime unsolved; the name of the victim is still unknown.

    a. bewildered   b. obtained   c. communicated   d. revived

_____communicate_____ 3. Letters are still my favorite way to ___ with faraway friends and family.

    a. fulfill   b. seize   c. communicate   d. humiliate

_____deceived_____ 4. Mel kept his wife from knowing he had lost his job. He ___ her by leaving the house each morning as if he were going to work.

    a. alerted   b. fulfilled   c. devoted   d. deceived

_____earnest_____ 5. To show how ___ he was about wanting the job, Ira offered to work for no pay for a week.

    a. timid   b. primary   c. hostile   d. earnest

_____emotions_____ 6. A raised voice can mean one of several ___: anger, excitement, happiness, or surprise.

    a. emotions   b. preys   c. burdens   d. fictions

_____legible_____ 7. It is hard for a right-handed person to write a ___ message using his or her left hand.

    a. severe   b. timid   c. legible   d. primary

_____investigate_____ 8. Unsatisfied with the way the local police were handling the murder case, the victim's family hired a detective to ___ it.

    a. revive   b. influence   c. investigate   d. exclude

_____fiction_____ 9. When my daughter said, "There is a monster under my bed," her story was not purely ___: there was a large spider hiding there.

    a. fiction   b. burden   c. function   d. excerpt

_____theory_____ 10. I realized my ___ that all dog lovers were nice people was wrong when I met Doreen. She is very nice to dogs, but nasty to human beings.

    a. prey   b. theme   c. function   d. theory

_____security_____ 11. To increase her feeling of ___ when she walks home from the bus stop at night, Elena learned karate.

    a. security   b. circumstances   c. burden   d. impulse

(Continues on next page)

_____*apparent*_____ 12. It's ___ that your shoes are muddy—you're leaving dirty footprints on the carpet.

    a. extravagant   b. hostile   c. apparent   d. timid

_____*extraordinary*_____ 13. Although many of our neighbors have gardens, Mr. Soo's is really ___. He grows thirty-pound watermelons, tomatoes as big as softballs, and flowers as beautiful as anything in a flower shop.

    a. hostile   b. extraordinary   c. misleading   d. monotonous

PART B

Write **C** if the italicized word is used **correctly**. Write **I** if the word is used **incorrectly**.

__C__ 14. Because my sister skipped assignments and classes, it's hard for me to *sympathize* with her disappointment over failing algebra.

__I__ 15. My boss *fulfilled* my request for a day off, saying, "No, you've had too much time off already."

__C__ 16. Someday I'd like to replace my old-fashioned camera with a new *automatic* one that does everything by itself, even advancing the film.

__I__ 17. Fay is so *extravagant* that she purposely finds fault with waiters so that she can refuse to leave them a tip.

__C__ 18. Some parents worry that "Barbie dolls," with their impossibly long legs and tiny waists, can *influence* little girls, making them feel bad about their own bodies.

__C__ 19. Dan is worried about his math test because he knows it is *crucial* to his grade for the course.

__C__ 20. It is more *economical* to buy a six-pack of sodas for $1.99 than to buy six single sodas at 50 cents each.

__C__ 21. Since he was a little boy, Jon has *devoted* himself to becoming a pilot. He reads constantly about airplanes and flying and saves all his money for flying lessons.

__I__ 22. I feel so tired that instead of getting up this morning, I would love to just *transfer* in bed.

__C__ 23. Having our grandfather live with us was not a *burden*. Not only was he easy to live with, but he was very helpful around the house.

__I__ 24. I was so excited when my parents *humiliated* me with a plane ticket to visit my sister in England.

__I__ 25. As Dan studied for his test, his family helped *distract* him by turning off the TV and keeping the house quiet and peaceful.

Score (Number correct) _____ × 4 = _____ %

Enter your score above and in the vocabulary performance chart on the inside back cover of the book.

UNIT FOUR: Test 2

PART A

Complete each item with a word from the box. Use each word once.

a. **abandon**	b. **circumstances**	c. **disregard**	d. **function**	e. **hinder**
f. **hostile**	g. **misleading**	h. **monotonous**	i. **perceive**	j. **prey**
k. **revive**	l. **seize**	m. **severe**		

function   1. It is the ___ of advertising to persuade you that you will be happier and better off if only you will buy a certain product.

abandon   2. Very young cats who have kittens will often ___ the babies instead of taking care of them.

severe   3. When children get chicken pox, the disease is just a minor problem, but for adults, chicken pox can be a ___ illness.

circumstances   4. Paula's parents live in unusual ___; although they have been divorced for years, they continue to live in separate parts of the same house.

misleading   5. It is ___ that we have a Morrisville address, since we actually live much closer to the town of Hendrix.

monotonous   6. I prefer a job that takes a lot of effort to one that is easy but ___, with little or no change from hour to hour and day to day.

disregard   7. Foolishly, Randy ___ed the fact that he is allergic to seafood, ate a lobster, and ended up in the hospital.

seize   8. Before I could take a bite of my grilled cheese sandwich, a hungry dog ___d it, pulling it out of my hand and gulping it down.

hinder   9. Luis does not let his lack of a car ___ him from getting to work; he rides his bicycle.

revive   10. Early in the season, the baseball team's chance of getting to the World Series was not good. But then the team ___d its hopes by winning eight games in a row.

perceive   11. Long before I entered the house, I could ___ that Mom was making her famous spaghetti sauce. Its wonderful smell was the clue.

prey   12. To catch its ___, the anteater sticks its tongue into an anthill.

hostile   13. Never run up to pet a dog you don't know. Move toward it slowly until you are sure it is not ___.

(Continues on next page)

PART B
Write **C** if the italicized word is used **correctly**. Write **I** if the word is used **incorrectly**.

_C_ 14. I will let my cousin move into my apartment only if he *assures* me it will be for no more than a week.

_I_ 15. Mr. Henderson does everything according to *impulse*. For example, when he decided to buy a car, he spent months comparing models and prices, reading articles in car magazines, and visiting car dealers.

_I_ 16. Anitra is the most *idle* one in her family—she does all of the cooking and cleaning by herself.

_I_ 17. Every group of friends seems to have one especially *timid* member who bosses the others around.

_C_ 18. In 1959, one film—*Ben Hur*—*dominated* the Academy Awards, winning 11 Oscars.

_I_ 19. The videotapes of the robbery showed that as it was going on, the night watchman was *alert* and snoring in his office.

_C_ 20. Although Marla was abused as a child, she has *overcome* that terrible experience and is a kind, loving parent herself.

_C_ 21. The sweater has bits of blue and green in it, but its *primary* color is red.

_C_ 22. Have you ever really had to write a paper on the *theme* "How I Spent My Summer Vacation"?

_I_ 23. Robert Frost's "Mending Wall" is a well-known poem whose *excerpt* warns us not to shut ourselves off from other people.

_C_ 24. "No bacon for me, thank you," said Ahmed. "We Muslims *exclude* pork from our diet."

_I_ 25. Scientists are working on a vaccine that will help people *obtain* the virus that causes AIDS.

Score   (Number correct) _____ × 4 = _____ %

Enter your score above and in the vocabulary performance chart on the inside back cover of the book.

UNIT FOUR: Test 3

PART A: Synonyms

In the space provided, write the letter of the choice that is most nearly the **same** in meaning as the **boldfaced** word.

  _b_ 1. **assure**   a) argue with   **b**) promise   **c**) run from   **d**) reach out to

  _a_ 2. **automatic**   a) operating by itself   **b**) money-saving   **c**) clear
                           d) ashamed

  _c_ 3. **bewilder**   a) discontinue   **b**) hide   **c**) confuse   **d**) examine

  _b_ 4. **circumstances** a) feelings   **b**) situation   **c**) hardships   **d**) enemies

  _d_ 5. **communicate**   a) take seriously   **b**) make strong   **c**) pay for   **d**) make known

  _d_ 6. **devote**   a) slow down   **b**) turn away   **c**) get rid of   **d**) give oneself

  _a_ 7. **distract**   a) pull attention away   **b**) point toward   **c**) get
                           d) make better

  _d_ 8. **emotion**   a) movement   **b**) victim   **c**) hardship   **d**) feeling

  _c_ 9. **excerpt**   a) sudden decision   **b**) effect   **c**) part of a work   **d**) whole

  _d_ 10. **fulfill**   a) hurry   **b**) embarrass   **c**) search for   **d**) carry out

  _d_ 11. **function**   a) knowledge   **b**) hardship   **c**) topic   **d**) use

  _a_ 12. **humiliate**   a) shame   **b**) give energy to   **c**) send   **d**) calm

  _b_ 13. **impulse**   a) position   **b**) sudden desire   **c**) heartbeat   **d**) difficulty

  _d_ 14. **influence**   a) say   **b**) activity   **c**) get   **d**) have an effect on

  _a_ 15. **investigate**   a) examine   **b**) ignore   **c**) punish   **d**) lose

  _c_ 16. **misleading**   a) proper   **b**) aware   **c**) giving the wrong idea   **d**) unfriendly

  _d_ 17. **obtain**   a) protect   **b**) explore   **c**) move   **d**) get

  _a_ 18. **perceive**   a) notice   **b**) grab   **c**) ignore   **d**) lie to

  _c_ 19. **prey**   a) hardship   **b**) subject   **c**) victim   **d**) struggle

  _b_ 20. **primary**   a) small   **b**) main   **c**) moving by itself   **d**) aware

  _a_ 21. **seize**   a) grab   **b**) tell   **c**) puzzle   **d**) convince

  _d_ 22. **sympathize**   a) ignore   **b**) slow down   **c**) leave out   **d**) feel pity

  _c_ 23. **theme**   a) difficulty   **b**) condition   **c**) main topic   **d**) hardship

  _a_ 24. **theory**   a) explanation   **b**) effect   **c**) activity   **d**) choice

  _d_ 25. **transfer**   a) puzzle   **b**) study closely   **c**) win   **d**) move

(Continues on next page)

PART B: Antonyms
In the space provided, write the letter of the choice that is most nearly **opposite** in meaning to the **boldfaced** word.

_d_ 26. **abandon**   a) make clear   b) surprise   c) lose   d) continue

_b_ 27. **alert**   a) patient   b) sleepy   c) serious   d) special

_b_ 28. **apparent**   a) not proper   b) hidden   c) difficult   d) unfriendly

_d_ 29. **appropriate**   a) least important   b) friendly   c) exact   d) not proper

_b_ 30. **burden**   a) truth   b) something easy to handle   c) something usual   d) thought

_b_ 31. **crucial**   a) not real   b) not important   c) not clear   d) not wanted

_c_ 32. **deceive**   a) tire   b) give away   c) tell the truth to   d) let go of

_d_ 33. **disregard**   a) know   b) throw away   c) make fun of   d) pay attention to

_d_ 34. **dominate**   a) accept as true   b) lie to   c) argue with   d) have a low position

_b_ 35. **earnest**   a) weak   b) dishonest   c) not fearful   d) not important

_d_ 36. **economical**   a) exciting   b) expected   c) expert   d) expensive

_d_ 37. **exclude**   a) set free   b) support   c) lose to   d) include

_c_ 38. **extraordinary**   a) friendly   b) careless   c) usual   d) important

_b_ 39. **extravagant**   a) troubled   b) money-saving   c) confident   d) not serious

_d_ 40. **fiction**   a) action   b) idea   c) subject   d) truth

_b_ 41. **hinder**   a) give away   b) help   c) change   d) lose

_d_ 42. **hostile**   a) not sincere   b) brave   c) not boring   d) friendly

_a_ 43. **idle**   a) busy   b) valuable   c) not proper   d) brave

_b_ 44. **legible**   a) not boring   b) unreadable   c) untruthful   d) not easy

_b_ 45. **monotonous**   a) unusual   b) interesting   c) true   d) easy to understand

_b_ 46. **overcome**   a) continue   b) lose to   c) have faith in   d) find fault with

_d_ 47. **revive**   a) make clear   b) pay attention   c) listen carefully   d) make weak

_d_ 48. **security**   a) relief   b) activity   c) anger   d) danger

_d_ 49. **severe**   a) sad   b) fast   c) new   d) mild

_b_ 50. **timid**   a) unclear   b) brave   c) important   d) fast

Score   (Number correct) _____ × 2 = _____ %

Enter your score above and in the vocabulary performance chart on the inside back cover of the book.

Unit Five

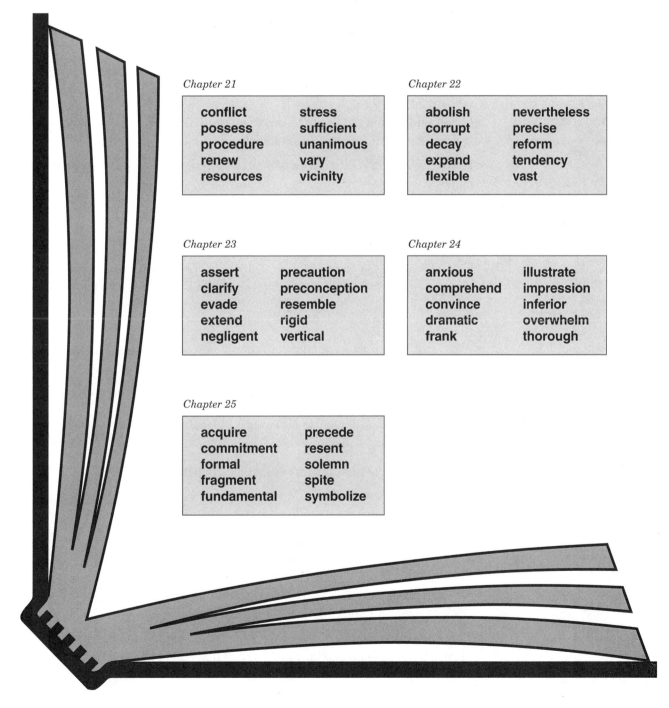

Chapter 21

conflict	stress
possess	sufficient
procedure	unanimous
renew	vary
resources	vicinity

Chapter 22

abolish	nevertheless
corrupt	precise
decay	reform
expand	tendency
flexible	vast

Chapter 23

assert	precaution
clarify	preconception
evade	resemble
extend	rigid
negligent	vertical

Chapter 24

anxious	illustrate
comprehend	impression
convince	inferior
dramatic	overwhelm
frank	thorough

Chapter 25

acquire	precede
commitment	resent
formal	solemn
fragment	spite
fundamental	symbolize

conflict	stress
possess	sufficient
procedure	unanimous
renew	vary
resources	vicinity

Ten Words in Context

In the space provided, write the letter of the meaning closest to that of each **boldfaced** word. Use the context of the sentences to help you figure out each word's meaning.

1 conflict
(kŏn′flĭkt′)
– *noun*

- When the **conflict** between the two diners became noisy, the restaurant manager asked them to settle their quarrel outside.
- Marsha's children often have a **conflict** about whose turn it is to put out the trash.

_a_ *Conflict* means 　　　a. fight.　　　b. joke.　　　c. duty.

2 possess
(pə-zĕs′)
– *verb*

- I can't understand the desire to **possess** very expensive cars and jewelry. If I had more money, I'd spend it on travel.
- People who spend time with young children need to **possess** plenty of patience.

_a_ *Possess* means 　　　a. to have.　　　b. to know.　　　c. to see.

3 procedure
(prə-sē′jər)
– *noun*

- What **procedure** should I follow to become a citizen?
- Even kindergarten students can learn the **procedure** for reporting an emergency: Dial 911, give your name and address, and describe the problem.

_b_ *Procedure* means 　　　a. answer.　　　b. steps.　　　c. support.

4 renew
(rĭ-nōo′)
– *verb*

- After helping to pay for their children's education, many parents barely have time to **renew** their savings in time for retirement.
- We need a good rain to **renew** the supply of water throughout this area. In the meantime, people are being asked not to water their lawns.

_c_ *Renew* means 　　　a. to change.　　　b. to upset.　　　c. to build up again.

5 resources
(rĭ-sôrs′əs)
– *noun*

- West Virginia's natural **resources** include coal and timber.
- A country's **resources** include its workers—the people who help to keep the economy strong.

_c_ *Resources* means 　　　a. plans.　　　b. expenses.　　　c. wealth.

6 stress
(strəs)
– *noun*

- My doctor said my headaches were caused by **stress**. He suggested that I think of ways to reduce the tension in my life.
- Troy and Angie are experiencing a lot of **stress**. Angie's mother is very sick, Troy just lost his job, and they just learned that Angie is going to have twins.

_b_ *Stress* means 　　　a. relief.　　　b. problems.　　　c. details.

7 sufficient
(sə-fĭsh′ənt)
– *adjective*

- The farmers were thankful that there was **sufficient** rain to save their crops.
- Brian's father told him, "When you bring the car home, make sure it has **sufficient** gas to get me to work tomorrow."

_c_ *Sufficient* means   a. less.   b. different.   c. enough.

8 unanimous
(yoō-năn′ə-məs)
– *adjective*

- The vote electing me president of the PTA was **unanimous**. In fact, there was no other candidate to vote for.
- The jury's decision was **unanimous**. Every juror believed that the woman on trial had robbed the beauty parlor after getting her hair cut.

_a_ *Unanimous* means   a. showing full agreement.   b. uncertain.   c. hard to understand.

9 vary
(vâr′ē)
– *verb*

- There are often great changes in weather along the coast. In one day, the temperature can **vary** by as much as forty degrees.
- Joan's lunches never **vary**. Every day, she eats a peanut butter and celery sandwich, pretzels, and a banana.

_b_ *Vary* means   a. to begin.   b. to change.   c. to disappear.

10 vicinity
(vĭ-sĭn′ĭ-tē)
– *noun*

- In the **vicinity** of the elementary school, the speed limit is fifteen miles an hour.
- The Johnsons decided not to buy the house they liked when they learned that there was a nuclear power plant in the **vicinity**.

_c_ *Vicinity* means   a. yard.   b. building.   c. neighborhood.

Matching Words with Definitions

Following are definitions of the ten words. **Print** each word next to its definition. If you look closely at each word in context, you will be able to figure out its meaning.

1.	*resources*	Whatever makes up the present and future wealth of a country, state, etc., including natural supplies and labor force
2.	*renew*	To fill up again; replace
3.	*vicinity*	The area near or around a place
4.	*conflict*	A quarrel or fight; disagreement
5.	*unanimous*	Showing full agreement
6.	*stress*	Mental or emotional tension; strain
7.	*vary*	To become different or to be different; change
8.	*sufficient*	As much as is needed
9.	*possess*	To own; have
10.	*procedure*	Method; the way in which something is done

CAUTION: Do not go any further until you are sure the above answers are correct. Then you can use the definitions to help you in the following practices. Your goal is eventually to know the words well enough so that you don't need to check the definitions at all.

➤ *Check 1*

Using the answer line, complete each item below with the correct word from the box.

a. **conflict**	b. **possess**	c. **procedure**	d. **renew**	e. **resources**
f. **stress**	g. **sufficient**	h. **unanimous**	i. **vary**	j. **vicinity**

_____*resources*_____ 1. A country's ___ include all of its minerals, such as coal, gold, and silver.

_____*unanimous*_____ 2. If there is no disagreement among jurors, we say that their decision is ___.

_____*conflict*_____ 3. Whether two people or groups are fighting with words or weapons, we can say they are having a ___.

_____*vicinity*_____ 4. If someone lives in the ___ of your home, you would call that person a neighbor.

_____*possess*_____ 5. If you are always patient, we can say that you ___ lots of patience.

_____*vary*_____ 6. Roses ___ greatly in color, size, and shape.

_____*procedure*_____ 7. A ___ is a process that often involves a series of steps.

_____*sufficient*_____ 8. If you say you have ___ time for an assignment, that means you have enough time to do it in.

_____*renew*_____ 9. To ___ my supply of clean towels, I'll have to do my laundry tonight.

_____*stress*_____ 10. Anything that puts pressure on our emotions, bodies, or minds can be called ___.

NOTE: Now check your answers to these questions by turning to page 250. Going over the answers carefully will help you prepare for the remaining practices, for which answers are not given.

➤ *Check 2*

Using the answer lines, complete each item below with **two** words from the box.

_____*conflict*_____
_____*stress*_____ 1–2. The ongoing ___ between the Millers and Smiths—an argument over the Smiths' noisy parties— has caused the Millers so much ___ that they are thinking of moving.

_____*vicinity*_____
_____*procedure*_____ 3–4. My father feels lucky that there is a surgeon in our ___ who has developed a special ___ for doing the type of operation that he needs.

_____*sufficient*_____
_____*unanimous*_____ 5–6. For certain trials, a majority vote among the jurors is not ___. Instead, the vote must be ___.

_____*possess*_____
_____*renew*_____ 7–8. According to one fairy tale, a king ___es a magic box full of gold coins; whenever the box becomes empty, it ___s its supply of coins.

_____*resources*_____
_____*vary*_____ 9–10. The natural ___ of the United States ___ depending upon the part of the country. For example, the Midwest is rich in farmland, and the Northeast has more coal.

➤ *Related Words*

Once you learn a new word, you can more easily understand many related words. Below are ten words related to the core words of this chapter. Use their definitions to help you write in the word that best completes each item.

a. **distress**, *noun*	Mental or physical suffering
b. **insufficient**, *adjective*	Not enough
c. **possession**, *noun*	Something that is owned
d. **stressful**, *adjective*	Producing tension
e. **variation**, *noun*	A change from what is usual

___*stressful*___   1. Even though a wedding is a happy event, it is also a ___ one for the people getting married and their families. For instance, it is common for families to argue about who gets invited and who does not.

___*possession*___   2. One of the museum's most valuable ___s is a five-thousand-year-old Chinese vase. Such vases are quite scarce°; there may be fewer than a dozen in the entire world.

___*insufficient*___   3. The trip to the shore was canceled when an ___ number of people signed up to go.

___*variation*___   4. For dinner, we had a ___ on the usual pork chops—it was Spicy Hawaiian Pork with Pineapple.

___*distress*___   5. When the movers dropped a box marked "Fragile," a look of ___ crossed Mrs. Henderson's face. She knew the accident had not been intentional°, but inside the box was a valuable statue which she had obtained° on a trip to Mexico.

f. **proceed**, *verb*	To go ahead
g. **renewable**, *adjective*	Always able to be supplied again
h. **suffice**, *verb*	To be enough
i. **unvarying**, *adjective*	Unchanging
j. **variety**, *noun*	A number of different things; mixture

___*suffice*___   6. Will five dollars ___ to pay for the taxi?

___*proceed*___   7. Turn left at Maple Avenue and ___ three blocks south.

___*renewable*___   8. Solar energy is ___; that is, we can always get more of it.

___*variety*___   9. The local college offers a ___ of adult classes, including yoga, oil painting, self-defense, and Chinese cooking.

___*unvarying*___   10. On the long car trip, the family drove past many miles of corn fields, and the children grew tired of the ___ view. That's when I pulled out the games I had brought along to help the children overcome° boredom.

➤ *Word Work*

A. In the space provided, write the letter of the word that most closely relates to the situation in each item.

__a__ 1. When you arrive at the doctor's office, tell the receptionist your name and sign the check-in chart.

   a. procedure   b. vary   c. vicinity

__b__ 2. There is enough chili for everyone to have a second helping, and even a third.

   a. stress   b. sufficient   c. conflict

__c__ 3. A hard day at work and a flat tire on the way home left Lou with a pounding headache.

   a. renew   b. resources   c. stress

__a__ 4. All the judges agreed that Evelyn should be named winner of the talent contest.

   a. unanimous   b. renew   c. possession

__b__ 5. The state has attracted investors because of its mineral rights and its well-trained workers.

   a. conflict   b. resources   c. vicinity

B. In the space provided, write the letter of the choice that best completes each item.

__c__ 6. The roommates have a **conflict** over housecleaning. They

   a. agree on how clean the room should be.
   b. hire someone else to clean the room.
   c. disagree over how clean the room should be.

__a__ 7. The boss's mood **varies**, so the boss's employees

   a. never know what kind of mood he will be in.
   b. know that he is generally in a good mood.
   c. think that he is usually in a good mood.

__b__ 8. Because our house is in the **vicinity** of many great restaurants, we

   a. have to travel a long way to find a good restaurant.
   b. don't have to travel far to find a good restaurant.
   c. can't find any good restaurants.

__b__ 9. A quality that Tony **possesses** is a good sense of humor. Tony

   a. finds it hard to see the funny side of things.
   b. is easily able to laugh at things.
   c. gets angry when people laugh at him.

__c__ 10. The store's supply of milk was **renewed** today. The store

   a. is out of milk.
   b. has ordered more milk.
   c. has a fresh supply of milk.

➤ *Word Parts*

A. The suffix *-ful* mean "producing ___" or "full of ___."

> *Examples:* *stress* — tension   *joy* — great happiness
>   *stressful* — producing tension   *joyful* — full of great happiness

On each answer line, write the word from the box that means the same as the *italicized* words.

a. **beautiful**	b. **playful**	c. **stressful**
d. **thankful**	e. **wasteful**	

_____*wasteful*_____   1. "All you can eat" restaurants encourage people to be *producing waste*, piling far more food on their plates than they really want or need.

_____*beautiful*_____   2. Although the outside of an oyster shell is rather ugly, the inside is *full of beauty*, with its pale milky rainbow of colors.

_____*thankful*_____   3. When my car broke down on a dark road far from my home, I was *full of thanks* that a police officer quickly arrived and offered me a ride to town.

_____*stressful*_____   4. Most people find it *producing stress* to have to speak in front of a large group.

_____*playful*_____   5. Our boss may seem overly serious, but when she's not busy, she can be quite *full of play*, laughing and telling jokes.

B. The prefix *com-* or *con-* means "with" or "together."

> *Examples:* *conflict* — a quarrel with someone
>   *communicate°* — to exchange information together

On each answer line, write the word from the box that best completes the item.

f. **communicate°**	g. **complicate°**	h. **conflict**
i. **confront°**	j. **contrast°**	

_____*conflict*_____   6. Thelma had a ___ with her neighbors over their dogs' getting into her garbage cans.

_____*complicate*_____   7. The more people you invite, the more you will ___ our job of preparing for the party.

_____*contrast*_____   8. There's a big ___ between the two Williams brothers. One is very outgoing and friendly, and the other is quite shy.

_____*confront*_____   9. When the Carveys didn't pay their rent for the third month in a row, the landlord actually came to their door to ___ them.

_____*communicate*_____   10. In the 1800s, it must have been very difficult to ___ with people who lived far away. Today we are all lucky to have phones and good mail service.

➤ *Final Check*

Read the passages carefully. Then fill in each blank with the word that best fits the context.

A. Traveling with Children

a. **conflict**	b. **stress**	c. **unanimous**
d. **vary**	e. **vicinity**	

Whether I'm driving in the (1)_____*vicinity*_____ of home or farther away, the trip seems to last longer if my kids are in the car. The minute we're on the road, the baby begins to cry and the older children start a major (2)_____*conflict*_____. These fights (3)_____*vary*_____ from time to time, but they often have something to do with one of four primary° complaints:

1. One kid is in the front seat when it's another kid's turn.

2. Someone who had a window seat last time got one again.

3. One of the gang hates the music that another has turned on. (No single radio station has won the (4)_____*unanimous*_____ approval of the children.)

4. One child feels another "is looking at me funny."

Now that I think about it, maybe I can preserve° the peace and lower the level of (5)_____*stress*_____ in my life by making the kids take a bus!

B. Saving Earth's Natural Supplies

f. **possess**	g. **procedure**	h. **renew**
i. **resources**	j. **sufficient**	

Once some of Earth's valuable (6)_____*resources*_____ are used up, it will be impossible to (7)_____*renew*_____ them. For example, coal will someday be used up and gone forever.

We do, however, (8)_____*possess*_____ other important supplies that can be used over and over. Paper, metals, plastics and glass can be turned into new products again and again by means of recycling. If we don't recycle, who knows what severe° shortages and garbage problems will result? It's up to each of us to have (9)_____*sufficient*_____ interest and foresight° to learn about the recycling methods in our communities and then to follow those (10)_____*procedure*_____s.

➤ *Questions for Discussion*

1. Describe a time when you were in **conflict** with a friend or family member. What were you arguing about? Did you find a way to settle the argument?

2. After you woke up this morning, what **procedure** did you go through to get ready for your day?

3. How do you **renew** the food supplies in your cupboard and refrigerator? Are you very organized, writing lists for once-a-week shopping trips? Or do you shop a little bit every day?

4. What do you eat for breakfast? Is it usually the same thing, or do you **vary** the foods you choose?

5. Name a few of your favorite places in the **vicinity** of your home.

➤ *Ideas for Writing*

1. Write about a time that you were in **conflict** with one or more other people. What was the argument about? Did you experience a lot of **stress** as a result of the conflict? How was the conflict finally settled?

2. Write about a close friend. What qualities does your friend **possess** that make you like him or her so much?

Check Your Performance			**CHAPTER 21**
Activity	*Number Right*	*Points*	*Total*
Check 2	_____	× 10 =	_____
Related Words	_____	× 10 =	_____
Word Work	_____	× 10 =	_____
Word Parts	_____	× 10 =	_____
Final Check	_____	× 10 =	_____

Enter your scores above and in the vocabulary performance chart on the inside back cover of the book.

CHAPTER

22

abolish	nevertheless
corrupt	precise
decay	reform
expand	tendency
flexible	vast

Ten Words in Context

In the space provided, write the letter of the meaning closest to that of each **boldfaced** word. Use the context of the sentences to help you figure out each word's meaning.

1 **abolish**
(ə-bŏl′ĭsh)
– *verb*

- With our advanced farming methods, why can't we **abolish** hunger?
- One way for a school district to save money is to **abolish** summer vacation and hold classes all year round.

b *Abolish* means   a. to make longer.   b. to get rid of.   c. to pay for.

2 **corrupt**
(kə-rŭpt′)
– *adjective*

- A **corrupt** police officer went to prison for selling the drugs he took in a raid.
- The country was run by by a **corrupt** ruler who robbed the rich and poor alike.

a *Corrupt* means   a. not honest.   b. respected.   c. poor.

3 **decay**
(dĭ-kā′)
– *verb*

- Teeth that are brushed and flossed regularly are not likely to **decay**.
- Leaves fall from the trees, **decay**, and become part of the forest floor.

c *Decay* means   a. to increase.   b. to bend.   c. to rot.

4 **expand**
(ĭk-spănd′)
– *verb*

- The grocery is buying the shop next door so that it can **expand** enough to double its space.
- During a heavy rain, that little creek **expands** into a fast-moving river.

c *Expand* means   a. to bend.   b. to break down.   c. to grow.

5 **flexible**
(flĕk′sə-bəl)
– *adjective*

- The lamp has a **flexible** neck that can be bent in any direction you need light.
- Lily is the kind of child who is upset at any change of plan, while Ashley is more **flexible** and able to enjoy doing something unexpected.

a *Flexible* means   a. able to bend or change.   b. long or tall.   c. useless.

6 **nevertheless**
(nĕv′ər-thə-lĕs′)
– *adverb*

- Too much sun can cause skin cancer; **nevertheless**, many people want a deep suntan.
- The doll is old and tattered, but the little boy loves it **nevertheless**.

c *Nevertheless* means   a. rarely.   b. because of that.   c. even with that.

7 precise
(prĭ-sīs′)
– *adjective*

- In baking, it is important to be **precise** when measuring ingredients.
- We found the house easily, thanks to our host's **precise** directions.

_a_ *Precise* means   a. exact.   b. busy.   c. strong.

8 reform
(rĭ-fôrm′)
– *verb*

- Does serving time in prison **reform** people or only keep them off the streets?
- Training classes can **reform** dogs so that they don't jump on people and pull on their leashes.

_b_ *Reform* means   a. to annoy.   b. to make better.   c. to confuse.

9 tendency
(tĕn′dən-sē)
– *noun*

- Fishermen have a **tendency** to to tell big stories about the fish they almost caught.
- I have a bad **tendency** to put off doing work until the last minute.

_c_ *Tendency* means   a. hard work.   b. limit.   c. habit.

10 vast
(văst)
– *adjective*

- Lake Superior is so **vast** that you could easily mistake it for an ocean.
- The library has a **vast** collection of books for adults, but not so many for children.

_c_ *Vast* means   a. well-known.   b. gradual.   c. very big.

Matching Words with Definitions

Following are definitions of the ten words. **Print** each word next to its definition. If you look closely at each word in context, you will be able to figure out its meaning.

1.	*expand*	To spread out; get larger
2.	*decay*	To gradually break down; rot
3.	*nevertheless*	In spite of that; even so
4.	*corrupt*	Dishonest; crooked
5.	*reform*	To cause or persuade to behave better
6.	*abolish*	To put an end to
7.	*precise*	Exact; correct; accurate
8.	*tendency*	A leaning toward thinking or behaving in a certain way
9.	*vast*	Very large in size, amount, or area
10.	*flexible*	Able to bend or be bent; able to change or be changed easily

CAUTION: Do not go any further until you are sure the above answers are correct. Then you can use the definitions to help you in the following practices. Your goal is eventually to know the words well enough so that you don't need to check the definitions at all.

➤ *Check 1*

Using the answer line, complete each item below with the correct word from the box.

a. **abolish**	b. **corrupt**	c. **decay**	d. **expand**	e. **flexible**
f. **nevertheless**	g. **precise**	h. **reform**	i. **tendency**	j. **vast**

_____*precise*_____ 1. I don't know Hank's ___ age, but I guess he's in his mid-fifties.

_____*nevertheless*_____ 2. The sun is shining brightly; ___, it is quite chilly outside.

_____*decay*_____ 3. The house is beginning to ___. Its windows are broken, and its paint is peeling off.

_____*expand*_____ 4. The high school is going to ___ by adding more classrooms.

_____*flexible*_____ 5. My grandfather's hands are stiff when he wakes up, but later in the day they grow more ___.

_____*vast*_____ 6. Scholars, writers, and researchers from all over the world visit the Library of Congress in Washington, D.C., to make use of its ___ collection of books and papers on every topic imaginable.

_____*corrupt*_____ 7. Former employees told reporters about ___ practices in the supermarket, such as soaking spoiling hams in bleach to get rid of the bad smell.

_____*reform*_____ 8. Eli used to answer the phone by yelling, "Who is this?" but a few lessons in phone manners ___ed him so that he now says "Hello?" politely.

_____*tendency*_____ 9. I have a ___ to talk loudly and quickly when I am nervous.

_____*abolish*_____ 10. The restaurant's owner decided to ___ the smoking section and make the entire restaurant smoke-free.

NOTE: Now check your answers to these questions by turning to page 250. Going over the answers carefully will help you prepare for the remaining practices, for which answers are not given.

➤ *Check 2*

Using the answer lines, complete each item below with **two** words from the box.

_____*tendency*_____
_____*nevertheless*_____ 1–2. Elena has a ___ to be careless and messy at home; ___, she is always neat and careful at work.

_____*reform*_____
_____*abolish*_____ 3–4. Many people feel that to ___ politicians and improve politics, it is necessary to ___ all gifts of money from groups that wish to influence° lawmakers.

_____*vast*_____
_____*decay*_____ 5–6. The housing project is so ___ that you can get lost walking around in it, and it's so poorly cared for that the buildings are starting to ___.

_____*corrupt*_____
_____*expand*_____ 7–8. The ___ crime boss wants his his evil business to ___ even more; he plans to add gambling operations to his drug business.

_____*flexible*_____
_____*precise*_____ 9–10. During their trip out West, Mom and Dad kept their plans very ___, so we didn't have a ___ idea of where they were at any time.

➤ *Related Words*

Once you learn a new word, you can more easily understand many related words. Below are ten words related to the core words of this chapter. Use their definitions to help you write in the word that best completes each item.

a. **abolition**, *noun*	Getting rid of something
b. **corruption**, *noun*	Making someone bad or dishonest
c. **expansion**, *noun*	Making something larger
d. **incorruptible**, *adjective*	Not able to be made dishonest
e. **reformatory**, *noun*	A school for young people who have broken the law

_____*expansion*_____ 1. The ___ of the car factory will create forty-five new jobs.

_____*corruption*_____ 2. The pastor of that church says that rock music is bad because it leads to the ___ of children.

_____*reformatory*_____ 3. Because he was only 15 when he committed his crime, Brian was sent to a ___ rather than to the state prison.

_____*incorruptible*_____ 4. Everyone respects Judge Mayer because he is fair, honest, and ___.

_____*abolition*_____ 5. One of the most important effects of the Civil War was the ___ of slavery in the United States.

f. **expandable**, *adjective*	Able to become larger
g. **imprecise**, *adjective*	Not correct; not exact
h. **inflexible**, *noun*	Not willing to change
i. **precision**, *noun*	Exactness; correctness
j. **vastness**, *noun*	Great size

_____*inflexible*_____ 6. My boss is ___; she wants to do things only one way—her way.

_____*expandable*_____ 7. During her pregnancy, Midori often wore sweatpants because of their stretchy, ___ waistline.

_____*imprecise*_____ 8. The bench that I built rocked back and forth because I made ___ measurements before I began cutting.

_____*precision*_____ 9. During operations, surgeons must make every movement with great ___, or they might do more harm than good. Nobody wants an awkward° surgeon.

_____*vastness*_____ 10. When I lie outside on a summer night, looking up at the sky filled with stars, I begin to think about the ___ of the universe and the smallness of our Earth. Is it possible that we are the sole° planet to have intelligent life?

➤ *Word Work*

A. In the space provided, write the letter of the word that most closely relates to the situation in each item.

_a_   1. The world's largest desert, the Sahara, covers 3½ million square miles of North Africa.

   a. vast   b. corrupt   c. flexible

_c_   2. Some people put their food scraps in a compost heap, where the food slowly rots and turns into rich fertilizer for the garden.

   a. precise   b. expand   c. decay

_c_   3. Because the speeding driver gave him fifty dollars, the policeman who stopped him did not write a ticket.

   a. tendency   b. vast   c. corrupt

_b_   4. The yoga instructor can bend her legs up so far that her ankles rest on her shoulders.

   a. nevertheless   b. flexible   c. reform

_a_   5. If I'm not careful, I often speak before I think.

   a. tendency   b. reform   c. expand

B. In the space provided, write the letter of the choice that best completes each item.

_a_   6. If a school **abolishes** its football team, the football players will probably

   a. be upset.   b. be more popular.   c. win more games.

_c_   7. A business is likely to **expand** when it is

   a. not honest.   b. closing.   c. doing very well.

_a_   8. I love chocolate ice cream; **nevertheless**,

   a. I am not going to have any.
   b. I am going to take a large helping.
   c. it is my favorite flavor.

_c_   9. An example of a **precise** measurement of time is

   a. a few minutes.   b. several hours.   c. forty-three seconds.

_b_ 10. A thief who **reforms** himself

   a. commits more thefts.
   b. stops stealing.
   c. begins hurting people as well as stealing.

➤ *Synonyms and Antonyms*

A. Synonyms. Write the letter of the word or phrase that most nearly means the **same** as each boldfaced word.

_a_ 1. **reform**

    a. make better   b. make more difficult

    c. make sure   d. get bigger

_b_ 2. **tendency**

    a. thought   b. habit of acting in a certain way

    c. fear   d. making something larger

_d_ 3. **decay**

    a. build   b. continue

    c. disappear   d. spoil

_d_ 4. **precise**

    a. helpful   b. unclear

    c. dishonest   d. exact

_c_ 5. **nevertheless**

    a. because   b. perhaps

    c. despite that   d. sometimes

B. Antonyms. Write the letter of the word or phrase that most nearly means the **opposite** of each boldfaced word.

_c_ 6. **corrupt**

    a. small   b. helpless

    c. honest   d. stiff

_a_ 7. **flexible**

    a. stiff   b. small

    c. gone   d. not correct

_d_ 8. **vast**

    a. many   b. broken

    c. incorrect   d. tiny

_b_ 9. **expand**

    a. grow stronger   b. get smaller

    c. break   d. build

_d_ 10. **abolish**

    a. end   b. become used to

    c. like   d. create

➤ *Final Check*

Read the passages carefully. Then fill in each blank with the word that best fits the context.

A. More Fat, Anyone?

a. **decay**	b. **expand**	c. **nevertheless**
d. **precise**	e. **vast**	

We know that fatty and sugary foods are bad for us. (1)____*Nevertheless*____, we love to eat them. Demand for food with (2)_____*vast*_____ amounts of fat and sugar is high.

To meet the demand for fat, many fast-food giants offer more and bigger high-fat menu items. Pizza Hut sells its Triple Decker Pizza, a health nightmare with as much fat as a stick and a half of butter! McDonald's offers a super-fat triple cheeseburger. And Taco Bell sells a variety° of fatty bacon products. To make matters worse, the fast-food chains offer sugar-filled ice cream, shakes, soda, pies, and cookies that make us fatter and cause our teeth to (3)_____*decay*_____. Although fat and sugar are not wholesome° for the customer, they are certainly good for the financial health of the fast-food chains.

Why do we disregard° what science teaches us about a good diet? Researchers cannot explain the (4)_____*precise*_____ reasons why we ignore what we know about healthy eating, but one thing is certain. As long as our appetite for fat and sugar continues to increase, our waistlines will continue to (5)_____*expand*_____.

B. Is Prison Effective?

f. **abolish**	g. **corrupt**	h. **flexible**
i. **reform**	j. **tendency**	

There's a lot of disagreement about how to (6)_____*reform*_____ criminals and make them good citizens. Today, most of them are sent to prison. But many people believe that serving time in prison does not really make a person less likely to commit another crime. They point out that in prison, a person may spend months or years in the company of more hardened criminals. Will a prisoner in such company come out of jail with the (7)_____*tendency*_____ to be honest? Not likely, they say—instead, the prisoner will probably learn only how to be more (8)_____*corrupt*_____.

In addition, many people want to (9)_____*abolish*_____ the death penalty. They believe it is just as wrong to kill a killer as it was for him or her to commit murder in the first place.

Even if you agree with these points, the question remains of how to deal with people who harm others. Some people want prison changed from a place where people are just locked up to a place where prisoners can obtain° an education, job training, and counseling. They want to see the system become (10)_____*flexible*_____ enough to adjust to a prisoner's needs, rather than treat everyone the same. They want to see prisons influence° prisoners in positive ways.

➤ *Questions for Discussion*

1. Tell about a home or building that has started to **decay**. What were the causes of the problem, and what could have been done to avoid it? What do you think will become of that home or building?

2. If you could **expand** one room in your home, which would it be? How would you use the increased space?

3. Do you know someone whom you would describe as having a **flexible** personality? How has this person shown that he or she is willing to change?

4. Think of a process in which it is important to be **precise**. What would you need to be exact about in order to do this process successfully? What would happen if you were not precise?

5. Do you believe that prison actually **reforms** criminals? Why or why not? Can you think of a better way to deal with people who have broken the law?

➤ *Ideas for Writing*

1. If you had unlimited power, what is one thing that you would **abolish** from the world? Write in a serious or humorous style about something you would get rid of if you had **vast** power.

2. Why do you think that some people grow up to be honest, while others become **corrupt**? Are there reasons why certain people have a **tendency** to commit dishonest acts? Write about why a person growing up may become an honest or a dishonest adult.

Check Your Performance			**CHAPTER 22**
Activity	*Number Right*	*Points*	*Total*
Check 2	_____	× 10 =	_____
Related Words	_____	× 10 =	_____
Word Work	_____	× 10 =	_____
Synonyms and Antonyms	_____	× 10 =	_____
Final Check	_____	× 10 =	_____

Enter your scores above and in the vocabulary performance chart on the inside back cover of the book.

assert	precaution
clarify	preconception
evade	resemble
extend	rigid
negligent	vertical

Ten Words in Context

In the space provided, write the letter of the meaning closest to that of each **boldfaced** word. Use the context of the sentences to help you figure out each word's meaning.

1 **assert**
(ə-sûrt′)
– *verb*

- The mayor **asserted** in court that he never took bribes, but the jury did not believe him.
- Every once in a while, the newspapers sold in supermarkets **assert** that Elvis Presley is alive and hiding somewhere.

_c_ *Assert* means   a. to doubt.   b. to fear.   c. to state strongly.

2 **clarify**
(klăr′ə-fī′)
– *verb*

- Mr. Patel is a great math teacher. He can **clarify** even the hardest problems so that everyone can understand.
- I didn't understand my health insurance plan, so I asked someone at the insurance company to **clarify** it for me.

_a_ *Clarify* means   a. to explain.   b. to create.   c. to stop.

3 **evade**
(ĭ-vād′)
– *verb*

- Our dog will do anything to **evade** a bath. Once we get him near the tub, we have to shut the bathroom door, or he will escape.
- In my favorite cops-and-robbers movie, the robbers tried to **evade** the police by leaving through a hole in the roof. However, their plan failed— the police were waiting on the roof!

_b_ *Evade* means   a. to break down.   b. to get away from.   c. to find.

4 **extend**
(ĭk-stĕnd′)
– *verb*

- We had so much fun camping that we **extended** our vacation one more day.
- "Because many students are having trouble finishing this project on time," said the instructor, "I will **extend** the deadline by one more week."

_a_ *Extend* means   a. to make longer or later.   b. to make clear.   c. to escape.

5 **negligent**
(nĕg′lĭ-jənt)
– *adjective*

- Our neighbor is **negligent** with her dog—she lets it run loose and dig in other people's yards.
- I was **negligent** in caring for my new plant, and it died.

_b_ *Negligent* means   a. friendly.   b. paying too little attention.   c. surprised.

6 **precaution**
(prĭ-kô′shən)
– *noun*

- We took the **precaution** of having the car tuned up before we began our long trip.
- As you walk in the woods, wear long pants as a **precaution** against poison ivy.

_c_ *Precaution* means   a. cure for a problem.   b. something stated.   c. step taken to be safe.

7 preconception
(prē′kən-sĕp′shən)
– *noun*

- From her voice on the phone, I had a **preconception** of my brother's girlfriend as being rather unfriendly.
- Our **preconception** that the party would be boring was completely wrong. Once we got there, we had a great time.

__b__ *Preconception* means   a. wish.   b. judgment made without experience.   c. statement of fact.

8 resemble
(rĭ-zĕm′bəl)
– *verb*

- A certain worthless mineral is known as "fool's gold" because it **resembles** real gold. Both minerals are shiny yellow.
- Eating wild mushrooms can be dangerous because a poisonous mushroom sometimes **resembles** one that is safe.

__b__ *Resemble* means   a. to be better than.   b. to look the same as.   c. to be easier to find than.

9 rigid
(rĭj′ĭd)
– *adjective*

- Modeling clay is **rigid** when it is cold, but once it warms in your hands it becomes softer and easier to work with.
- The guards outside the palace stood stiffly—they looked as **rigid** as poles.

__c__ *Rigid* means   a. not heavy.   b. hard to beat.   c. not bending.

10 vertical
(vûr′tĭ-kəl)
– *adjective*

- Clothes with **vertical** stripes generally make the wearer look taller and thinner.
- The dark **vertical** lines of the telephone poles looked striking against the background of the snowy field.

__c__ *Vertical* means   a. very clear.   b. curving.   c. up-and-down.

Matching Words with Definitions

Following are definitions of the ten words. **Print** each word next to its definition. If you look closely at each word in context, you will be able to figure out its meaning.

1. ___preconception___   An opinion formed before having enough information or experience
2. ___resemble___   To look like or be similar to; be like
3. ___clarify___   To make clear or easy to understand
4. ___precaution___   Something done in advance to avoid a problem
5. ___negligent___   Careless
6. ___assert___   To state positively, often without proof
7. ___evade___   To escape or avoid through clever action
8. ___vertical___   In a straight up-and-down line; upright
9. ___rigid___   Stiff; not bending
10. ___extend___   To make longer in time or later in time

CAUTION: Do not go any further until you are sure the above answers are correct. Then you can use the definitions to help you in the following practices. Your goal is eventually to know the words well enough so that you don't need to check the definitions at all.

➤ *Check 1*

Using the answer line, complete each item below with the correct word from the box.

a. **assert**	b. **clarify**	c. **evade**	d. **extend**	e. **negligent**
f. **precaution**	g. **preconception**	h. **resemble**	i. **rigid**	j. **vertical**

clarify	1. A good math teacher can ___ a difficult problem.
assert	2. The people who want to build the mall ___ that it will mean more business for local stores, but the local stores owners do not believe them.
rigid	3. The children found a ___ board to use as a bridge over the creek.
evade	4. Eli was a poor worker—he ___d responsibility whenever possible.
extend	5. The instructor ___ed the test so everyone had time to finish.
preconception	6. Before tasting spinach, many kids have the ___ they will not like it.
resemble	7. Expensive silk roses ___ real roses.
negligent	8. It was ___ of you to play soccer in the house—you must have known you could break something.
precaution	9. Remember to put on sunblock lotion as a ___ against sunburn.
vertical	10. As we got closer to New York City, we saw the ___ shape of the tall Empire State Building against the bright summer sky.

NOTE: Now check your answers to these questions by turning to page 250. Going over the answers carefully will help you prepare for the remaining practices, for which answers are not given.

➤ *Check 2*

Using the answer lines, complete each item below with **two** words from the box.

negligent _precaution_	1–2. It was ___ of the town to open a swimming pool without taking the ___ of hiring a lifeguard first.
resemble _preconception_	3–4. Because Krista ___s her sister physically, I had the ___ that she would have a similar personality, but the two girls are actually very different.
clarify _evade_	5–6. A reporter said the mayor's views on taxes were unclear, and he asked the mayor to ___ her ideas. However, the Mayor ___d the question by saying, "Who can think about taxes when our basketball team is about to win the state championship?"
assert _extend_	7–8. The new advertisements for the motor oil ___ that using the oil is guaranteed to ___ the life of your car.
rigid _vertical_	9–10. To make a playhouse, Mac began with four ___ pieces of wood. He stuck one end of each deep in the ground, so that each piece of wood was in a ___ position.

➤ *Related Words*

Once you learn a new word, you can more easily understand many related words. Below are ten words related to the core words of this chapter. Use their definitions to help you write in the word that best completes each item.

a. **clarification**, *noun*	Explanation
b. **conception**, *noun*	An idea or thought
c. **extension**, *noun*	An increase in time
d. **negligence**, *noun*	Carelessness
e. **rigidity**, *noun*	Stiffness; inability or unwillingness to change

_____negligence_____   1. The children were scolded for their ___ in leaving the cover off the ant farm and letting all the ants escape.

_____extension_____   2. My boss gave me a two-day ___ to my vacation so that I can go on a ten-day trip with my family.

_____clarification_____   3. Many students had trouble understanding the science assignment, so the instructor took some class time for a ___.

_____conception_____   4. A young child's ___ of heaven is a place where angels live on clouds.

_____rigidity_____   5. I found Emmet hard to live with because of his ___. He found it almost impossible to accept change and other people's ways of doing things.

f. **assertion**, *noun*	A statement made positively but without proof
g. **assertive**, *adjective*	Able to stand up for oneself and say what one thinks or wants
h. **clarity**, *noun*	Clearness of thought and choice of words
i. **evasion**, *noun*	The act of avoiding something
j. **resemblance**, *noun*	Similar appearance

_____assertive_____   6. Jay should be more ___. If he is served the wrong meal in a restaurant, he eats it rather than speaking up to say there has been a mistake.

_____assertion_____   7. Few people believed the man's ___ that he had been kidnapped by aliens.

_____resemblance_____   8. Bok choy is a popular Chinese vegetable that has a ___ to cabbage, to which it is related.

_____clarity_____   9. It is very helpful when a textbook is written with great ___.

_____evasion_____   10. The businessman avoided paying taxes for years, but he was finally caught and went to jail for tax ___. He had been so dishonest with so many people that nobody sympathized° with him or felt sorry to see him go to prison.

➤ *Word Work*

A. In the space provided, write the letter of the word that most closely relates to the situation in each item.

___*a*___ 1. A hotel clerk claims that she has love letters written to her by a well-known politician.

      a. assert   b. extend   c. clarify

___*c*___ 2. Before it is cooked, spaghetti is hard and breaks instead of bending.

      a. evade   b. negligent   c. rigid

___*c*___ 3. When the phone rang, the mother ran into the house to answer it, leaving her two-year-old alone by the pool.

      a. vertical   b. clarify   c. negligent

___*b*___ 4. In the middle of his fifth-grade year, Ben began to think that he was going to have a terrrible time in sixth grade.

      a. precaution   b. preconception   c. resemble

___*b*___ 5. The sunflower grew six feet tall, straight up into the air.

      a. evade   b. vertical   c. clarify

B. In the space provided, write the letter of the choice that best completes each item.

___*b*___ 6. After someone **clarifies** a problem, it should be

      a. a mystery.
      b. easier to understand.
      c. even more troubling.

___*a*___ 7. Because a snowstorm arrived during the furniture sale, the sale was **extended**, so people

      a. had more time to shop during the sale.
      b. could not buy furniture.
      c. had to pay full price for the furniture.

___*c*___ 8. A **precaution** against slipping on your icy sidewalk is

      a. an injury, such as a broken bone.
      b. an ice storm.
      c. spreading plenty of sand or salt over the ice.

___*c*___ 9. Two people who are likely to **resemble** one another physically are

      a. best friends.
      b. members of the same soccer team.
      c. brothers.

___*c*___ 10. People **evade** questions that they

      a. are happy to answer truthfully.
      b. did not hear.
      c. do not want to answer.

➤ *Word Parts*

A. The prefix *ex-* can mean "beyond" or "out."

Examples: *extraordinary°* — beyond the ordinary
excerpt° — a part that is taken out of a whole work

On each answer line, write the word from the box that best completes the item.

a. **excerpt°**	b. **exclude°**	c. **extend**
d. **external°**	e. **extraordinary°**	

_____*extend*_____ 1. Since so many people had something to say, the meeting was ___ed another thirty minutes.

_____*excerpt*_____ 2. A TV show titled *That's Entertainment* includes ___s from many wonderful musical films.

_____*exclude*_____ 3. When the children play, they prefer to ___ Hank because he is such a bully.

_____*external*_____ 4. You are supposed to cut off the ___ layer of the kiwi fruit before eating it.

_____*extraordinary*_____ 5. Mrs. Martin is an ___ woman. She has brought up four wonderful children by herself and also built a fine career at a bank where she is now a vice president.

B. The prefix *pre-* often means "before."

Examples: *precaution* — something done beforehand to avoid a problem
preserve° — to protect or keep in good condition, before there's a problem

On each answer line, write the word from the box that best completes the item.

f. **preconception**	g. **preheat**	h. **prepare**
i. **preserve°**	j. **pretest**	

_____*prepare*_____ 6. To ___ for the trip, I have to wash and pack a lot of clothes.

_____*pretest*_____ 7. Sometimes the math instructors gives students a ___ to help them see if they are ready for the real test.

_____*preheat*_____ 8. The brownie recipe says to ___ the oven to 350 degrees.

_____*preserve*_____ 9. To ___ her wedding dress for her daughter, Mrs. Henry keeps it covered in plastic and in a box.

_____*preconception*_____ 10. New college students often have the ___ that instructors will remind them about assignments and tests. But in college, students must keep track of such things themselves.

➤ *Final Check*

Read the passages carefully. Then fill in each blank with the word that best fits the context.

A. She Changed My Mind

a. **clarify**	b. **extend**	c. **preconception**
d. **resemble**	e. **rigid**	

When I entered a Catholic school as a third-grader, I was very scared. The teachers were nuns, and although I had never known any nuns myself, I had a (1)_____*preconception*_____ of what a nun would be like. I pictured a hostile° woman dressed in a strange robe and sitting stiffly, as (2)_____*rigid*_____ as the ruler in her hand, and frowning when I forgot the answers to her questions. I imagined her deciding to (3)_____*extend*_____ my school day by several hours after everyone else went home.

By the time I actually arrived in the classroom, I would not have been surprised if the teacher had fire coming out of her nostrils. Imagine my surprise, then, when I saw a pretty young woman standing at the front of the classroom. "Good morning!" she said cheerily. "My name is Sister Mary Elizabeth." I stared at her in surprise. She (4)_____*resemble*_____d my favorite aunt. Her face was not cold as I had expected, but warm and smiling. When she stopped by my desk later that morning to (5)_____*clarify*_____ an arithmetic problem, she knelt beside me and gave my ponytail a gentle, playful tug. One day in class was sufficient° for me to fall in love with Sister Mary Elizabeth and to realize how little I had really known about nuns.

B. So Sue Me

f. **assert**	g. **evade**	h. **negligent**
i. **precaution**	j. **vertical**	

"I'll sue!" This threat is all too often carried out. Americans have a strong tendency° to bring one another to court.

Take the case of the teenager who walked down the street, listening to music through the headphones of his personal stereo. He came to a curb and stepped into the street. A car running through a red light nearly hit him. Because he was listening to music, he had not heard the car coming. Did he sue the (6)_____*negligent*_____ driver? No—he sued the maker of the stereo. He claimed the stereo should have come with a note telling him to take the (7)_____*precaution*_____ of removing the stereo when he was crossing a street.

Another well-known case involved a similar circumstance°. A woman sued a fast-food chain for serving her coffee that was too hot. She spilled the coffee in her own lap, burned herself, and (8)_____*assert*_____ed that the restaurant was to blame.

What is next? Should ice-cream cones carry warning labels saying, "Keep the cone in a (9)_____*vertical*_____ position or else the ice cream might fall off"? It seems that suing someone else has become yet another way for people to (10)_____*evade*_____ taking responsibility for their own actions.

➤ *Questions for Discussion*

1. What is one responsibility you have in your life—around the house, at school, or at work—that you would like to **evade**? What are some ways you could try to escape that responsibility?

2. Tell about an incident you have witnessed in which you believe someone acted in a **negligent** way. In what way was the person careless? What happened, or could have happened, because he or she was negligent?

3. What are some **precautions** that you take to keep from becoming a victim of crime? Explain how the things you do help keep you safe from crime.

4. Describe a time when you formed a **preconception** of someone or something that turned out to be incorrect. Where did you get the ideas that led to your opinion? Was your preconception more positive or more negative than the opinion you formed after you had more information?

5. Who are the two people in your family (or a family you know) who **resemble** each other the most? In what ways are they alike? Are they similar in looks alone or also in the way that they act?

➤ *Ideas for Writing*

1. Most people are lucky if they can go away for one or two weeks of vacation in a year. Imagine that somehow you have been able to **extend** your vacation to last an entire month—and that you have plenty of money to spend on it. Write a description of how you would spend your month.

2. Pretend that you are a scientist from Mars who has been sent to study the planet Earth. Your assignment today is to look out one window and describe all the **vertical** objects that you see. Since your Martian boss has never visited Earth, you will have to carefully **clarify** what each object is and what it does.

Check Your Performance			CHAPTER 23
Activity	*Number Right*	*Points*	*Total*
Check 2	_____	× 10 =	_____
Related Words	_____	× 10 =	_____
Word Work	_____	× 10 =	_____
Word Parts	_____	× 10 =	_____
Final Check	_____	× 10 =	_____

Enter your scores above and in the vocabulary performance chart on the inside back cover of the book.

anxious	illustrate
comprehend	impression
convince	inferior
dramatic	overwhelm
frank	thorough

Ten Words in Context

In the space provided, write the letter of the meaning closest to that of each **boldfaced** word. Use the context of the sentences to help you figure out each word's meaning.

1 anxious
(ăngk′shŭs)
– *adjective*

- Dean was **anxious** about his new job. He worried about doing well and whether he would like his supervisor.
- You seemed **anxious** before the test, but you look more relaxed now.

_b_ *Anxious* means   a. sure.   b. troubled.   c. late.

2 comprehend
(kŏm′prĭ-hĕnd′)
– *verb*

- Although my Japanese friend knew English pretty well when she came to this country, she did not **comprehend** such slang terms as "cool" and "gross."
- I cannot **comprehend** how a computer works, but at least I understand how to use one for writing papers.

_c_ *Comprehend* means   a. to believe.   b. to remember.   c. to understand.

3 convince
(kən-vĭns′)
– *verb*

- The lawyer is sure she can **convince** the jury that her client is innocent.
- Cindy tried to **convince** her roommate that she had not stolen her necklace, but her roommate still did not believe her.

_b_ *Convince* means   a. to learn from.   b. to cause to believe.   c. to keep from.

4 dramatic
(drə-măt′ĭk)
– *adjective*

- To hold our attention, our gym teacher used **dramatic** movements, such as waving her arms or jumping.
- Mr. Johnson prefers not to be noticed when he enters a room, but Mrs. Johnson enjoys making **dramatic** entrances, such as by swirling a bright purple cape around her shoulders.

_c_ *Dramatic* means   a. distant.   b. usual.   c. attracting attention.

5 frank
(frăngk)
– *adjective*

- Mrs. Robins told her doctor, "Please be **frank** with me. If you know what is wrong with me, please tell me the truth."
- "To be **frank**," my sister said to me, "your new hairdo looks as if you had stuck your finger into an electrical socket."

_b_ *Frank* means   a. careful.   b. honest.   c. worried.

6 illustrate
(ĭl′ə-strāt′)
– *verb*

- Whenever Mrs. Fine wanted to teach us a new word, she **illustrated** its use in a sentence.
- Pastor Gibson **illustrated** his point about forgiving by telling a story about one victim who learned to forgive his attacker.

_a_ *Illustrate* means   a. to explain with an example.   b. to change.   c. to make difficult.

7 impression
(ĭm-prĕsh′ən)
– *noun*

- My first **impression** of Leroy was that he was loud and rude, but spending time with him showed me that under all the noise was a warm, friendly person.
- I had the **impression** that Vicky was coming on the ski trip, but at the last minute I learned that she had never really planned to come.

  _c_ *Impression* means   a. argument.   b. rule.   c. opinion.

8 inferior
(ĭn-fîr′ē-ər)
– *adjective*

- Silver is considered to be **inferior** to gold, but I still prefer silver jewelry.
- Joan's basketball skills are **inferior** to those of the other team members, but the coach believes Joan will improve quickly.

  _b_ *Inferior to* means   a. just like.   b. worse than.   c. new to.

9 overwhelm
(ō′vər-hwĕlm′)
– *verb*

- You will **overwhelm** children if you give too many instructions at one time.
- A gang of teens **overwhelmed** the old man, holding him down while they took his money.

  _b_ *Overwhelm* means   a. to encourage.   b. to overpower.   c. to watch.

10 thorough
(thûr′ō)
– *adjective*

- After a **thorough** search of every corner of my apartment, I finally found my glasses—in my pocket.
- Before signing up your children at a day-care center, do a **thorough** check of how kind and well-trained the staff are.

  _b_ *Thorough* means   a. quick.   b. careful.   c. exciting.

Matching Words with Definitions

Following are definitions of the ten words. **Print** each word next to its definition. If you look closely at each word in context, you will be able to figure out its meaning.

1.	_frank_	Honest and open; sincere
2.	_inferior_	Lower in value or quality
3.	_thorough_	Complete; very carefully done
4.	_comprehend_	To understand completely
5.	_illustrate_	To make clear, as with an example, picture, or demonstration°
6.	_anxious_	Worried; troubled; fearful about what might happen
7.	_dramatic_	Having very exciting, interesting qualities; striking; very noticeable
8.	_impression_	A belief, opinion, or thought—often based on little information
9.	_convince_	To persuade by argument or proof
10.	_overwhelm_	To make mentally, emotionally, or physically helpless with too much of something; overpower

CAUTION: Do not go any further until you are sure the above answers are correct. Then you can use the definitions to help you in the following practices. Your goal is eventually to know the words well enough so that you don't need to check the definitions at all.

➤ *Check 1*

Using the answer line, complete each item below with the correct word from the box.

a. **anxious**	b. **comprehend**	c. **convince**	d. **dramatic**	e. **frank**
f. **illustrate**	g. **impression**	h. **inferior**	i. **overwhelm**	j. **thorough**

_____ *comprehend* _____ 1. If you say that you ___ a math problem, it means you understand it well.

_____ *inferior* _____ 2. A grade of C is ___ to a B.

_____ *impression* _____ 3. Your first ___ of people is the same thing as your first opinion of them.

_____ *overwhelm* _____ 4. Too much confusing work would ___ anyone.

_____ *thorough* _____ 5. It usually takes more time to do a ___ job than a sloppy one.

_____ *anxious* _____ 6. Something frightening or troubling makes people ___.

_____ *dramatic* _____ 7. A ___ outfit is unusual and will attract attention.

_____ *frank* _____ 8. A ___ person is likely to tell you just what he or she thinks of your new hairdo, instead of giving you false compliments.

_____ *convince* _____ 9. It should take proof to ___ a jury that someone is guilty.

_____ *illustrate* _____ 10. A good way to make an idea more clear is to ___ it in some way. To do so, you might use an example or a picture.

NOTE: Now check your answers to these questions by turning to page 250. Going over the answers carefully will help you prepare for the remaining practices, for which answers are not given.

➤ *Check 2*

Using the answer lines, complete each item below with **two** words from the box.

_____ *dramatic* _____
_____ *impression* _____
1–2. Karla's bright lipstick, false eyelashes, and ___ red dress gave me the ___ that she liked to attract attention to herself.

_____ *anxious* _____
_____ *comprehend* _____
3–4. Many people would feel ___ about moving to a foreign country, especially if they did not ___ the language.

_____ *frank* _____
_____ *illustrate* _____
5–6. My boss is so ___ that she will often tell us stories about her own mistakes to ___ her instructions.

_____ *convince* _____
_____ *inferior* _____
7–8. A mother in the shoe store was trying to ___ her child not to choose a certain pair of shoes. "You like them because they have your favorite cartoon character on them," she explained, "but they are so ___ to this other pair that they will fall apart in a month."

_____ *overwhelm* _____
_____ *thorough* _____
9–10. "Don't let this big exam ___ you," said the instructor. "We've done a ___ job of reviewing the material, and I'm sure you will all do well."

➤ *Related Words*

Once you learn a new word, you can more easily understand many related words. Below are ten words related to the core words of this chapter. Use their definitions to help you write in the word that best completes each item.

a. **anxiety**, *noun*	Worry; fear
b. **comprehension**, *noun*	Understanding
c. **conviction**, *noun*	A strong belief
d. **frankness**, *noun*	Honesty
e. **impress**, *verb*	Affect; influence°

_____frankness_____   1. "You're right; I was speeding," the driver told the police officers, hoping to please them with his ___.

_____anxiety_____   2. As I waited to hear how badly my car was damaged, I tried to control my ___.

_____conviction_____   3. My mother always had a ___ that you should help people less fortunate than yourself.

_____comprehension_____   4. The lecture on the planets and stars was beyond the ___ of many people in the audience.

_____impress_____   5. What adults do may ___ young children. For instance, if an adult they respect smokes, they are likely to think that smoking must be OK.

f. **drama**, *noun*	A play, or an event having exciting, play-like qualities
g. **dramatize**, *verb*	To turn into a play
h. **illustrator**, *noun*	A person who creates pictures for books, magazines, etc.
i. **inferiority**, *noun*	Poor quality as compared with something else
j. **impressive**, *adjective*	Having a strong positive effect

_____illustrator_____   6. Some wonderful children's books were created by a famous husband-and-wife team; she is the writer, and he is the ___.

_____inferiority_____   7. In many ads, advertisers will talk about the ___ of other brands compared with their own. Of course, they always assert° that their own product is the best.

_____drama_____   8. Other drivers often slow down and stare at an accident, attracted by the ___ of the scene.

_____dramatize_____   9. The TV movie ___d the life of Cesar Chavez, who fought for the rights of migrant workers. He tried to reform° the way farm employers treat their workers.

_____impressive_____   10. The high-school basketball player's performance was so ___ that several college teams wanted the player to join them.

➤ *Word Work*

A. In the space provided, write the letter of the word that most closely relates to the situation in each item.

a. **anxious**	b. **dramatic**	c. **frank**
d. **illustrate**	e. **inferior**	

_d_ 1. As Tri Lee described how North and South Vietnam were once divided, he drew a map of the country on the blackboard.

_a_ 2. Sara chewed her nails and tapped her foot as she waited to learn if she had passed the test.

_e_ 3. I bought these two shirts on the same day. One still looks like new, but the other has faded and is tearing at the seams.

_c_ 4. "I think I should tell you that I've been in prison," said Tom. "I hope you will still consider me for the job."

_b_ 5. In the movie *Aladdin*, Prince Ali makes a grand entrance into the city, surrounded by soldiers, elephants, dancers, and musicians.

B. In the space provided, write the letter of the choice that best completes each item.

_b_ 6. Hana did a **thorough** job of cleaning her room. Hana

  a. dusted the room b. spent a long time c. cleaned the room once
   a little.   carefully cleaning.   a month.

_a_ 7. The magician **convinced** the audience that he could read minds. The audience

  a. believed   b. laughed at   c. paid no attention
   the magician.   the magician.   to the magician.

_b_ 8. On the first day of school, all the new faces and instructions **overwhelmed** Emmy. Emmy

  a. was pleased with the new experience.
  b. was confused by being faced with so much that was new.
  c. gained a better view of herself.

_c_ 9. Paul quickly **comprehended** the instructions for building the model. When it comes to building models, it seems that Paul is

  a. not interested. b. not experienced. c. skillful.

_b_ 10. Ivan's main **impression** of his girlfriend's father was that he had a pleasant smile. Ivan and his girlfriend's father

  a. were close friends. b. had seen each other c. had never met face to face.
        only briefly.

➤ *Synonyms and Antonyms*

A. Synonyms. Write the letter of the word or phrase that most nearly means the **same** as each boldfaced word.

_c_ 1. **convince**

    a. point out   b. study

    c. persuade   d. fear

_b_ 2. **dramatic**

    a. helpful   b. striking

    c. confusing   d. not well-known

_c_ 3. **illustrate**

    a. have faith   b. work hard

    c. explain   d. argue

_a_ 4. **impression**

    a. belief   b. proof

    c. news   d. honesty

_c_ 5. **overwhelm**

    a. delay   b. make clear

    c. overpower   d. overwork

B. Antonyms. Write the letter of the word or phrase that most nearly means the **opposite** of each boldfaced word.

_a_ 6. **anxious**

    a. calm   b. forgetful

    c. busy   d. lonely

_d_ 7. **comprehend**

    a. pretend   b. know

    c. find   d. misunderstand

_d_ 8. **frank**

    a. certain   b. expert

    c. humorous   d. dishonest

_c_ 9. **inferior**

    a. far away   b. well-known

    c. better   d. simple

_d_ 10. **thorough**

    a. truthful   b. risky

    c. sensible   d. incomplete

➤ *Final Check*

Read the passages carefully. Then fill in each blank with the word that best fits the context.

A. Fear of Public Speaking

a. **anxious**	b. **convince**	c. **inferior**
d. **overwhelm**	e. **thorough**	

I get (1)_____*anxious*_____ even thinking about getting up in front of the whole class to give my history report. I don't know why I'm so worried. I guess I'm afraid that I will humiliate° myself. I have done a (2)_____*thorough*_____ job of preparing my report—I don't think I've left anything important out. I guess I compare myself with others and worry about whether my work is (3)_____*inferior*_____ to theirs. I hope that my fears won't (4)_____*overwhelm*_____ me and prevent me from doing a good job. I'll have to (5)_____*convince*_____ myself that as long as I have made an effort, my report will be OK.

B. Mrs. Thornton's Condition

f. **comprehend**	g. **dramatic**	h. **frank**
i. **illustrate**	j. **impression**	

Adults should be honest with children. I can (6)_____*illustrate*_____ this point by telling how I and my fellow first-graders suffered when our teacher had a baby. It wasn't that we didn't like babies or that we didn't like Mrs. Thornton. Most of us loved them both. The problem was that we did not realize she was pregnant, so her (7)_____*dramatic*_____ growth frightened us. Could that happen to us some day? Would we balloon up for no reason? Also, we were worried about her. But even when we made our concern evident° by asking what was happening to her, she gave us only silly answers like "I guess I ate too much breakfast!"

Finally, one day she didn't appear at school. Instead, our principal simply announced, "Mrs. Thornton will not be your teacher anymore." We were left with the (8)_____*impression*_____ that something awful had happened to her. We were fearful and sad. Fortunately, the substitute teacher who took Mrs. Thornton's place saw our tearful faces and realized we did not (9)_____*comprehend*_____ the situation. She explained that Mrs. Thornton had just had a baby and that she was fine and very happy. But we could have been saved a great deal of worry and fear if the adults in our lives had just been more (10)_____*frank*_____ with us and had clarified° the situation.

➤ *Questions for Discussion*

1. Did you ever try to **convince** a friend to give up a bad habit? What was the habit, and what did you do to convince your friend to give it up?

2. Tell about a time when your first **impression** of a person or a situation (perhaps a job or a school) turned out to be mistaken.

3. Do you know people who seem to like to make other people feel **inferior** to them? How do they do it?

4. Talk about a time when work or other responsibilities **overwhelmed** you. How were you overwhelmed, and how did you react?

5. How might someone go about doing a very **thorough** job of studying the words in this chapter? Name specific steps that the person could take.

➤ *Ideas for Writing*

1. Write about a time when you were **frank** about your feelings, even though someone else might not like what you said. How did you feel about speaking out honestly? Did the experience make you feel **anxious**? How did other people respond°?

2. Write about a specific° quality of someone you know. Begin by explaining that quality in general. Then go on to use an example to **illustrate** what you mean. For instance, you might write about how stubborn someone is. Your example might be one particular event that showed the person's stubbornness in a **dramatic** way.

Check Your Performance   **CHAPTER 24**

Activity	Number Right	Points	Total
Check 2	_____	× 10 =	_____
Related Words	_____	× 10 =	_____
Word Work	_____	× 10 =	_____
Synonyms and Antonyms	_____	× 10 =	_____
Final Check	_____	× 10 =	_____

Enter your scores above and in the vocabulary performance chart on the inside back cover of the book.

acquire	precede
commitment	resent
formal	solemn
fragment	spite
fundamental	symbolize

Ten Words in Context

In the space provided, write the letter of the meaning closest to that of each **boldfaced** word. Use the context of the sentences to help you figure out each word's meaning.

1 acquire
(ə-kwīr′)
– *verb*

- While living in England, Brad **acquired** a little bit of an English accent.
- Before going on the trip, I **acquired** a good pair of hiking boots.

__b__ *Acquire* means   a. to appreciate.   b. to get.   c. to do without.

2 commitment
(kə-mĭt′mənt)
– *noun*

- Nita has made a **commitment** to stop smoking this year.
- The Greens made a **commitment** to give 5 percent of their income to charity.

__a__ *Commitment* means   a. promise.   b. piece.   c. symbol.

3 formal
(fôr′məl)
– *adjective*

- Because my boss is a rather **formal** person, I never call him by his first name or try to joke with him.
- A **formal** wedding can be very expensive, so Julie and Ed have decided on a casual wedding in the park.

__b__ *Formal* means   a. interesting.   b. traditional and proper.   c. full of hope.

4 fragment
(frăg′mənt)
– *noun*

- Don't go into the kitchen barefoot. I broke a glass, and there may still be a **fragment** on the floor.
- Scientists digging up an ancient city found a piece of pottery which they think is a **fragment** of a bowl.

__c__ *Fragment* means   a. whole.   b. copy.   c. small part.

5 fundamental
(fŭn′dĕ-mĕn′tl)
– *adjective*

- A **fundamental** rule of water safety is this: Don't go swimming alone.
- One must learn the **fundamental** operations of arithmetic before going on to algebra.

__c__ *Fundamental* means   a. based on fun.   b. unusual.   c. needing to be learned first.

6 precede
(prĭ-sēd′)
– *verb*

- Do you think that friendship **precedes** love in a relationship? Or does love come first?
- On the East Coast, the 11 o'clock news **precedes** the *Tonight Show*, which begins at 11:30.

__a__ *Precede* means   a. to come before.   b. to be part of.   c. to stand for.

7 resent
(rĭ-zĕnt′)
– *verb*

- The voters **resent** the fact that the mayor made promises he did not keep after his election.
- People often **resent** being given advice they did not ask for.

_a_ *Resent* means   a. to feel bitter about.   b. to feel better about.   c. to feel frightened by.

8 solemn
(sŏl′əm)
– *adjective*

- The fire chief told some jokes to get the children's attention. But when he began to speak about not playing with matches, he became **solemn**.
- The group of laughing children became **solemn** when they heard that their friend had been injured.

_c_ *Solemn* means   a. hard to understand.   b. silly.   c. serious.

9 spite
(spīt)
– *noun*

- Turning against her former friend, the girl said with **spite** in her voice, "Everyone thinks you're a real loser."
- The disk jockeys' **spite** toward each other was obvious—each of them said nasty things about the other on the air.

_b_ *Spite* means   a. puzzlement.   b. hate.   c. sense of humor.

10 symbolize
(sĭm′bə-līz′)
– *verb*

- In ancient Egypt, a picture of a small circle with a dot in the middle **symbolized** the sun.
- During World War II, holding two fingers up in a V stood for victory; during the 1960s, it **symbolized** peace.

_b_ *Symbolize* means   a. to be like.   b. to stand for.   c. to point toward.

Matching Words with Definitions

Following are definitions of the ten words. **Print** each word next to its definition. If you look closely at each word in context, you will be able to figure out its meaning.

1. _____formal_____ Proper; not casual; according to custom or tradition

2. _____commitment_____ A promise to do something; pledge

3. _____acquire_____ To get through one's own actions; gain something as one's own

4. _____fundamental_____ Basic; forming a foundation; essential

5. _____fragment_____ A small piece broken off something whole

6. _____resent_____ To feel angered and injured by

7. _____spite_____ An unfriendly feeling that causes one to want to hurt or shame another

8. _____symbolize_____ To stand for; be a symbol of

9. _____solemn_____ Serious and respectful

10. _____precede_____ To come before

CAUTION: Do not go any further until you are sure the above answers are correct. Then you can use the definitions to help you in the following practices. Your goal is eventually to know the words well enough so that you don't need to check the definitions at all.

➤ *Check 1*

Using the answer line, complete each item below with the correct word from the box.

a. **acquire**	b. **commitment**	c. **formal**	d. **fragment**	e. **fundamental**
f. **precede**	g. **resent**	h. **solemn**	i. **spite**	j. **symbolize**

_____*fragment*_____ 1. When I dropped the blue china vase, it broke into ___s.

_____*commitment*_____ 2. The neighbors' ___ to keep their street beautiful shows in their neat lawns and lovely flower gardens.

_____*formal*_____ 3. Instead of having a ___ class, the instructor and students held a picnic.

_____*acquire*_____ 4. Every year, the library ___s about two hundred new books.

_____*spite*_____ 5. Pamela felt such ___ toward her ex-husband that she went through their family photographs and cut his picture out of every one of them.

_____*resent*_____ 6. I ___ the way my roommate cooks late-night snacks and then leaves dirty dishes for me to clean up.

_____*precede*_____ 7. When I go to a movie theater, I try to get there early enough so that I can see the ads that ___ the film.

_____*solemn*_____ 8. Jerome is usually lighthearted, but he becomes ___ when he talks about his brother's struggle with mental illness.

_____*fundamental*_____ 9. There are lots of rules about good manners, but the ___ idea behind them all is this: Treat people the way you wish they would treat you.

_____*symbolize*_____ 10. At the Academy Awards, many actors wore little red ribbons to ___ their concern for people living with AIDS.

NOTE: Now check your answers to these questions by turning to page 250. Going over the answers carefully will help you prepare for the remaining practices, for which answers are not given.

➤ *Check 2*

Using the answer lines, complete each item below with **two** words from the box.

_____*acquire*_____
_____*symbolize*_____ 1–2. To remind themselves of why they are saving money, Sam and Christi ___d a dollhouse to ___ the real house they hope to buy someday.

_____*solemn*_____
_____*commitment*_____ 3–4. Everyone was very ___ at the much-loved doctor's funeral. Many people expressed their ___ to carrying on his good works and keeping his memory alive.

_____*precede*_____
_____*formal*_____ 5–6. On graduation day, the principal's speech, which ___s the handing out of diplomas, is always very ___. But afterward, one of the teachers gives a casual, funny talk.

_____*spite*_____
_____*fragment*_____ 7–8. When Ray was ordered to share his toy with his sister, he showed his ___ by breaking the toy into pieces and handing the ___s to the girl.

_____*resent*_____
_____*fundamental*_____ 9–10. Maya ___s the fact that Will told her secret to other people. By doing that, he broke a ___ rule of friendship.

➤ *Related Words*

Once you learn a new word, you can more easily understand many related words. Below are ten words related to the core words of this chapter. Use their definitions to help you write in the word that best completes each item.

a. **acquisition**, *noun*	Something that has been gotten; something owned
b. **formality**, *noun*	An act done only to follow a rule
c. **fragmented**, *adjective*	Broken up
d. **solemnity**, *noun*	Seriousness
e. **symbol**, *noun*	Something that stands for something else

___*formality*___ 1. My sister apologized for asking to see my driver's license when I wrote a check at the store where she worked. "It's just a ___," she said, "but the boss gets mad if I don't do it for everybody."

___*fragmented*___ 2. My mother's family is so ___ that she doesn't even know where some of her brothers and sisters live.

___*solemnity*___ 3. When I heard the tone of ___ in my mother's voice, I knew something important had happened.

___*symbol*___ 4. A red heart is a ___ of love or friendship; on Valentine's Day, people put hearts on Valentine's cards, hang them in windows, and make heart-shaped cakes.

___*acquisition*___ 5. Myra collects stamps, so every time I visit her I have to look at her newest ___.

f. **commit**, *verb*	To seriously agree (to doing something)
g. **predecessor**, *noun*	One who held a position or job before another
h. **resentment**, *noun*	Bad feelings due to a sense of having been hurt
i. **spitefully**, *adverb*	In a manner filled with meanness
j. **symbolic**, *adjective*	Using symbols

___*resentment*___ 6. Still angry over her parents' divorce, Alma felt great ___ toward her new stepmother.

___*predecessor*___ 7. The new cook at the restaurant is not as good as his ___.

___*commit*___ 8. If you are going to join the basketball team, you must ___ to practicing twice a week.

___*symbolic*___ 9. At some weddings, the newlyweds each take a candle and then use it to light a third candle, a ___ way of showing that their two lives are being joined.

___*spitefully*___ 10. Angry that he hadn't gotten the raise he asked for, Marv ___ dropped a paper clip into the office copying machine and jammed it.

➣ *Word Work*

A. In the space provided, write the letter of the choice that best completes each item.

_c_ 1. The cosmetic company has made a **commitment** never to test its products on animals. The company

    a. never used to test its products on animals, but now does.
    b. is looking into the idea of testing its products on animals.
    c. has promised not to test its products on animals.

_b_ 2. The mood in the courtroom was **solemn**. People in the courtroom had heard something very

    a. exciting.   b. serious.   c. funny.

_c_ 3. Somehow or other, the reporter **acquired** a copy of the secret paper. The reporter had

    a. lost a copy of the paper.   b. sold a copy of the paper.   c. gotten a copy of the paper.

_a_ 4. Since their discussion, Ana has **resented** Mark. Ana

    a. is angry about what Mark said.
    b. agrees with what Mark had to say.
    c. forgot what Mark said.

_b_ 5. Devon's voice was full of **spite** as he spoke to his teammate. Devon

    a. admired his teammate.
    b. was angry with his teammate.
    c. was entertained by his teammate.

B. Write each word next to the examples that best match it.

a. **formal**	b. **fragment**	c. **fundamental**
d. **precede**	e. **symbol**	

_a_ 6. A dance with the men in tuxedoes and the women in long dresses
    Bowing to the queen
    Standing up when an older person enters the room

_b_ 7. A broken glass
    A piece of an old dish
    Scraps of torn-up paper

_d_ 8. A before B
    January before February
    President Kennedy before President Johnson

_e_ 9. The color red means anger
    In a letter, a row of *XXX*'s means kisses
    The bald eagle stands for the United States

_c_ 10. Beginning Spanish
    The ABCs
    Food, shelter, clothing

➤ *Analogies*

Each item below starts with a pair of words in CAPITAL LETTERS. For each item, figure out the relationship between these two words. Then decide which of the choices (*a*, *b*, *c*, or *d*) expresses a similar relationship. Write the letter of your choice on the answer line. (All the repeated words in these items are from this unit.)

_b_ 1. PRECEDE : FOLLOW ::

   a. hurry : rush   b. earlier : later
   c. speak : talk   d. bother : annoy

_d_ 2. SPITE : BITTERNESS ::

   a. insult : compliment   b. abolish° : keep
   c. love : hate   d. friendship : affection

_a_ 3. ACQUIRE : OWN ::

   a. get : possess°   b. clarify° : confuse
   c. locate : lose   d. buy : sell

_d_ 4. SOLEMN : PLAYFUL ::

   a. funny : laughter   b. fun : party
   c. ugly : talented   d. exciting : boring

_d_ 5. FRAGMENT : WHOLE ::

   a. law school : lawyer   b. fixed : broken
   c. dog : German shepherd   d. page : book

_a_ 6. HONEST : CORRUPT° ::

   a. early : late   b. fundamental : basic
   c. start : begin   d. symbolize : flag

_c_ 7. OIL : RESOURCES° ::

   a. hate : love   b. give : gift
   c. uncle : relatives   d. coal : mine

_d_ 8. FLEXIBLE° : RIGID° ::

   a. old : ancient   b. ball : bat
   c. food : grapes   d. peace : war

_b_ 9. VERTICAL° : TELEPHONE POLE ::

   a. sufficient° : enough   b. flat : table
   c. cold : summer   d. gray : black

_b_ 10. EXTEND° : SHORTEN ::

   a. frank° : honest   b. easy : difficult
   c. precise° : exact   d. wear : necklace

➤ *Final Check*

Read the passages carefully. Then fill in each blank with the word that best fits the context.

A. Wacky Weddings

a. **commitment**	b. **formal**	c. **fundamental**
d. **precede**	e. **symbolize**	

The ingredients needed for a wedding are pretty basic. They include two people who have decided to get married and someone qualified to marry them. But from the (1)_____*fundamental*_____ ingredients, people create an amazing variety° of ceremonies. Some weddings are very (2)_____*formal*_____. In those, the bride and groom wear traditional outfits—a fancy white dress for her, a tuxedo for him—and have bridesmaids and groomsmen. During such customary° weddings, the groom (3)_____*precede*_____s the bride down the aisle, and afterward, they leave hand in hand. But some people like their weddings to be playful rather than traditional. One man and woman got married while dressed as clowns. Another couple were married while riding a roller coaster. Yet others have said "I do" while they were skydiving or ice skating.

Is an "offbeat" wedding any less meaningful than a traditional one? The couples that choose very different weddings say no. They say the most important thing is the (4)_____*commitment*_____ that they are making to one another. In the case of the two clowns, they said that their unusual wedding (5) _____*symbolize*_____d their desire to keep fun in their marriage.

B. The Cost of Hatred

f. **acquire**	g. **fragment**	h. **resent**
i. **solemn**	j. **spite**	

An old story illustrates° the nature of (6)_____*spite*_____ and the terrible effects such meanness can have on people. There were two merchants in a village. They had grown up together, and each always (7)_____*resent*_____ed what the other did. No one could remember why the two men had first quarreled. But by the time they were middle-aged, their hatred of one another influenced° their lives greatly. Neither could bear to see the other happy or successful. If one of them (8)_____*acquire*_____d a new house, the other had to get a bigger, better one. If one man's shop did well, the other was furious until his did better. One day, one of the men dropped on old jar that had been sitting on a shelf for years. It broke into (9)_____*fragment*_____s. Immediately, a mighty genie appeared. "Oh, lucky man!" said the genie. "You have a great opportunity, for I will grant you any wish. But first I must give you one small warning. Whatever you wish for yourself, your enemy will receive in double measure. If you wish for a million dollars, he will receive two million. If you ask for a golden castle, he will have two." The man became (10)_____*solemn*_____ and thought deeply. There were many wonderful things he could ask for, but he could not bear to think of his lifelong enemy receiving twice as much as he did. Finally he thought of an answer to his problem. A sickly smile spread over his face as he made his wish. "I wish, genie," he said, "that you would beat me half to death."

➤ *Questions for Discussion*

1. Of all the things that you have **acquired** in your life, what is one of the most meaningful? Where and how did you get it? Is it something that is valuable in terms of money, or does it have another kind of value to you?

2. Think of one **commitment** you have made. It could have been to study harder, to break a bad habit, or to get more exercise. What led you to make that promise? Were you able to live up to it?

3. Describe a **formal** ceremony that you have seen. During that ceremony, how did people speak and act that was unlike the way they would normally behave?

4. Think of a time when you **resented** another person's words or behavior. What did he or she do that angered you? How did you respond°?

5. The world is full of things that **symbolize** other things or ideas. For example, a diamond ring on a woman's left hand may symbolize her engagement. What are some other common things that stand for something else?

➤ *Ideas for Writing*

1. Pretend that you are an archeologist a thousand years from now. You are digging up the area that used to be your bedroom and finding **fragments** of things you once owned. Write about what you find there. What would a scientist learn or guess about life today by studying your room?

2. Write about an experience that left you feeling full of **spite** toward someone. What happened to stir up that angry feeling? In the time that **preceded** the experience, had you liked or disliked the other person? Afterward, did you express your anger, or did you keep it to yourself?

Check Your Performance **CHAPTER 25**

Activity	Number Right	Points	Total
Check 2	_____	× 10 =	_____
Related Words	_____	× 10 =	_____
Word Work	_____	× 10 =	_____
Analogies	_____	× 10 =	_____
Final Check	_____	× 10 =	_____

Enter your scores above and in the vocabulary performance chart on the inside back cover of the book.

UNIT FIVE: *Review*

The box at the right lists twenty-five words from Unit Five. Using the clues at the bottom of the page, fill in these words to complete the puzzle that follows.

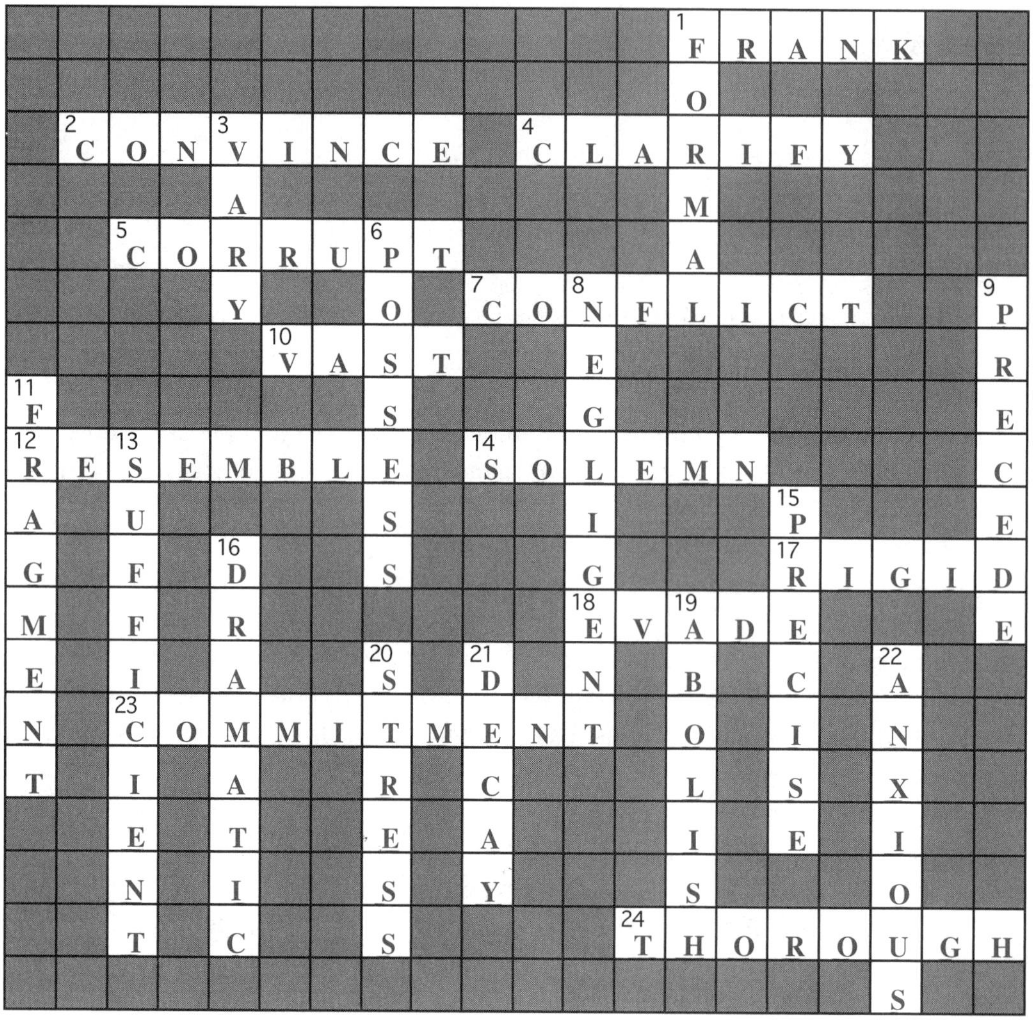

Word list:

- abolish
- anxious
- clarify
- commitment
- conflict
- convince
- corrupt
- decay
- dramatic
- evade
- formal
- fragment
- frank
- negligent
- possess
- precede
- precise
- resemble
- rigid
- solemn
- stress
- sufficient
- thorough
- vary
- vast

(Crossword grid with answers:)

1 ACROSS: FRANK
2 ACROSS: CONVINCE
4 ACROSS: CLARIFY
5 ACROSS: CORRUPT
7 ACROSS: CONFLICT
10 ACROSS: VAST
12 ACROSS: RESEMBLE
14 ACROSS: SOLEMN
17 ACROSS: RIGID
18 ACROSS: EVADE
23 ACROSS: COMMITMENT
24 ACROSS: THOROUGH

1 DOWN: FORMAL
2 DOWN: CONVEY / (COYNCE...)
3 DOWN: VARY
6 DOWN: POSSESS
8 DOWN: NEGLIGENT
9 DOWN: PRECEDE
11 DOWN: FRAGMENT
13 DOWN: SUFFICIENT
15 DOWN: PRECISE
16 DOWN: DRAMATIC
19 DOWN: ABOLISH
20 DOWN: STRESS
21 DOWN: DECAY
22 DOWN: ANXIOUS

ACROSS

1. Honest and open; sincere
2. To persuade by argument or proof
4. To make clear or easy to understand
5. Dishonest; crooked
7. A quarrel or fight; disagreement
10. Very large in size, amount, or area
12. To look like or be similar to
14. Serious and respectful
17. Stiff; not bending
18. To escape or avoid through clever action
23. A promise to do something
24. Complete; very carefully done

DOWN

1. Proper; not casual; according to custom or tradition
3. To become different or to be different; change
6. To own; have
8. Careless
9. To come before
11. A small piece broken off something whole
13. As much as is needed
15. Exact; correct; accurate
16. Having very exciting, interesting qualities; striking; very noticeable
19. To put an end to
20. Mental or emotional tension; strain
21. To gradually break down; rot
22. Worried; troubled; fearful about what might happen

UNIT FIVE: Test 1

PART A
Choose the word that best completes each item and write it in the space provided.

procedures   1. Some of the new ___ for treating cancer are quicker and less unpleasant than older ones.

     a. vicinities   b. fragments   c. conflicts   d. procedures

unanimous   2. In court, the decision of the jury must be ___. If even one juror has a different opinion, the decision doesn't count.

     a. negligent   b. vertical   c. solemn   d. unanimous

vicinity   3. When we lived in the ___ of a railroad, we got so used to the noise of trains that we stopped noticing it.

     a. resources   b. vicinity   c. precaution   d. tendency

vary   4. Marie's moods ___ with the weather. She's cheerful when the sun shines and gloomy when it's cloudy.

     a. decay   b. precede   c. abolish   d. vary

stress   5. Even good events can create ___ in people's lives. For example, researchers have found that there's even more strain in getting married than in being fired from one's job.

     a. fragment   b. stress   c. resource   d. precaution

illustrate   6. To ___ how much smell affects taste, our teacher had us eat a banana while smelling an onion.

     a. evade   b. illustrate   c. resent   d. overwhelm

inferior   7. Emily went through life feeling ___ to her brother, who she believed was more intelligent and talented than she could ever be.

     a. inferior   b. negligent   c. thorough   d. formal

abolish   8. The new principal wants to ___ report cards. The kids love the idea of having no report cards, but the teachers do not.

     a. abolish   b. corrupt   c. overwhelm   d. expand

evade   9. When Jared's father asked, "What time did you come in last night?" Jared tried to ___ the question by answering, "I wasn't wearing a watch."

     a. comprehend   b. resent   c. evade   d. symbolize

rigid   10. When I take jeans off the clothesline, they often feel ___, so I shake them or put them in the clothes dryer for a few minutes to make them soft again.

     a. anxious   b. dramatic   c. fundamental   d. rigid

(Continues on next page)

_____dramatic_____ 11. Myrna's purple and black living room is certainly ___, but I prefer something a little less showy.

        a. corrupt   b. flexible   c. precise   d. dramatic

_____impression_____ 12. From the smile on Rico's face, you might have the ___ that he has no problems. The truth is, however, that his parents are both quite ill, and he lost his job two weeks ago.

        a. commitment   b. precaution   c. impression   d. fragment

_____acquired_____ 13. The Masons were not very happy when their daughter ___ a nose-ring.

        a. extended   b. reformed   c. acquired   d. preceded

PART B

Write **C** if the italicized word is used **correctly**. Write **I** if the word is used **incorrectly**.

___C___ 14. I used to be *anxious* about going to the dentist, but then I started going to Dr. Craine. He's so funny and nice that I just can't feel afraid of him.

___I___ 15. Ms. Acosta is respected for being a *corrupt* teacher—she'll make you work hard, but you'll gain a lot from her course.

___I___ 16. It is impossible to cut the steak with these plastic forks and knives—they are so *flexible* that they snap into pieces as soon as you press hard on them.

___C___ 17. Because I missed the first fifteen minutes of the movie, I didn't really *comprehend* the rest of the story.

___C___ 18. Even though the police believe that Frank robbed the liquor store, they don't yet have *sufficient* evidence to arrest him.

___I___ 19. Parties at the Schroeders' house are rather *formal*, with guests taking off their shoes, helping themselves to food out of the refrigerator, and generally acting at home.

___I___ 20. I was *frank* enough to tell Edna that she looked lovely in her new purple dress, even though I really thought it made her look like an eggplant.

___C___ 21. After angrily tearing up her boyfriend's letter, Elaine wanted to read it again, so she glued the *fragments* back together.

___I___ 22. Whenever Mr. Fletcher goes for a walk, he *precedes* his dog. The dog runs ahead, pulling Mr. Fletcher by the leash.

___C___ 23. Mac did a *thorough* job of cleaning our windows; they seem almost invisible.

___C___ 24. The natural *resources* of South Africa include gold and diamonds.

___I___ 25. The teacher wanted to *overwhelm* his new students, so he gave them just a little homework at first.

Score   (Number correct) _____ × 4 = _____%

Enter your score above and in the vocabulary performance chart on the inside back cover of the book.

UNIT FIVE: Test 2

PART A
Complete each item with a word from the box. Use each word once.

a. **assert**	b. **conflict**	c. **convince**	d. **decay**	e. **expand**
f. **fundamental**	g. **precaution**	h. **precise**	i. **renew**	j. **resemble**
k. **solemn**	l. **symbolize**	m. **tendency**		

_____conflict_____ 1. Two robins in the yard were having a noisy ___ over a worm that they both wanted to eat.

_____decay_____ 2. In a forest, fallen trees ___ until they become part of the earth on the forest floor.

_____precise_____ 3. When making a pair of pants, your measurements have to be ___ if you want the pants to fit well.

_____tendency_____ 4. Small dogs are quick and lively; large dogs have a ___ to be quiet and slow-moving.

_____assert_____ 5. The TV ad ___s that this little eight-pound vacuum cleaner does a better job than many full-size vacuums.

_____expand_____ 6. When Buck plans to eat a big dinner, he wears a pair of pants with a waist that ___s.

_____precaution_____ 7. Ella is so worried about a house fire that every time she leaves home, she takes the ___ of unplugging all the lamps, the toaster, and the TV.

_____resemble_____ 8. In my opinion, the smell of blue cheese ___s the smell of an old running shoe.

_____convince_____ 9. Even though I had homework to do, Raoul ___d me I should go skating with him instead, telling me, "The exercise will wake up your brain."

_____fundamental_____ 10. My parents were not strict about housekeeping, but they did have two ___ rules: we had to make our beds every morning, and we were never allowed to leave unwashed dishes overnight.

_____renew_____ 11. Some paper companies are taking steps to ___ the forests they are cutting down, so that in the future, the forests will still be there.

_____solemn_____ 12. Although everyone was ___ at my grandfather's funeral, there was laughter at the luncheon afterward, when people began telling loving, funny stories about him.

_____symbolize_____ 13. In many Christian religions, the dove is used in stories and pictures to ___ peace.

(Continues on next page)

PART B
Write **C** if the italicized word is used **correctly**. Write **I** if the word is used **incorrectly**.

_I_ 14. The thing that prisoners *possess* most is freedom.

_C_ 15. In some companies, workers can *extend* their workday by two hours and then enjoy three-day weekends.

_C_ 16. The day was hot and sunny; *nevertheless*, almost no one showed up to use the city swimming pool.

_I_ 17. It is a shame how spending time with the wrong people has *reformed* Nathan. He used to be a nice guy, but now he's rude and not exactly honest.

_C_ 18. Most department stores have a few computer games for sale, but you have to go to a computer store for a really *vast* selection of games.

_I_ 19. When Thomas tried to explain how the accident happened, he was so excited and confused that he only *clarified* the story.

_I_ 20. Bonnie is a *negligent* baby sitter, always making sure the children are safely in bed and the house is cleaned up before the parents come home.

_C_ 21. Although I had the *preconception* that Mrs. Arnold would be a difficult person to work for, I soon came to like her very much.

_I_ 22. I painted a line from the left edge of the wall all the way over to the right edge, and then I covered that *vertical* line with a colorful border design.

_I_ 23. The police arrested a man who wrote a *commitment* describing how he had robbed the video store.

_C_ 24. I *resent* what my brother did—after I told him what I was going to buy for our mother's birthday, he rushed out and bought it first, so I had to come up with a new idea.

_I_ 25. Judging from the way Tina and Frank keep smiling and winking at one another, there seems to be a good deal of *spite* between them.

Score	(Number correct)	_____	× 4 =	_____ %

Enter your score above and in the vocabulary performance chart on the inside back cover of the book.

UNIT FIVE: Test 3

PART A: Synonyms

In the space provided, write the letter of the choice that is most nearly the **same** in meaning as the **boldfaced** word.

_a_ 1. **assert**   a) state as true   b) put limits on   c) give one's time
d) make more difficult

_b_ 2. **commitment**   a) location   b) promise   c) opinion   d) difficulty

_a_ 3. **convince**   a) persuade   b) differ   c) listen carefully   d) own

_c_ 4. **decay**   a) own   b) look for   c) break down   d) replace

_d_ 5. **evade**   a) stand for   b) struggle   c) make clear   d) avoid

_c_ 6. **fragment**   a) unfriendly feeling   b) a snack   c) piece of a whole
d) true statement

_d_ 7. **fundamental**   a) careless   b) bored   c) stiff   d) basic

_c_ 8. **illustrate**   a) replace   b) stand for   c) show through example   d) get

_d_ 9. **impression**   a) argument   b) piece   c) effort   d) belief

_a_ 10. **nevertheless**   a) even so   b) afterward   c) because   d) even better

_b_ 11. **overwhelm**   a) receive   b) overpower   c) understand   d) come before

_b_ 12. **possess**   a) lie about   b) own   c) differ   d) show

_a_ 13. **precaution**   a) something done to prevent a problem   b) something done to fix a
problem   c) a problem   d) a result

_c_ 14. **preconception**   a) truth   b) decision   c) opinion formed before knowing
about something   d) area nearby

_b_ 15. **procedure**   a) part of a whole   b) way of doing something   c) reason   d) goal

_a_ 16. **reform**   a) make better   b) replace   c) learn about   d) prevent

_b_ 17. **renew**   a) mention again   b) make new again   c) ignore   d) make clear

_b_ 18. **resemble**   a) be ahead   b) be similar to   c) worry about   d) improve

_c_ 19. **resent**   a) replace   b) rot   c) feel angry at   d) differ

_d_ 20. **resources**   a) something missing   b) period of time   c) enough
d) wealth of a country

_a_ 21. **solemn**   a) serious   b) noticeable   c) complete   d) careless

_d_ 22. **symbolize**   a) show   b) make use of   c) get larger   d) stand for

_b_ 23. **tendency**   a) anger   b) habit   c) tension   d) belief

_a_ 24. **unanimous**   a) in full agreement   b) quarreling   c) carefully done   d) basic

_a_ 25. **vicinity**   a) neighborhood   b) wealth   c) promise   d) opinion

(Continues on next page)

PART B: Antonyms
In the space provided, write the letter of the choice that is most nearly **opposite** in meaning to the **boldfaced** word.

_b_ 26. **abolish**   a) differ   b) create   c) give away   d) ignore

_c_ 27. **acquire**   a) make worse   b) escape   c) lose   d) see

_d_ 28. **anxious**   a) dishonest   b) tired   c) careless   d) relaxed

_c_ 29. **clarify**   a) include   b) correct   c) confuse   d) grow strong

_c_ 30. **comprehend**   a) enjoy   b) give away   c) misunderstand
d) remain the same

_d_ 31. **conflict**   a) anger   b) loss   c) profit   d) agreement

_b_ 32. **corrupt**   a) useful   b) honest   c) loose   d) careless

_a_ 33. **dramatic**   a) not noticeable   b) brightly colored   c) careful   d) careless

_d_ 34. **expand**   a) agree   b) confuse   c) begin   d) become smaller

_c_ 35. **extend**   a) begin   b) give away   c) shorten   d) make worse

_b_ 36. **flexible**   a) flat   b) stiff   c) incomplete   d) careless

_c_ 37. **formal**   a) attractive   b) not sincere   c) casual   d) troubled

_b_ 38. **frank**   a) careless   b) dishonest   c) loose   d) not enough

_b_ 39. **inferior**   a) recent   b) better   c) far away   d) serious

_d_ 40. **negligent**   a) not enough   b) lacking respect   c) incorrect   d) careful

_d_ 41. **precede**   a) get smaller   b) grow   c) happen again   d) come after

_c_ 42. **precise**   a) not serious   b) not complete   c) not exact   d) not common

_c_ 43. **rigid**   a) dull   b) rude   c) bending   d) correct

_d_ 44. **spite**   a) reaction   b) action   c) growth   d) friendly feeling

_a_ 45. **stress**   a) relaxation   b) argument   c) question   d) idea

_a_ 46. **sufficient**   a) not enough   b) not easy   c) not true   d) not basic

_d_ 47. **thorough**   a) not proper   b) harmful   c) boring   d) not complete

_b_ 48. **vary**   a) confuse   b) stay the same   c) disappear   d) make worse

_a_ 49. **vast**   a) small   b) changing   c) unpleasant   d) better

_d_ 50. **vertical**   a) small   b) better   c) not interested   d) horizontal

Score   (Number correct) _____ × 2 = _____ %

Enter your score above and in the vocabulary performance chart on the inside back cover of the book.

A. Limited Answer Key

Important Note: This answer key contains the answers for the "Check 1" activity that is on the third page of each chapter. You should not look at these answers until you have tried your best to pick the word that belongs in each sentence of this activity.

If you use the answer key correctly, it will help you learn and remember the words in the chapter. It will also help you prepare for the other activities and tests, for which the answers are not given. To make this key easier to use, the titles of each chapter's readings are written after the chapter number.

Chapter 1 (Johnny Appleseed; The Lovable Leech?)

1. transform
2. fertile
3. preference
4. surplus
5. peculiar
6. solitary
7. principal
8. challenge
9. suitable
10. dependent

Chapter 2 (Finding Fault—And What to Do About It; What Do Your Hobbies Reveal About You?)

1. frustration
2. deliberate
3. Excessive
4. indicate
5. attitude
6. fragile
7. category
8. analyze
9. critical
10. contrast

Chapter 3 (Fixing Up Furniture; Barbara's Date with Her Cousin)

1. desperate
2. evident
3. accompany
4. scarce
5. dispose of
6. rejection
7. preserve
8. determine
9. pursue
10. restore

Chapter 4 (The Vacuum-Cleaner Salesman; Peace at Last)

1. reduction
2. betray
3. exaggerate
4. abundant
5. neutral
6. comparison
7. demonstrate
8. distinct
9. inhabit
10. dispute

Chapter 5 (Study Skills to the Rescue!; How to Control Children)

1. unstable
2. utilize
3. aggravate
4. considerable
5. obnoxious
6. intentional
7. coincide
8. interference
9. humane
10. cease

Chapter 6 (Toasters; A Mean Man)

1. reliable
2. advise
3. minimum
4. penalize
5. originate
6. current
7. deprive
8. hesitate
9. objection
10. maintain

Chapter 7 (A Special Memory; Watch Your Manners!)

1. endure
2. classify
3. recollect
4. astonish
5. exclaim
6. abrupt
7. eager
8. complex
9. horizontal
10. consent

Chapter 8 (Big Brothers and Sisters; Kevin's First Date)

1. potential
2. vanish
3. variety
4. appeal
5. wholesome
6. adequate
7. establish
8. customary
9. respond
10. awkward

Chapter 9 (Differences in a Gym Program; Teaching A Lesson)

1. discipline
2. ultimate
3. resort
4. vague
5. interpret
6. propose
7. eliminate
8. furthermore
9. emphasis
10. brutal

Chapter 10 (Knowing How to Argue; A Change of School, A Change of Heart)

1. linger
2. anticipate
3. occur
4. reluctant
5. version
6. specific
7. miserable
8. accustomed
9. misinterpret
10. revise

Chapter 11 (Coming Out of a Coma; The Office Doughnut Contest)

1. internal
2. external
3. maximum
4. remedy
5. incredible
6. conscious
7. objective
8. protest
9. assume
10. exhaust

Chapter 12 (The People's Choice; The Christmas Wars)

1. triumph
2. artificial
3. counsel
4. frequency
5. complicate
6. conscience
7. temporary
8. represent
9. transparent
10. detect

Chapter 13 (What's Your Type?; What a Circus!)

1. withdraw
2. detract
3. strive
4. trait
5. foresight
6. tolerance
7. intense
8. interval
9. substance
10. prosper

Chapter 14 (Practicing Kindness; The Stinking Rose)

1. consistent
2. significant
3. evaluate
4. observe
5. random
6. cope
7. phrase
8. sole
9. practical
10. approximately

Chapter 15 (A Modern Fairy Tale; Wolf Children)

1. shallow
2. authentic
3. harsh
4. concept
5. disrupt
6. thrive
7. remote
8. confront
9. eligible
10. characteristic

Chapter 16 (A Mismatched Couple; A Campaign to Become Class President)

1. transfer
2. burden
3. influence
4. extravagant
5. sympathize
6. apparent
7. fulfill
8. security
9. economical
10. automatic

Chapter 17 (The Famous Detective; Why So Quiet?)

1. appropriate
2. deceive
3. communicate
4. bewilder
5. theory
6. investigate
7. legible
8. earnest
9. fiction
10. emotion

Chapter 18 (Fear of Speaking; Do You Believe in Magic?)

1. humiliate
2. distract
3. assure
4. revive
5. impulse
6. crucial
7. perceive
8. hostile
9. timid
10. extraordinary

Chapter 19 (The Miracle Runner; One of Those Days)

1. alert
2. primary
3. idle
4. theme
5. overcome
6. abandon
7. devote
8. circumstances
9. function
10. dominate

Chapter 20 (Pregnancy and Alcohol; A Criminal with a Tail)

1. misleading
2. prey
3. exclude
4. hinder
5. severe
6. monotonous
7. obtain
8. excerpt
9. seize
10. disregard

Chapter 21 (Traveling with Children; Saving Earth's Natural Supplies)

1. resources
2. unanimous
3. conflict
4. vicinity
5. possess
6. vary
7. procedure
8. sufficient
9. renew
10. stress

Chapter 22 (More Fat, Anyone?; Is Prison Effective?)

1. precise
2. nevertheless
3. decay
4. expand
5. flexible
6. vast
7. corrupt
8. reform
9. tendency
10. abolish

Chapter 23 (She Changed My Mind; So Sue Me)

1. clarify
2. assert
3. rigid
4. evade
5. extend
6. preconception
7. resemble
8. negligent
9. precaution
10. vertical

Chapter 24 (Fear of Public Speaking; Mrs. Thornton's Condition)

1. comprehend
2. inferior
3. impression
4. overwhelm
5. thorough
6. anxious
7. dramatic
8. frank
9. convince
10. illustrate

Chapter 25 (Wacky Weddings; The Cost of Hatred)

1. fragment
2. commitment
3. formal
4. acquire
5. spite
6. resent
7. precede
8. solemn
9. fundamental
10. symbolize

B. Dictionary Use

It isn't always possible to figure out the meaning of a word from its context, and that's where a dictionary comes in. Following is some basic information to help you use a dictionary.

HOW TO FIND A WORD

A dictionary contains so many words that it can take a while to find the one you're looking for. But if you know how to use guide words, you can find a word rather quickly. *Guide words* are the two words at the top of each dictionary page. The first guide word tells what the first word is on the page. The second guide word tells what the last word is on that page. The other words on a page fall alphabetically between the two guide words. So when you look up a word, find the two guide words that alphabetically surround the word you're looking for.

* Which of the following pair of guide words would be on a page with the word *litigate*?

    liquid / litter   **lodger / longhand**   **light / lily**

The answer to this question and the questions that follow are given on the next page.

HOW TO USE A DICTIONARY LISTING

A dictionary listing includes many pieces of information. For example, here is a typical listing. Note that it includes much more than just a definition.

> **thun•der** (thŭn′dər) *n.* **1.** The explosive sound following an electrical charge of lightning. **2.** Any loud, resounding noise. — *v.* **3.** To give forth thunder. **4.** To make a loud, resounding noise like thunder. **5.** To utter loudly or threateningly.

Key parts of a dictionary entry are listed and explained below.

Syllables. Dots separate dictionary entry words into syllables. Note that *thunder* has one dot, which breaks the word into two syllables.

* To practice seeing the syllable breakdown in a dictionary entry, write the number of syllables in each word below.

    out•pa•tient   *3*   **Mis•sis•sip•pi**   *4*   **re•frig•er•a•tor**   *5*

Pronunciation guide. The information within parentheses after the entry word shows how to pronounce the entry word. This pronunciation guide includes two types of symbols: pronunciation symbols and accent marks.

Pronunciation symbols represent the consonant sounds and vowel sounds in a word. The consonant sounds are probably very familiar to you, but you may find it helpful to review some of the sounds of the vowels—*a, e, i, o,* and *u.* Every dictionary has a key explaining the sounds of its pronunciation symbols, including the long and short sounds of vowels.

    Long vowels have the sound of their own names. For example, the *a* in *pay* and the *o* in *no* both have long vowel sounds. Long vowel sounds are shown by a straight line above the vowel.

    In many dictionaries, the *short vowels* are shown by a curved line above the vowel. Thus the *u* in the first syllable of *thunder* is a short *u*. The pronunciation chart on the inside front cover of this book indicates that the short *u* has the sound of *u* in *up*. It also indicates that the short *a* has the sound of *a* in *hat*, that the short *e* has the sound of *e* in *ten*, and so on.

* Which of the words below have a short vowel sound? Which has a long vowel sound?

    camp (kămp) *short*   **pie** (pī) *long*   **silk** (sĭlk) *short*

Another pronunciation symbol is the *schwa* (ə), which looks like an upside-down *e*. It stands for certain rapidly spoken, unaccented vowel sounds, such as the *a* in *above*, the *e* in *item*, the *i* in *easily*, the *o* in *gallop*, and the *u* in *circus*. More generally, it has an "uh" sound, like the "uh" a speaker makes when hesitating (as in *ago*) or "ih" (as in *item*). Here are three words that include the schwa sound:

in•fant (ĭn′fənt)   **bum•ble** (bŭm′bəl)   **de•liv•er** (dĭ-lĭv′ər)

• Which syllable in *thunder* contains the schwa sound, the first or the second? _____*second*_____

Accent marks are small black marks that tell you which syllable to emphasize, or stress, as you say a word. An accent mark follows *thun* in the pronunciation guide for *thunder,* which tells you to stress the first syllable of *thunder.* Syllables with no accent mark are not stressed. Some syllables are in between, and they are marked with a lighter accent mark.

• Which syllable has the stronger accent in *ultimatum*? _____*third*_____

ul•ti•ma•tum (ŭl′tə-mā′təm)

Parts of speech.   After the pronunciation key and before each set of definitions, the entry word's parts of speech are given. The parts of speech are abbreviated as follows:

noun—*n.*   pronoun—*pron.*   adjective—*adj.*   adverb—*adv.*   verb—*v.*

• The listing for *thunder* shows that it can be two parts of speech. Write them below:

_____*noun*_____   _____*verb*_____

Definitions.   Words often have more than one meaning. When they do, each meaning is usually numbered in the dictionary. You can tell which definition of a word fits a given sentence by the meaning of the sentence. For example, the word *copy* has several definitions, including these two: **1.** To make a copy of. **2.** To imitate.

• Show with a check which definition (1 or 2) applies in each sentence below:

The boy learned to swear by *copying* his father.   1 ___   2 _✓_

The students *copied* the homework assignment into their notebooks.   1 _✓_   2 ___

Other information.   After the definitions in a listing in a hardbound dictionary, you may get information about the *origin* of a word. Such information about origins, also known as *etymology,* is usually given in brackets ([ ]). And you may sometimes be given one or more synonyms or antonyms for the entry word. *Synonyms* are words that are similar in meaning to the entry word; *antonyms* are words that are opposite in meaning.

WHICH DICTIONARIES TO OWN

You will find it useful to own two recent dictionaries: a small paperback dictionary to carry to class and a hardbound dictionary, which contains more information than a small paperback version. Among the good dictionaries strongly recommended are both the paperback and the hardcover editions of the following:

The American Heritage Dictionary
The Random House College Dictionary
Webster's New World Dictionary

ANSWERS TO THE DICTIONARY QUESTIONS

Guide words: *liquid / litter*   Accent: stronger accent on third syllable *(ma)*
Number of syllables: 3, 4, 5   Parts of speech: noun and verb
Vowels: *camp, silk* (short); *pie* (long)   Definitions: 2; 1
Schwa: second syllable of *thunder*

C. Word List